The Politics of Faction

The Politics of Faction

Christian Democratic Rule in Italy

Alan S. Zuckerman

New Haven and London   Yale University Press

1979

Designed by John O.C. McCrillis
and set in Press Roman type.
Printed in the United States of America by
The Murray Printing Co., Westford, Massachusetts.

Published in Great Britain, Europe, Africa, and Asia (except Japan) by Yale University Press, Ltd., London. Distributed in Australia and New Zealand by Book & Film Services, Artarmon, N.S.W., Australia; and in Japan by Harper & Row Publishers, Tokyo Office.

Library of Congress Cataloging in Publication Data
Zuckerman, Alan, 1945-
  The politics of faction.

  Bibliography: p.
  Includes index.
  1. Partito della democrazia cristiana. 2. Patronage, Political–Italy.
3. Italy–Politics and government–1945- I. Title
JN5657.D43Z8   320.9'45'092   78-23838
ISBN 0-300-02285-9

For My Parents

Edith and Udah Jacob Zuckerman

Who Have Given Me So Much of Themselves

Contents

Tables

Preface

What follows is a work with a particular set of goals, which may be set out very briefly and generally. At its heart is a theoretical challenge: to show that various elements of Italian politics form a pattern which may be accounted for by a logically coherent argument. To some degree, I also provide a case study of Italian politics. Events in that country are detailed over a number of years. However, I make no effort to provide a complete description of those events. Logically speaking, that is impossible. Theoretically speaking, even if possible, it would be unnecessary. I do not try to locate each grain of sand on the beach of Italian politics, but to set out the general contours, to locate the dunes, if not each footprint.

My argument uses a limited set of explanatory factors. Thus, when analyzing cabinet coalitions and policy-making, for example, I generally ignore the role of the Communist and Neo-Fascist parties because they do not enter into my explanation of the patterns. I do not maintain, however, that others could not develop arguments that use these parties to explain those elements of Italian politics. Indeed, Sartori and Di Palma do just that.[1] I make no claim that mine is the exclusive interpretation. Indeed, there need be no single explanation, but different ones derived from alternative theoretical positions. My claims are three: (1) to have accounted for a set of political phenomena in Italy by showing them to be logically related in an argument that entails their existence; (2) to have done so with hypotheses that may be applied to other cases; and (3) where I have done preliminary testing—namely in Japan and India—to have shown that my argument fits there as well, to have located in those countries the phenomena that are logically entailed by my argument.

Put simply, I develop an argument and take its hypotheses as far as I can. I do not deal with all elements of Italian politics. Rather, my goal has been to show that much of it can be accounted for by a limited set of explanatory factors.

Stated most generally, I contend that the predominance of a particular form of political group within the political elite leads to specific characteristics on various political dimensions. The political group that stands at the center of my analysis may be defined by the bases of its cohesion: personal loyalty and the exchange of limited goods and services—namely, appointments, contracts, jobs, and votes. Its analysis may be approached from various perspectives, and although terms abound to signify the same underlying phenomenon, I use the conceptual labels political clientele and clientelist faction. This political group reflects the members' belief that it is in their mutual and exclusive self-interest to act together. It may be distinguished from political groups whose members cohere to bring about the interests of a broad category of people, which some call categoric groups.[2] It is also markedly different from the political group whose members are tied by the shared desire to benefit the society as a whole.[3]

I use the way that the group forms and persists as a determinant of its competitive goals and behavior. Thus, I will examine other characteristics, such as social background or beliefs, only when they pertain to how the members of the political elite form competing groups. I propose to emphasize purposefully the analytical links in the argument, even where they appear to overlook otherwise relevant factors. In chapter 2, I will detail hypotheses concerning the group's tactics and strategies in contests for the control of authoritative positions and policies in parliament, the cabinet, the bureaucracy, and within the political parties. I will attempt to account for the presence of these groups and to specify the consequences of their predominance for the patterns of cabinet formation and persistence, the content and process of policy, and the regime's stability as well.

Who is the political elite? An answer to this often debated question should precede the analysis of the groups within it. However, I will avoid a direct response to the issue, by not defining the boundaries of the concept. Rather, I will examine those who are certain to be found within the walls of the "data container,"[4] no matter which conceptualization is used. Thus, I will retain the distinction between those continuously involved in political competition and those whose participation is at most sporadic. In my analysis, the former will be the political elite.[5] My assumption is that to focus on those who control or openly seek to control governing positions examines individuals within the political elite, even if it does not examine all those within the category.

In sum, my concern is neither within issues which cut wide

swaths through a population nor with the cohesion of similarly affected individuals into voters, nominal members of political parties, rioters, or revolutionaries. This particular segment of society is circumscribed not by the laws of citizenship and suffrage rights but by the more exclusive requirements needed to enter the club of political contestants, those who directly compete to control and occupy governing positions. My goal is to explore the effects of a particular form of political group within the political elite on various characteristics of the political system.

The research on Italy combines various sources into a description of political clienteles among the public and political elite. In addition to my own fieldwork and interviews, I have used the published field studies of anthropologists and the results of mass surveys and aggregate statistical analyses. The Italian portion of the Almond and Verba five-nation study has been used extensively.[6] To provide rough but useful measures of differences in economic development, I have aggregated their survey responses into four geographic and socioeconomic categories: north, center, south, and islands. The date of the survey introduces specific costs and benefits. Since 1959, Italy has been characterized by much internal migration, particularly from the south and the islands to the north. Hence, Almond and Verba's survey responses are of limited utility in a description of contemporary Italy. At the same time, they are particularly good for comparing the behavior and norms of Italians at a time when north-south differences were more likely. To bring the description based on survey responses up to date, I have reported the results of work of Barnes and Sani for the years 1968 and 1972.[7] My third source is information on the use of preference votes by the electorate. The Italian form of proportional representation allows voters to select their "preferred" candidates from the party's list in each election district. The use of this option may be taken to indicate a voter's tie to a particular candidate, as well as to indicate the extent of a candidate's local following. Candidates interested in positions within their party, especially but not exclusively Christian Democrats, strive to accumulate preference votes to demonstrate their political power. Typically, preference votes are gathered through the exchange of such particularistic goods as jobs and favors. Preference voting is a rough indicator of the presence and strength of political clienteles in an area.

Depicting national patterns from field studies and mass surveys carries with it a high margin of error. Most field studies describe areas left behind by waves of internal migration to the cities of Italy. At the same time, few studies shed light on the presence or absence of political clienteles in those cities. Using survey responses to show the presence of clientelist norms and practices runs into a compound problem. Italians appear unwilling to reveal their thoughts, and recent evidence documents changes in the values that they do express. Examining clientelist factions within the political elite avoids some of these problems. It means that the analysis need not center on remote villages or questionable surveys. It displays evidence that is perhaps even more germane to the argument than political clienteles among voters. Most important, it permits the description of clientelist factions to be linked to the analyses of their consequences for political competition, policy-making, and regime stability.

The description of the clientelist factions within the Christian Democratic party utilizes varied sources of information in the world of Italian political activists. Most generally, it reflects my sustained observation for a decade through weekly newsmagazines and daily newspapers. Most specifically, it reflects two extended periods of fieldwork during two years. Between July 1968 and September 1969, I studied the workings of the highest decision-making bodies of the party—through interviews with twenty of the twenty-seven elected members of the Central Directorate—observed sessions of the National Council and the 1969 Party Congress, and held discussions and nonstructured interviews with informed observers, party functionaries, and delegates to the National Congress. To explore potential north-south differences within the party and to explore the local-national links of the political clienteles, I also examined the Christian Democratic party structure in Potenza, a relatively poor, nonindustrial province in the mountains of Basilicata (and the locus of Banfield's "Montegrano"); Vicenza, a relatively prosperous, mixed industrial and agricultural province in the Veneto; and Milan, the center of industrial Italy. Both Potenza and Vicenza are the homes of national leaders of clientelist factions. In each province, I interviewed two-thirds of the approximately 35 members of the highest decision-making body, the party committee in Potenza and Vicenza and directorate in Milan, observed section meetings, and distributed a mailed questionnaire to party members. In the summer of 1972, I returned to the field to examine directly the role of clientelist factions in contests for the control of cabinet positions and local changes in Potenza and Vicenza. In late autumn of 1974, at the time of the fall of the last Móro government, I returned once again and interviewed a number of national party leaders.

I have synthesized these interviews, discussions, and observations into a picture of the Christian Democratic party and its factions. With few exceptions my information combines into a remarkably consistent picture of the different units of the party. Hence, there was no need to provide summary statistics of the interview responses. Where a respondent depicted a rather different party structure, I have noted it. Since these divergent views were few, I have generally drawn together my sources and quoted the most interesting responses.

The initial methodological and analytic focus grew out of the contributions of the Workshop in Comparative Politics, directed by Harry Eckstein and Ted Gurr at Princeton University.[8] Within this framework, my focus has been on relations among "superordinates" (leaders), particularly their bases of internal conflict and their modes of decision-making and the relations between party leaders and members, particularly their abilities to influence each other. My emphasis on the party factions arose from their obvious importance within the structure and process of the party's governing itself and Italy. In turn, the Workshop's focus on a social unit's authority patterns drew my attention to the theoretical importance of the clientelist structure of most of the factions.

Acknowledgments

I began the research armed with a theoretical perspective, interview schedule, questionnaires, and little else. If the product is now a book, it has as much to do with the help of loved ones, friends, colleagues, and teachers as my own persistence. That it is a book gives me the privilege of thanking them publicly.

Before all others, I must acknowledge the assistance of many Italians who made the fieldwork not only possible but enjoyable. Dottor Angelo Sferrazza opened many doors into the Christian Democratic party. He introduced me to Onorevole Angelo Sanza, then party secretary in Potenza, now member of the Chamber of Deputies. Together they gave me the guidance and encouragment that comes from friendship as well as intellectual curiosity. E. A. Bayne of the Center for Mediterranean Studies, Dottor Giovanni Di Capua of Agenzia R.A.D.A.R., Professor Alberto Spreafico then of C.O.S.P.O.S., and Dottor Antonio Boccia provided crucial research help. The party leaders that I interviewed in Rome, Potenza, Vicenza, and Milan put up with the stumblings of a curious American, sporting a tape recorder and an accent, who prodded them with questions about their party. They were always gracious. I trust that I have accurately conveyed and interpreted what they told me.

While a graduate student at Princeton University, I studied with two masters of social science, Harry Eckstein and Marion J. Levy, Jr. They tried to teach me the demands and beauty of the systematic and general analysis of politics. I hope that my work approaches their standards. Joseph LaPalombara, Alberto Spreafico, and Alan Stern helped to focus my research on the Christian Democratic party. Joseph LaPalombara also provided critical comments on and encouragement for different portions of this work. Eric Nordlinger, Gianfranco Pasquino, and Raphael Zariski read each line of an earlier draft. Their comments convinced me that I was getting somewhere with my analysis. My colleagues at Brown University provided an encouraging environment. David Pusateri and Howard Pearl were most able research assistants, and Ruby Campbell and Lee Boileau were patient and kind as they typed many versions of the manuscript. Finally, a year on sabbatical at Tel Aviv University enabled me to complete the study.

My research has benefited from several financial sources. Princeton's Workshop in Comparative Politics, directed by Harry Eckstein and Ted Robert Gurr, supported the initial year of fieldwork. Brown University's faculty summer stipend and travel funds brought me back to the field at a later date.

When I began, Roberta was Ricki and Gregory was a toddler. Since then, Ezra and Shara have joined us. Roberta and I have come to understand some of the demands and joys of life. If that were all, it would suffice.

Netanyah, Israel

1. Political Competition

The study of political competition is characterized by particular theoretical questions and research foci. Stated most generally, it examines the modes by which individuals translate private demands into public policy and control the authoritative decision-making positions: the characteristics of allies and foes, of leaders and followers; the bases for the selection of each; how the members of the different competing groups interact; and the attributes of the competitive systems. Each of these descriptive questions elicits attempts at explanation as well.

The extension of suffrage rights to all adults colors the study of democracies, particularly the ways that the masses have participated in contests for the control of authoritative positions and policies. The literature exhibits predominant interest in the most frequent and public competitive attitudes and behavior of large segments of a citizenry: elections and civil violence. It devotes major resources to the study of political divisions and cleavages and to that institution developed to structure mass political competition, the political party. In doing so it typically presumes that the behavior of the masses determines the modes and consequences of political competition—that is (1) the frequency and severity of political violence; (2) elections; (3) the distribution of seats in parliaments and the formation of cabinets; (4) the efficiency of policy-making; and (5) the persistence of regimes. It typically ignores the independent significance of political elites. As a consequence, it encounters serious theoretical difficulties.

Mass and Elite Political Competition

Within this widely accepted theoretical framework, there is general agreement that when persons maintain intense loyalties to social divisions, the resulting polarized cleavage system will produce violent political conflict. Differences emerge over which cleavage type is most likely to be held intensely and to result in polarization.

In the analysis of mass democracies, the greatest amount of scholarly attention has been directed to exploring the effects of

1

social class cleavages on political conflict. Marx provides the point of analytical commencement. He explains and predicts violent political conflict that produces social transformations by the actions of political movements based on social classes. However, Marx's conceptualization of social class raises difficulties. Classes are distinguished from the general category of social and political division by their *membership sources* (perceptions of mutual interest derived from similar relationships to the means of production), by their *size* (they necessarily encompass large portions of the national society), and by their *goals* (they engage in political conflict to effect the "objective" interests of the membership).[1] The result is a most limited denotation of the concept. There have been few, if any, examples of it. Hence, Marx's link between social class and revolutionary violence is difficult to test.

Attempts to broaden the denotation of social class by reducing the number of defining characteristics have not produced powerful explanatory statements. Certainly, class defined in terms of occupation or income level does not point to a particularly revolutionary social group. As a result, other hypotheses have been suggested to link social class and the characteristics of political conflict. Lipset relates variations in the intensity of perceived membership in a social class to the rigidity of status demarcation lines.[2] Where barriers between the classes decline, as in Western Europe, Lipset argues, there is a reduction in the intensity of class-related feelings. The result is a politics of bargaining rather than revolution.[3]

Rose and Urwin replace Marx's hypothesis with its converse. After noting that religion is a more frequent basis of socially cohesive parties than is social class in Western Europe and the United States, they posit:

> *If class cohesive parties predominate, then regime strains are likely to be low.* This hypothesis assumes that class cohesion makes for bargaining politics. Class is defined by occupation, an economic characteristic, and reflects the significance of market considerations. . . . While social scientists have argued that these economic considerations ought to lead to political conflict, it would be more parsimonious to assume that economic differences should lead to economic conflict.[4]

If Marx's hypothesis—that social class-based political cleavages are likely to become intense, to lead to polarization and to revolutionary violence—finds little support, do other cleavage types have a greater probability of producing those consequences? The literature provides no accepted answers. Marx's profound impact on the literature of the social sciences has generally riveted scholarly attention on social class and its consequences.

There have been, however, efforts to explore the consequences on political conflict of other cleavage types. Particular attention has been given to cultural differences. An example already noted is Rose's and Urwin's comparison of the varied social bases of political parties. In joint work with Rokkan and on his own, Lipset has explored this issue. Contrasting cleavages in developed and developing areas, Lipset generalizes:

> If we now turn to an examination of the sources of party cleavage in contemporary democratic countries, it is clear that the role relationships which have proved most likely to generate stable lines of party support are largely aspects of stratification, as between higher and lower orders of status, income and power, or aspects of cultural differences, as between specified groups which vary widely in their view of the nature and values of the good society.[5]

He relates each type of cleavage to its "prototypical political party"—"class parties" and ":religious parties," in turn, and to a mode of "political controversy." Class parties are likely to engage in the "politics of collective bargaining"; the conflict of religious parties leads to instability.[6] Though Lipset associates each prototype with societies at different levels of development (class parties predominate in economically developed stable polities and the other in developing areas), other scholars make no such link. Rose and Urwin argue, for example, that the predominance of parties based on religious and communal ties is likely to lead to regime strains, regardless of the level of economic development.[7] Though some evidence indicates that conflict between religious, communal, or ethnic groups is difficult to resolve without violence, there is also indication that the presence of specific political conditions will result in the politics of bargaining and compromise between such groups.[8]

In sum, there are contrasting hypotheses linking types of political cleavage with the characteristics of political conflict. However, no preponderance of evidence supports any one of them.

An important problem with attempts to link types of political cleavage and types of political conflict is that societies are rarely characterized by the presence of just one cleavage. Partially as a result, a large body of analysis uses the pattern of how members are distributed in the different cleavages as an explanatory variable.[9] Rae and Taylor summarize the arguments of Simmel, Ross, and Coser that the cross-cutting cleavages reduce conflict:

> This reduction of conflict could occur in two ways. One is through the modification of individual attitudes and behavior—not only through cross-pressures at election time . . . but by reducing the intensity of individual political feelings in general. . . . Secondly, the more cross-cutting there is, the smaller the number of persons who are in the same group in both cleavages, and hence the more difficult it is to build a coalition or potential conflict group containing only individuals who have no link with the opposition, i.e., who agree on all their membership.[10]

Lipset's work highlights the classic argument as well as some of its emendations. In his analysis, the prime determining factor of political violence and instability is the presence of intensely held political attitudes and beliefs. Intensity, in turn, is determined by the pattern of the distribution of political opinions throughout a society: the tendency to adopt extremist positions varies inversely with the individual's frequency of interaction with those of opposing political views and, consequently, the intensity of political conflict will decline as the frequency of interaction increases.

This distribution of political opinions is conducive to stable democracies, according to Lipset.

> The available evidence suggests that the chances for stable democracy are enhanced to the extent that groups and individuals have a number of cross-cutting, politically relevant affiliations. To the degree that a significant proportion of the population is pulled among conflicting forces, its members have an interest in reducing the intensity of political conflict.[11]

More recently, Lipset has added the independent significance of the number of political parties to the analysis. He associates two-party systems with low political intensity and the politics of compromise and multiparty systems with the magnification of political differences and ideological political conflict.[12]

Thus, the literature includes arguments linking a membership pattern of cross-cutting cleavages with political conflict characterized by the absence of violence, bargaining, compromise, and stability. A system of reinforcing cleavage is associated with intensely held political attitudes, extremist positions, inability to compromise, instability, and violence. In all, this literature produces a rich harvest of explanatory hypotheses. If these propositions are to be tested, however, it is necessary that the types of cleavage distribution systems describe particular cases. This has proved difficult.

Dahl summarizes the results of studies of political cleavage distribution. Distinguishing between the social, psychological, and political dimensions of cleavage, he concludes:

> None of the countries examined in this book closely approaches the pattern . . . [of] full-scale political polarization, where sharp political, socioeconomic, and political dualisms all coincide.[13]

In addition, Rae and Taylor contend that examples of cross-cutting cleavages are equally difficult to find:

> Unfortunately, it is evident that virtually all extant cleavage systems result in some cross-cutting and that none result in complete cross-cutting; the pertinent question is not whether cleavages cross-cut each other, but rather how much they cross-cut each other.[14]

Thus, it would seem that no matter how intuitively plausible the hypotheses that contrast the consequences of cross-cutting and reinforcing cleavages may appear, this approach needs emendations.[15] One suggestion, offered by Dahl and Rae and Taylor, is to improve the empirical precision of the concepts. This would permit the necessary but more complex task of measuring the degrees and kinds of partially cross-cutting and reinforcing cleavage systems. In turn, this would enable the testing of hypotheses using the particular distributions found. For example, is a mix of religion and class and ethnicity and similar variables more or less likely to prove volatile, to underpin institutionalized parties? How do the patterns affect party strategies?

Another suggestion overturns the theoretical cart of this literature. It rejects the presumption that the characteristics of the masses are the primary determinants of the forms and consequences of political competition. In its place, it puts the distinction between mass political competition, as exemplified by elections, rebellions, and letter-writing campaigns, and elite political competition, as exemplified by cabinet coalition politics and bargaining over the content of policy proposals. It argues: (1) the two realms are best analyzed separately—mass characteristics should be used to explain mass behavior and elite characteristics to explain elite behavior; or (2) the attributes of the political elite may be used to explain both spheres of political competition.

The difference between the two approaches may be seen by contrasting Dahl's and Mosca's conceptualizations of the political elite. Because Dahl contends that the behavior of the masses influences the behavior of the elite and because Mosca's analysis reverses the causal connection, the two scholars see the same phenomena but draw different theoretical conclusions.

Mosca's "ruling class" and Dahl's "political stratum" are defined in generally the same way. "In New Haven, as in other political systems," writes Dahl, "a small stratum of individuals is much more highly involved in political thought, discussion, and action than the rest of the population."[16] Dahl proceeds to describe the leaders of New Haven in terms strikingly similar to Mosca's initial definition of the ruling class: "In any durable association of more than a handful of individuals, typically a relatively small proportion of the people exercises relatively great direct influence over all the important choices bearing on the life of the association."[17] Compare this to Mosca: "In all societies— from societies that are very meagerly developed and have barely attained the dawnings of civilization, down to the most advanced and powerful societies—two classes of people appear—a class that rules and a class that is ruled. The first class, always less numerous, performs all political functions, monopolizes power and enjoys the advantages that power brings."[18]

The crucial theoretical difference between the studies lies in how they use the variable characteristics of the political elite (which is the same as ruling class or political stratum). This is evident in the theorizing over the effects of mass elections on the political elite. In the first part of the *Elementi*, Mosca contends that mass elections destroy the balance of diverse social and political forces within the political elite. In its place, elections bring the dominance of a single political force, professional politicians skilled in competitive intrigue. As a consequence, the political elite increases in cohesion; the only divisions that occur are linked to particularistic goals and power games.[19] Dahl's theoretical views yield opposing conclusions. Mass elections serve to divide a formerly united political elite. Because control of governing positions requires electoral success, the leaders must vie for the votes of competing social groups.[20] At the heart of the theoretical split is Mosca's argument that mass political demands are organized and controlled by political activists and Dahl's contention that the leaders must respond to mass claims.

Although the theoretical utility of separating the realms of political activists and mass politics and of analyzing elite arrangements apart from the electorate's characteristics is typically associated with Mosca, it also surfaces in Weber's writings:

> In all political associations which are somehow extensive, that is, associations going beyond the sphere and range of the tasks of small rural districts where power-holders are periodically elected, political organization is necessarily managed by men interested in the management of politics. This is to say that a relatively small number of men are primarily interested in political life and hence interested in sharing political power. They provide themselves or their proteges as candidates for election, collect the financial means, and go out vote-grabbing.[21]

Thus the political elite does not merely reflect the demands and the characteristics of the masses. Rather, the political activists directly affect the ways in which political competition and policy-making are carried out, as well as the content of policies and the outcome of elections. If so, then a typology of the characteristics of the political elite would be useful to account for the variations in these elements of political competition. It might use the following (or other) explanatory factors: (1) their general and political beliefs and the intensity with which they hold those values; (2) the pattern of group formation within the political elite—Do they typically divide into persistent groups or not? If they do, how are the groups structured?; (3) the tie between divisions within the political elite and the political parties—How constrained are they by the bonds of party loyalty and organization? How do the parties, or other groups, link activists at various places of the country?

Where answers to these questions locate patterns, they may be formulated into hypotheses linked to the characteristics of political competition. Which types are associated with stable voting patterns? Which types with political cleavages based on social bonds? They could also be linked to competition within the political elite. How do they affect contests for cabinet positions, for the control of policies in the parliament, cabinet, and bureaucracy? The different types could as well be tied to variations in the persistence of particular regimes as a whole.

One such effort was set out by Weber. In *Politics as a Vocation,* he distinguishes those for whom politics is materially and ideally their life (professionals) from those who are not dependent for their existence on political activities: "Either politics can be conducted 'honorifically' and then, as one usually says, by 'independent,' that is wealthy men, and especially by rentiers. Or, political leadership is made accessible to propertyless men who must then be rewarded.[22] The latter are divided into those who "live for" politics (to control power or to serve a cause) and those who "live off" politics. Those on salaries, whether in political parties or government bureaucracies, and political bosses exemplify the politician who lives off politics. Fundamental to Weber's analysis is the attachment of the political boss to the control of government offices, through patronage and the spoils system. In his analysis of the United States, he writes:

> What does this spoils system, the turning over of federal offices to the following of the victorious candidate, mean for the party formations of today? It means that quite unprincipled parties oppose one another; they are purely organizations of job hunters drafting their changing platforms according to the chances of vote-grabbing.[23]

Both Weber and Mosca associate the rise in importance of professional politicians with the spread of universal suffrage.[24]

Thus, the political followings of local notables, the earliest form of political associations, were replaced by the rise of mass democracies and the importance of individuals dedicated to winning electoral contests.

> The rule of notables and guidance by members of parliament ceases. "Professional" politicians *outside* the parliaments take organization in hand. They do so either as "entrepreneurs"— the American boss and the English election agent are, in fact, such entrepreneurs—or as officials with a fixed salary. Formally, a fargoing democratization takes place. . . . Naturally power actually rests in the hands of those who, within the organization, handle the work *continuously.*[25]

Although Weber's distinction between professionals and amateurs examines both the bases of group cohesion and personal incentives, much recent work has emphasized the personality characteristics of activists as the means of establishing a typology. The most influential of such efforts is the work of James Q. Wilson:

> An amateur is one who finds politics *intrinsically* interesting because it expresses a conception of the public interest. The amateur politician sees the political world more in terms of ideas and principles than in terms of persons. Politics is the determination of public policy, and public policy ought to be set deliberately rather than as the accidental by-product of a struggle for personal power. . . .[26]
>
> The professional, on the other hand—even the "professional" who practices politics as a hobby rather than as a vocation—is preoccupied with the outcome of politics in terms of winning or losing. Politics, to him, consists of concrete questions and specific persons who must be dealt with in a manner that will "keep everybody happy" and thus minimize the possibility of defeat at the next election. . . .[27]

Other recent analyses have examined variations in the social background characteristics of political elites, particularly of high government officials. However, the presumption that there is a causal link between social background and behavior has come under massive attack. For example, "Linking 'social background' at one end and 'behavior' at the other is a string of corridors

labeled 'experiences,' 'character orientations,' 'attitudes,' and
'interests' with many connecting arrows."[28] Furthermore, tests
have shown no association between social background characteristics and elite behavior.[29]

As a result, some have moved beyond this highly mechanistic
analysis to provide detailed studies of elite values. Edinger and
Searing have offered links between the study of political elites and
theories of socialization[30] and Putnam in his studies of elites in
western Europe has provided systematic interpretations of elite
political culture drawn from interviews with high party and
government officials.[31] Still others have rejected the utility of
direct analyses of elite goals. In its place, they have substituted a
set of presumed goals, particularly the control of governing positions, and have explained the outcome of competition within the
political elite from these assumptions. This approach characterizes
both those who take political parties and those who take individuals to be the relevant units of analysis.[32]

Here, I have shifted to examples that not only describe the
political elite, but use their characteristics as explanatory variables.
Thus, Sartori contends that the type of elite conflict depends on
the attitudes and goals of the elite as do the types of political
cleavage and the characteristics of mass conflict.[33] Similarly, Di
Palma emphasizes the autonomous position of political elite characteristics as determinants of political conflict and the activation
of cleavages into mass divisions.[34] Others use the political elite
along with other explanatory factors. Lijphart, in his study of
consociational democracies, links nonviolent mass conflict and
elite cooperation, which in turn is associated with elite willingness
to compromise.[35] The latter, Lijphart argues, is dependent on the
characteristics of political cleavage. In a more detailed and complex argument, Nordlinger accounts for nonviolent mass conflict
and elite cooperation in sharply divided societies by elite willingness to avoid conflict, and partially explains the latter by the
characteristics of the elite-mass relations within the segments.[36]

Although of relatively recent importance, this research is characterized by areas of theoretical agreement. Elite cooperation is
hypothesized to be a crucial determinant of mass nonviolence.
Elite attitudes, competitive goals, and decision rules determine
elite cooperation or noncooperation. The literature has areas of
theoretical disagreement, especially concerning the effects of polit-

ical cleavage on elite values. It also contains examples of conceptual imprecision, such as "willingness to compromise." On the whole, it presents a theoretical alternative in the analysis of political competition: mass characteristics are not the primary determinants. As all theoretical efforts, it requires the specification of concepts and the elaboration of hypotheses with wide-ranging explanatory power.

2. Factions, Clienteles, and Political Competition

The analysis of clientelist factions may be approached from two points.[1] The first draws heavily on economic modes of thought. It argues for the ubiquity of relationships based on exchange of personal and tangible favors. Where these ties reach into the government, public officials and policies become corrupted. Its particular concern is with eliminating or at least weakening what are seen as selfish political arrangements. This approach is much less concerned with explaining how and where these bonds develop into persistent political groups. Hence, its arguments are of greater use in analyzing the consequences of these groups than in specifying the reasons for their presence.

The second approach focuses on the hierarchical form of group that results from these ties. Its typical examples are the bonds between landlords and peasants, political bosses and voters. Because these are frequently seen as unusual relationships the literature devotes more effort to explaining their presence than to examining their consequences for other political phenomena. By drawing together these two theoretical sources, conceptual clarity is increased and the hypotheses developed by each approach can be applied to the general concept.

Clientelist Factions: A Conceptual and Theoretical Elaboration

> Two neighbors may agree to drain a meadow which they possess in common, because it is easy for them to know each other's mind; and each must perceive that the immediate consequence of his failing in his part is abandoning the entire project. But it is very difficult, and indeed impossible, that a thousand persons should agree on any such action; it being difficult for them to concern so complicated a design, and still more difficult for them to execute it; while each seeks a pretext to free himself of the trouble and expense and would lay the whole burden on others. Political society easily remedies both these inconveniences. Magistrates . . . prevent . . . failure because they find no interest in it, either immediate or remote. Thus bridges are built, harbors opened, ramparts raised, canals formed, fleets equipped, and armies disciplined, everywhere by the care of government.[2]

Hume's problem lies at the center of the economic analysis of politics. Given presumptions of individual actors seeking to maximize narrow self-interest, what will effect the production of items which are in the interest of all but no one in particular? To use the technical language of recent work, how does one account for the production of "collective goods"? (That is, "any good that cannot be withheld from any member of a specified group once it is supplied to one member of that group.")[3] Hume sets forth government as that combination of roles and structures which brings about action in the general interest, as it raises men above their "human infirmities." Because it acts in the collective interest, government is to be obeyed and praised: "Of all men that distinguish themselves by memorable achievements, the first place of honor seems due to legislators and founders of states who transmit a system of laws and institutions to secure the peace, happiness and liberty of future generations."[4]

Hume's analysis also directs attention to particularistic elements in governmental activities. Once outfitted, navies may defend all, and once erected, bridges may serve all, but they are not built from collective goods nor located on collective sites. Navies require specific goods and services, ranging from selecting and building bases and ships to sewing uniforms; bridge-building requires comparable decisions. Each of these and related choices redounds to the benefit of some, whether contractors, workers, or real-estate owners, and to the detriment of others. It follows that some will be more concerned with the control of those particular outcomes and with the distribution of limited rather than collective goods. Indeed, the argument that some will combine to control government resources and thereby to further selfish interests derives from the assumptions of Hume's own analysis. He argues that such action runs counter to the general interest in the supply of collective goods and is to be condemned:

> As much as legislators and founders of states ought to be honored and respected among men, as much ought the founders of sects and factions to be detested and hated, because the influence of faction is directly contrary to that of laws. Factions subvert government, render laws impotent and beget the fiercest animosities among men. . . .[5]

Raymond Wolfinger's distinction of two types of *homo politicus* helps clarify the particular political group to be examined.

Wolfinger separates the machine politician, "primarily interested in the control over the sources of patronage" and "relatively indifferent to public policy," from the political leader primarily concerned with the content of policy.[6] The crucial difference between the two types is underlined in the story told by Wolfinger about the two kinds of supporters of New Haven's reform mayor, Richard Lee: "The three men had lunched well together and, mellowed by several martinis, the politician addressed the academics somewhat as follows:

> You know, we've worked pretty hard on this campaign and gone through a lot together. I like you fellows and appreciate your help, but there's something I can't figure out: what are you after?
> Why, we want to see Dick elected.
> I know, we all do, but what's in it for *you?* We're all friends, you can be frank with me.
> That's all we want, just to put Dick in city hall.
> Aw, come one, you guys don't have to give me that. What do you want? Jobs? Contracts?

"And so it went. The two intellectuals were unable to persuade the politician that their only aim was to elect Lee. The politician was unable to believe that two grown men, much less distinguished ones, would devote all that time and energy to a cause from which they did not hope to profit personally."[7]

Nor must one presume the presence of political actors seeking only to maximize personal self-interest in order to argue for the frequent occurrence of groups tied by the exchange of tangible favors.[8] Given a limited number of decision-makers and interested groups (such as shipbuilders and bridge contractors), the familiarity and friendship that necessarily follow from frequent dealings may extend to the perception of mutual obligation and loyalty. F. G. Bailey makes the general point: "Any continued series of transactions between the same partners will tend to engender a moral relationship. This, indeed is the dilemma of a bureaucracy. Bureaucrats should treat their 'clients' in a completely universalistic fashion: as members of the public and not as friends or enemies. But continued transactions create friends and enemies among the public, and the bureaucrats become improperly obliging or disobliging, making room for forms of nepotism and even corruption."[9] Finally, one of Wolfinger's New Haven politicians makes a related argument: "If two people can do the job and one of them is a friend of yours, why not take the friend?"[10] Some will always be concerned solely and always with private gains, even at the expense of public goals. This is so whether or not one begins with the presumption that individuals seek always to advance their own particular concerns. Friendship and habit as well as greed corrupt public office.

It follows from these arguments that the manipulation of public goods—whether positions or policies—for private ends is to be found in all political situations.[11] Examples abound, from the sale of judgeships to the passage of laws that favor specific persons, from rigged bids on government contracts to employment in return for political support. All are reflected in what Wolfinger labels machine politics: "the manipulation of certain *incentives* to partisan political participation; favoritism based on political criteria in personnel decisions, contracting and the administration of the laws."[12]

General propositions about the political consequences of these ties may be derived from this literature. Before concerning themselves with collective goods, individuals will seek to further their own interests. To do so, they will try to control governing positions as ends in themselves and to occupy other posts and affect the distribution of government resources. In saying that these ties are ubiquitous, this literature does not deal with variations in the scope and extent of their presence. It does not, a particular flaw for my concerns, specify when the ties become the bases of persistent political groups. The point is not to account for the sale of a judgeship, however frequent, but to show when the arrangement is part of an ongoing structural tie and to specify the consequences of such groups. The focus is on Wolfinger's "political machine," defined as "an organization that practices machine politics, that is, attracts and directs its members by means of these incentives."[13] Although machine politics may be found everywhere, political machines are not. Thus, if this literature allows some of the consequences of political machines to be outlined it does not specify when and where political machines will form and prosper.

This form of political group, however, has been the subject of many studies. Although the literature shares areas of theoretical convergence, the different sources are reflected in the diverse terms used to signal its presence. Machines and political machines join with personalist factions, factions of interest and affection, factions of convenience, and limited factions, as well as patron-client ties, political clienteles, and clientelist factions, to signal with varying degrees of consistency a concept that connotes a political group tied by the exchange of particularistic rewards and personal loyalty. To use the hypotheses of the various sources, I will first show that they deal with the same political group by passing through two thickets. Some of the relevant literature is not familiar to students of political competition. The term political clientele and its associated hypotheses are not typically used in much of political science. It must be carefully defined to avoid confusion. In addition, very little of the literature, whatever its source, deals with political clienteles within the political elite. Much of it focuses on the ties between political activists and those outside the spheres of politics. For both reasons, I will sort through the various strands to clarify the concept's meaning and theoretical importance.

Clientelism (and its related terms, patron-client ties and dyadic alliances) is used to refer to the social grouping of markedly unequal individuals (called patrons and clients) in "personalized reciprocal relationships."[14] The tie is based on personal loyalty, obligation, and the exchange of unequal goods and services. In Carl Landé's words:

> The distinguishing feature of archetypal patron-client relationships is a broad but imprecise spectrum of mutual obligations consistent with the belief that the patron should display an almost parental concern for and responsiveness to the needs of his client, and that the latter should display almost filial loyalty to his patron. . . .[15]

Eric Wolfe notes that the patron

> provides economic aid and protection against both the legal and illegal exaction of authority. The client, in turn, pays back in more intangible assets. These are, first, demonstrations of esteem. . . . A second contribution by the client to the patron is offered in the form of information on the machinations of others. A third form of offering consists in

the promise of political support. Here the element of power emerges which is otherwise masked by reciprocities for the client not only promises his vote or strong arm in the political process, he also promises—in effect—to entertain no other patron than the one from whom he has received goods and credit.[16]

In one concrete example of the patron-client tie, that of the landlord and "his" peasants, the landlord provides land to farm, the necessary tools, and protection. The client works the land, provides the patron with a portion of the produce as well as esteem and devotion and his body for errands and possible political contests. In another frequently cited example, the patron's position is based not on his ownership of land and the tools to work it, but on his control of access to the society's center and its political and economic resources. While the clients provide roughly similar resources for the patron as in the first case, the patron's mediator-gatekeeper role serves as the basis of his position.[17]

The characteristics of clienteles may be further clarified by describing two closely related social groupings: friendship and asymmetric dependency relationships. Julian Pitt-Rivers comments on the close analytic and empirical links between friendship and clientelism and their importance in parts of Spain:

> It is a commonplace that you can get nothing done in Andalusia save through friendship. It follows then that the more friends a man can claim the greater his sphere of influence; the more influential his friends are the more influence he has. . . . .So while friendship is in the first place a free association of equals, it becomes in a relationship of economic inequality the foundation of the system of patronage. . . . The relationship of the *padrino* and *hombre de confianza* [client] is a kind of lopsided friendship, from which the element of *simpatia* is by no means excluded. . . .[18]

When the aspect of personal dependency and protection is stressed to the exclusion of all others, the patron-client relationship is replaced by a social grouping typified by the Mafia. Eric Hobsbawm discusses the blending of these two forms of social cohesion in Sicily:

> In lawless communities power is rarely scattered among an anarchy of competing units, but clusters round local strongpoints. Its typical form is patronage, its typical holder the private magnate or boss with his body of retainers and dependents and the network of "influence" which surrounds him and causes men to put themselves under his protection.[19]

Closely related to but distinct from both patron-client relations and the Mafia is the system of *caciquismo* in the Spanish countryside.[20] In sum, it is possible to develop a continuum of personalized reciprocal relationships based on the variation of the perceived equality of the partners. At one pole is friendship's free association of equals and at the other extreme the personal dependency of one partner on the other in the Mafia relationship. Located at the mid-point is the patron-client tie. Caciquismo stands between it and the Mafia.

Clientelism was first conceptualized and described by anthropologists. It is not surprising, therefore, that most patron-client ties examined have been in the villages of nonindustrial areas. As it has emerged from the anthropological literature, the study of political clienteles (that is, groups with the structure of clienteles that seek to influence or control a social unit's authoritative decision-making positions) exhibits related strands of research interest. The most common focus is on patron-client ties as they are used in the village politics of small-scale societies. Another cluster of studies reflects the decline in local political isolation and the rise in state intervention by examining the transformation of existing clienteles into groups engaged in extralocal political competition. Of particular importance here is that the basis of the patron role remains tied to the control of traditional resources. Voting with the patron becomes another requirement of clienthood. Examples of this type of political clientele have been most frequently located in societies undergoing extensions of suffrage and the early phases of mass politicization.[21]

A third area is the analysis of political groups with the structural characteristics of clienteles in which the bases of patronage have shifted to control of government resources. By far, the most frequently cited instance is the political machine. As do Wolfinger and many others, Scott points to the crucial role of particularistic, material rewards in the formation and maintenance of the political machines. Scott surveys literature describing the applicability of the machine model to parts of Africa and Asia, as well as to the United States.[22] As with most studies of clienteles, these types have been described with particular regard to the relations between political leaders and their local level bases, especially voting support.

The research overlap between studies of political clienteles and what are sometimes called personalist factions is evident in many areas. Duverger's description of caucus-based political parties peopled and led by local notables (whether the Conservative parties' aristocrats, industrial magnates, and bankers or the tradespeople, lesser industrialists, civil servants, teachers, lawyers, journalists, and writers of the Liberal parties) parallels the examples of traditional patron-client groupings engaged in electoral competition.[23] In addition, Duverger's contention that caucus-based parties were most prominent in Europe at the end of the nineteenth and beginning of the twentieth centuries further dovetails with the location of political machines during the early phases of mass politicization. In a related manner, many authors have found affective, personalist factions in the Indian and Japanese parties.[24] Sartori[25] and Passagli[26] stress the distinction between factions of principle and personalist factions of convenience in Italy though they differ on the causes of the latter. Passigli, in particular, labels the personalist factions clienteles. Studies of political parties in other European democracies have stressed this distinction and have noted the importance of personalist party factions as have numerous studies of the Soviet Union. Linden's analysis of political conflict during Khrushchev's tenure is but one example that takes the *shefstvo* as a primary unit of Soviet political competition.[27] To reiterate, the literature on political machines in the United States belongs on this list.[28]

Efforts to classify these political groups are also present. Duverger's analysis of personal oligarchies within political parties suggests types of factions of convenience within the political elite. Two important classes are distinguished: cliques and teams of leaders. The former are united by a "personal attachment to a dominant chief. . . . This leader's retinue has a monopoly of the positions of leadership and takes on the characteristics of an oligarchy."[29] The team's structure is markedly different:

> The distinctive feature of the team is the comparative equality that rules among its members, the fact that its bonds

develop a horizontally, not vertically. Such teams are formed in very different ways. Sometimes it happens that they are the result of a deliberate compact entered into by a few men, generally belonging to a new generation, who united in order "to shake the fruit tree," to win the positions of control from those in possession, and to monopolize them for their own advantage.[30]

He cites examples of each type as factions in political parties and movements and as machines in American parties.

Clientelist Factions and Political Clienteles: A Synthesis

It is now possible to set out the particular political group to be studied. It is *cohesive* based on the exchange of unequal goods and services and personal loyalty (personalized, reciprocal relationships). More concretely, members exchange jobs, contracts, positions, and personal ties for political support, especially votes. It is a *group*, in that the relationship persists in recognized form for relatively long periods of time. It is *political,* in that it seeks to control authoritative decision-making positions and policies. Thus, I use political group and faction synonymously. Because the group's structure distinguishes it from others within the general class of factions (political groups), it will be called a clientelist faction. At the same time, it may be set apart from patron-client ties and clienteles because it is engaged in political competition. For this reason, it may also be called a political clientele, and I will use clientelist faction and political clientele interchangeably.

The term *political machine* will be reserved for political clienteles that engage in mass elections. Thus, all political clienteles are not political machines, but all political machines are political clienteles. Analytically, a political machine is a class within the genus clientelist faction. Empirically, one link of a political clientele may be a political machine. In addition, much of what are called, by others, personalist factions, or factions of convenience, affection, and interest, are political clienteles. I will reserve the labels *personalist faction* and *faction of affection* for those political groups which cohere for reasons of personal loyalty without the exchange of material favors but, unlike Duverger's *team*, have asymmetric power relations.

The structural features of clientelist factions are characterized by (1) the dominance of the patron or boss—he has a preeminent position in the group's decision-making; others are obsequious to him; he may be arrogant to them; (2) each member is most concerned with his own personal gains, particularly as they pertain to the control of particularistic material goods; (3) patrons (leaders) and clients (followers) are personally loyal to each other—each perceives his own welfare is intimately tied to that of the other; and (4) the group is structured like a pyramid, built upon chains of personal ties.

The hierarchical character of this association sets it apart from other political groups, where "insofar as both leaders and followers are servants of the same cause, some sense of equivalence between them is created."[31] In political associations tied by adherence to a general policy or collective interest, several structural characteristics are to be expected: (1) a relatively greater emphasis on member equality in the internal organization of the faction, the normative claims of faction members, and the actual practices of the group; (2) personal gain is typically associated with the achievement of policy success; and (3) loyalty is less person-specific and more closely related to issue or policy agreement.

In addition, the literature suggests dimensions useful for a preliminary typology of political clienteles:

1. Location—Does the political clientele exist in such formal organizations as political parties, parliaments, government, or private bureaucratic agencies or in the villages of traditional societies? Does it operate at the national or local level of political competition or both? Does it engage in elections or limit its activities to the restricted arenas of elite political competition?

2. Institutionalization

a. Plasticity of structure—Does the clientelist faction have a formal leadership, headquarters and a bureaucratic organization? Does it have periodic meetings?

b. Persistence—Has it the ability to survive numerous political contests? What is the rate of membership flux?

3. Basis of leader-patron position—Does he control traditional resources: land and related occupations and instruments, access to markets and the society's center? Does he control government resources: positions, contracts, and

money? What is the mix of affective solidarity ties and the exchange of material rewards? Does the political clientele survive the lack of access to perquisites or is there bitter internal fighting?

The goal of this study is not to specify types of political clienteles as much as it is to theorize about the entire class. These dimensions will be used here only to categorize the examples in the literature. The political clienteles of anthropologists and political scientists differ primarily in regard to the patron's sources and the location of activities. In the work of the former, patronage is associated with the control of traditional resources, and political clienteles are most frequently studied in village politics and in local level elections. It is rare to find a patron-client chain traced to the national level and examined there. In the political science literature, the patron role is almost always based on the control of government resources. There political clienteles are typically located within formal organizations, particularly political parties.

In the chapters that follow, I will examine political clienteles institutionalized as Italian party factions. They may be distinguished from Key's factions of "friends and neighbors" by their institutionalization and greater dependence on particularistic exchanges.[32] Their relatively greater degree of faction—specific and personal loyalty as well as their institutionalization—sets them apart from the factions noted by Landé.[33] As is also the case in some examples of Duverger's elite cliques and the Russian *shefstvo*, these party factions differ both from traditional political clienteles in the sources of the patron position and from machines on the basis of their primary concern with elite political conflict rather than elections.

Of the two central theoretical issues of this study, the first seeks to account for the presence and persistence of clientelist factions. In pursuit of this problem, the theoretical links between elite and mass political groups must be examined. Changes in mass characteristics, particularly as they pertain to alterations in the economic and social structure, do not provide adequate explanations for the continued presence of clientelist factions. The second central issue seeks to explore the consequences for the patterns of political competition that result from the persistence of clientelist factions as competing political groups. This portion of my argument will rest on a view of elite political groups as having independent causal affects on numerous elements within a political system.

On the Occurrence and Demise of Clientelist Factions: Marx vs. Mosca and Weber

A recurrent theme in the literature associates the spread of mass democratization with the eventual collapse of clientelist factions and associated modes of political behavior. Where they are seen as instruments of court intrigue, these factions, it is argued, will be destroyed with the growth in the political importance of the masses. In this view, the masses are particularly concerned with general issues and the supply of collective goods. Where elections are the means of selecting governing personnel, the populace vote to eliminate the importance of selfish political groups. A more telling argument draws theoretical consequences from the necessarily limited size of political clienteles. Because they can only provide numerically limited items to relatively small proportions of the electorate, it should not be difficult to attract the excluded into political associations claiming to act in the interests of the entire society. When this argument is linked to the spread of industrialization and with it the growth of social class as a fundamental social cleavage, it yields the most common and important analysis of the rise and demise of machine and clientelist politics. It is an argument found in numerous case studies as well as general works, and best presented by Marx and his followers. Simply put, political clienteles emerge with the end of the traditional social order and die with the growth of industrialization and its rational politics of issues, particularly class.

Allum's analysis of Neopolitan politics exemplifies this position. He argues that the political characteristics of Naples are linked to the area's general social patterns which are neither *gemeinschaft* nor *gesellschaft:*

> Our model of political organization in transitional or intermediate social situations is the political boss and/or political machine. The political boss is a political entrepreneur who provides votes on his own account and at his own risk. . . .
> Since they are a mass of individuals who are incapable of organizing themselves, the boss organizes them into a political machine. Moreover, since he cannot count on tradi-

tional political ties to ensure loyalty, he must be in a position to obtain favours and advantages for them. . . .[34]

Allum agrees with Tarrow[35] and Graziano,[36] who explain the presence and persistence of clientelist factions in southern Italy by the area's incomplete industrialization. Because this argument uses the collapse of established social and political roles as explanatory factors, it can be generalized to account for the rise and fall of machines in U.S. cities. Thus, Scott associates machines with "the shaking loose of traditional deference patterns. . . . For the United States, large-scale immigration by basically peasant populations was the occasion for this change. . . . In other areas, the extension of suffrage rights and migration to cities marked this process."[37]

Similarly, but out of a different analytic tradition, Key associates the presence of machines (as well as factions of friends and neighbors) with the issueless politics found in areas of social disorganization and industrial underdevelopment.[38] Common to these arguments is the position that machines flourish where traditional behavior patterns have not yet been replaced by the rise of issues and social divisions that form political cleavages out of them. To cite James Q. Wilson: "The opportunities for machine organization decline as new loyalties to larger collectivities are gradually formed (to social classes, to the city as a whole, or to the race), as acculturation is accomplished, as economic opportunities widen, and as the supply of governmentally controlled incentives that can be awarded on a particularistic, rather than categorical, basis declines."[39]

Although Marx's arguments certainly expect the progress of industrialization to pave the way for class formation, he also analyzes factors that might block the rise of large class groupings:

> The journeymen and the apprentices were organized in each craft as it best suited the interest of the masters. The filial relationship in which they stood to their masters gave the latter a double power—on the one hand because of their influence on the whole life of the journeymen, and on the other because, for the journeymen who worked with the same master, it was a real bond, which held them together against the journeymen of other masters and separated them from these. And finally, the journeymen were bound to the existing order by their simple interest in becoming masters themselves.[40]

Still, his work provides a theoretical basis for these arguments. In *The Eighteenth Brumaire,* Marx sets forth the importance of the mode of economic activity and the strength of communications as determinants of class formation:

> The small peasants form a vast mass, the members of which live in similar conditions, but without entering into manifold relations with one another. Their mode of production isolates them from one another instead of bringing them into mutual intercourse. The isolation is increased by France's bad means of communication and the poverty of the peasants. . . . In this way, the great mass of the French nation is formed by simple addition of homologous magnitudes, much as potatoes in a sack form a sackful of potatoes. . . . In so far as there is merely a local interconnection among these small peasants, and the identity of their interests begets no unity, no national union, and no political organization, they do not form a class.[41]

Crucial to Marx's general analysis is that the "real bonds" of the master-apprentice relationship and the communications problems exemplified by the French peasantry will be replaced as capitalist industrialization overwhelms these stumbling blocks to mass organization. Affective bonds between master and apprentice are destroyed by the production necessities and brutalities of capitalist enterprises. Most important, the growth in size of the industrial working class and the technical feats of capitalism resolve the problems of mass communication. Dahrendorf's work exemplifies a strand of Marxist political theory which presumes that communications gaps no longer inhibit the formation of mass class organization.[42]

Gramsci's study of Italian social and political conditions during the early years of the century returns the focus to a society characterized by clientelist relations and weak class associations. His is the first explicitly Marxist analysis of clientelism. Gramsci centers on the major differences between northern and southern Italy and the role of southern intellectuals and rural bourgeoisie in maintaining the existing patterns:

> The intellectual strata of North and South differ in structure and origin: in the Mezzogiorno the predominant type is still the pettifogging lawyer (*paglietta*), who ensures contact between the peasant masses and the landowners and the State

apparatus. In the North the dominant type is the factory "technician," who acts as a link between the mass of the workers and the management. . . .[43]

In Gramsci's view, the government used the southern intellectuals to reduce the south to a colony of the North. It did so by feeding the intellectuals' particularistic demands at the expense of the general needs of the southern masses. The government, he continues, provided

> personal favours to the "intellectual" stratum of *paglietta* in the form of jobs in the public administration; of licence to pillage the local administration with impunity . . . i.e., incorporation of the most active Southern elements "individually" into the leading personnel of the State, with particular "judicial" and bureaucratic privileges, etc. Thus the social stratum, which could have organized the endemic Southern discontent, instead became an instrument of Northern policy, a kind of auxiliary private police. Southern discontent, for lack of leadership, did not succeed in assuming a normal political form. . . .[44]

This produced poorly differentiated social classes and consequently weak political parties. Gramsci characterizes the parties by their "lack of principle, opportunism, absence of organic continuity, imbalance between tactics and strategy, etc. The principal reason why the parties are like this is to be sought in the deliquescence of the economic classes, in the gelatinous social structure of the country. . . ."[45]

Gramsci's solution to the problem, the active political party which develops, solidifies, and unifies the social classes, points to a fundamental tension in Marxist analysis. Dahrendorf's argument rests on the presumption that the necessary social changes will occur and bring with them mass political organization along class lines.[46] Gramsci, the political activist, calls for the direct participation of the party to organize and direct its class base.[47] Both agree that such changes will overcome existing particularistic arrangements.

The mode of analysis first developed by Marx is especially important because it solves Hume's problem: the omnipresence of factions which destroy the government's ability to act in the general interest. The revolutionary class, because of its universal characteristics, acts not only in its own interests but for the general good of all:

> A class must be formed which has *radical chains,* a class in civil society which is not a class of civil society, a class which is the dissolution of all classes, a sphere of society which has a universal character because its sufferings are universal and which does not claim a *particular redress* because the wrong which is done to it is not a *particular wrong but wrong in general.* There must be formed a sphere of society which claims no *traditional* status but only a human status, a sphere which is not opposed to particular consequences but is totally opposed to the assumptions of the German political system; a sphere, finally, which cannot emancipate itself from all the other spheres of society, without, therefore, emancipating all these other spheres, which is, in short, a *total loss* of humanity and which can only redeem itself by a *total redemption of humanity.* This dissolution of society, as a particular class, is the *proletariat.* [emphasis in original] [48]

Gramsci's analysis places greater emphasis on the revolutionary political party. Still, it echoes this conclusion:

> The modern prince, the myth-prince, cannot be a real person, a concrete individual. It can only be an organism, a complex element of society in which a collective will, which has already been recognized and has to some extent asserted itself in action, begins to take concrete form. History has already provided this organism, and it is the political party— the first cell in which there come together germs of a collective will tending to become universal and total.[49]

In sum, whether explicitly derived from Marx or not, these analyses argue that clientelist arrangements are tied to early stages of industrialization and democratization. Existing as they do in a transitional stage of social and political development, they will be overwhelmed by the onward thrust of modernization.

These arguments contain crucial flaws.

1. Political clienteles have been located in areas where, given these arguments, they should not have been found. Although particular arrangements and ties may change, there is much

evidence that clientelism as a form of political association neither requires social disorganization nor is necessarily replaced with the spread of industrialization. In some instances patron-client ties and social class arrangements exist side by side and individuals choose to utilize one or the other for different purposes. In others, political clienteles persist in the face of other changes.

2. Of equal importance, there are numerous instances in which clientelism has infiltrated the "rational organizations" of industrial society. The many party factions and political machines noted previously are obvious examples of this point, as are the similar groupings within bureaucracies.

Those who do not simply assume the demise of political clienteles offer several explanations for their origins and persistence. One argument maintains the focus on the general characteristics of the society, particularly the supportive cultural norms. Beliefs, it is argued, do not merely reflect the prevailing social and economic relations. They have independent and lasting consequences of their own. Another approach uses political factors that affect the political elite as the key determinants. Clientelist factions are, in this view, associated with the availability of large amounts of the resources that sustain the groups, namely government positions and contracts. In presenting this particular argument, analysts deny the relevance of mass characteristics for competition within the political elite. They also show that the number of government positions open to political control has not declined.

It is useful to exemplify these approaches to the analysis of political clienteles. Which elements within the society and culture are used to account for clientelist factions? In suggesting some explanations for their frequent use in the societies of Southeast Asia, Landé notes:

> One is that peoples of these societies find models of dyadic structures in their cognatic kinship systems, and, therefore are inclined to favor dyadic alliances when they build larger structures with nonkinsmen.[50]

Boissevain observes the reinforcing presence of the structure of the Roman Catholic church in societies with a strong cult of saints as a determinant of clienteles and political clienteles.[51] Similarly, Myron Weiner, in his analysis of Indian political parties, argues that when individuals seek closely knit face-to-face groups, party factions of the clientelist type will be found.[52] Clientelist party factions in Japan are explained by Nakane and Scalapino and Masumi as continuations of the traditional mode of group formation and behavior which are highly resistant to the imported Western organization of political parties.[53]

In an analysis of an Irish political machine, Sacks argues that the most important explanation for its presence is in the general political culture:

> The combination of intense partisanship and the traditional view of government as venal and prone to favoritism has created the impression that friends of the government enjoy preferential access. This sense of access may or may not produce the desired results, such as imaginary patronage. Nevertheless, its existence is a factor of prime importance in understanding the ability of the local Donegal parties to hold their following intact.[54]

In a related argument, Boissevain emphasizes the norms of interpersonal relations. He singles out the tendency to distrust others as a determinant of clientelism:

> It is obvious that many of the conditions which give rise to the need for protection and hence patronage are simply the result of the successful operation of the patronage system. Patronage is to a large extent a self-perpetuating system of belief and action grounded in the society's value system.[55]

Thus, several sources locate the bases of political clienteles in the general value system.

What is the association between the overall political culture and elite political groups? The link may be forged in a number of ways: political activists may share the beliefs and practices of the general society which lead to the formation of patron-client ties and political clienteles. Like their neighbors, those engaged in political competition may be familiar with clientelist arrangements and reproduce them in their political dealings. Thus, where these patterns prevail—such as frequent use of dyadic arrangements or high levels of distrust—clientelist factions will abound within the political elite. In this view, the general characteristics of the society affect the nature of the groups within the political elite. These patterns, however, have independent consequences of their own, without particular regard to level of economic development.

An alternate view shifts the focus to political factors. It contends that clientelist factions may prevail within the political elite, without the presence of patron-client ties or the norms of clientelism in the society at large. Two factors are frequently cited as reasons: (1) relatively large numbers of positions open to control through political competition, and (2) few formal limitations on the frequency of contests for those positions. Linden and Sartori exemplify this argument. Linden associates the presence of clientelist factions in the Soviet Communist party with (1) the absence of defined and regularized methods of resolving problems of authority, control, and decision-making in the party; (2) the "logic of polity," which inclines the leader to seek absolute power over contending groups and which induces them to seek to inhibit or prevent his attempts, and (3) the traditional use of such factions at various levels of the CPSU.[56] Sartori suggests that the mere availability of government positions will foster clientelist factions. He contends that where elections within a party are ruled by proportional representation of all those competing, clientelist factions will be present.[57]

Assuring access to governing resources promotes the presence of political clienteles. If so, there is no reason to expect a decline in political clienteles. Indeed, on the face of it, it is surprising that so many have assumed a decline in government patronage opportunities. The growth in the number and scope of government activity in the economy has certainly increased the availability of contracts and other manifestations of indirect patronage. Schools and hospitals as well as bridges and navies provide opportunities for particularistic arrangements.

Nor can one argue that government positions are fewer and less desirable than in the past. Recent studies in the United States, the purported home of this demise, indicate a growth rather than a decline in the number of positions controlled through patronage arrangements. Pinto-Duschinsky contrasts evidence of declines in the proportion of government positions open to political control with the actual increase in the number of positions. He cites evidence that in 1884, 117,000 of 131,000 federal employees were exempt from merit rules; in 1970, 325,000 of 3,000,000 were exempt.[58] The result is an increase in number, but not in proportion. He writes,

> In summary, several factors have militated against the elimination of political patronage. First, the huge extension of government and the need for policy staffs has meant that the number of patronage jobs has not fallen nearly as fast as the percentage of such jobs. Second, huge numbers of political openings have been established under special categories (minority jobs, 'emergency' jobs, summer jobs). Third, civil-service regulations do not themselves eliminate political influence in jobs officially listed as 'civil service.' This has meant that large reservoirs of job patronage have remained. In addition, there has been a huge extension of pork-barrel and 'indirect patronage'[59]

If government resources provide the key, patronage arrangements do not appear to be on the way to a certain death. There is strong reason to suggest that clientelist factions will be found within the political elite, whether or not the values and behavior of the masses are conducive to clientelism.

Therefore, there is little evidence that factors said to cause a decline in political clienteles have done so. Indeed, these same factors—increase in democratization and economic development associated with the government—may have increased the presence of political clienteles. At the same time, there are those who argue that, by focusing on the general characteristics of a society, analysts have missed the most important determinants. Political factors within the arena of those who contest government positions best explain the presence and strength of clientelist factions.

This conclusion runs counter to the theoretical framework set forth by Marx and used by so many. However, it is in line with analyses of Max Weber and Gaetano Mosca. Stated most generally, both argue for the theoretical utility of separating political activists and the mass electorate and for positing two types of activists: amateurs and professionals. Both predict the increasing importance of professionals, whose desire to make politics their permanent source of income makes them especially prone to clientelist arrangements. Both also associate the rise of professionals with growth in industrialization and democratization.

Arguing directly counter to Marx, Mosca associates the rise of mass democracy not with the eventual demise of those who control government positions to further personal goals, but with an increase in their number and importance. In Mosca's analysis, universal suffrage fundamentally conditions the requirements for entering the ruling class. Most important, it makes it possible for those and only those skilled in electoral competition to control all governing positions:

> The truth is that the representative *has himself elected* by the voters, and, if that phrase seems too inflexible and too harsh to fit some cases, we might qualify it by saying that *his friends have him elected.* [60]

The control of government through elections requires appeals to the "common herd" and maintaining of followings through the use of particularistic ties. From this Mosca draws three crucial consequences: (1) many of the most qualified will be unwilling to debase themselves in electoral conflicts; (2) only those skilled in political intrigue and able to support their followings will be able to control governing positions; and (3) governments will be characterized by (a) the predominance of a single political force, (b) the absence of decisions in the general interest, and (c) the presence of constant interference in government by particularistic interests.[61] As a result, and particularly in Marxist regimes, to cite Weber, revolutionaries become "spoilsmen."[62]

Drawn together, the sources provide factors conducive to the formation and presence of clientelist factions: the general norms and behavior patterns of clientelism, and the formal rules and prizes in contests to control government positions. Thus, where many are in patron-client ties and the associated norms are widespread, clientelist factions will be found within the political elite and as links between the masses and political elite. Where these norms are found within the political elite or when the structure of political competition is conducive to their presence or both, clientelist factions will be found within the political elite, whether or not among the masses. These and other hypotheses accounting for the presence and persistence of clientelist factions may be set out in a formal argument.

> 1. Where there are large amounts of government resources available to control through political competition and few limits on those contests, political clienteles will be present.

2. Where the structure of political competition is less conducive—that is, where these factors are missing—clientelist factions will be found where patron-client ties and their associated norms abound in a society.[63]

3. Where there are both conducive political and social factors, political clienteles will pervade the political elite.

4. One or more of the following will lead to the presence of patron-client ties in a society: (a) highly valued and frequently found primary groups with dyadic structures; (b) pervasive norms of interpersonal distrust and the traditional use of clienteles as a social bond; or (c) fears of economic survival in areas of poverty.

In other words, in a society without patron-client ties, one should expect to find clientelist factions only where the particular political factors make for their presence. Where patron-client ties abound, clientelist factions will survive, even if it is difficult to control the relatively few government resources. Where there are patron-client ties and easy access to government patronage, political clienteles will pervade the political elite.

On the Consequences of Political Clienteles: Competition, Policy, and Regime Survival

A coordinate goal of my study is to specify the consequences for the structure of political competion, for the content of policies and how they are made, and for the persistence of the given regime of the predominance of political clienteles. Not surprisingly, those who assume the necessary demise of clientelist factions provide little help. However, Mosca and arguments taken from economic modes of analysis provide guidance. Both posit that clientelist factions will distort government policies to benefit their own particularistic ends. To cite Mosca:

> Discussion of governmental acts in our parliament and the control that representatives should exercise over governmental acts almost always go astray under the pressure of personal ambitions and party interests. . . . The natural desire to govern well is continuously thwarted by the no less natural desire to serve their own personal interests.[64]

Mosca adds a dynamic quality to this hypothesis. With no interference from outside forces, political clienteles will expand to drive out all other political groups. At the close of the first volume of the *Elementi,* Mosca asks what would happen if the situation were to persist. He answers that the mode of personalist rule would spiral, bring in more of these groups, isolate the ruling class, and bring about its downfall:

> The scions of today's celebrities in parliament, bank, and governmental positions would in fact attain with increasing ease the posts that are now occupied by their fathers, and a little world apart would come into being, a clique of influential families, into which it would be hard for newcomers to make their way. . . . But the contradiction between the spirit of institutions and the men who would be called upon to represent them would become more and more conspicuous, and the oligarchy, which would be governing in the name of the people and would never be able wholly to eschew the intrigues and hypocrisies that are inevitable in any parliamentary government, would drift farther and farther away from the sentiments of the people.[65]

Mosca specifies three results of the rule of selfish, personalist factions: the inability to govern in the general interest; laws and policies which benefit a specific subset of the population; growth in the control of governing positions by these factions. Taken together, these factors make it increasingly difficult for those without the skills of political intrigue but with the proper technical knowledge to control decision-making positions. As a result, entry into the ruling class, that is, the control of governing positions, is monopolized by the same individuals, who are increasingly cut off from the rest of society. The final product is a revolution led by those who had been barred from the ruling class, fostered by the loss of the will to govern by the old political elite.

In the following chapters, I describe conditions of contemporary Italy which closely resemble Mosca's predictions: the predominance of clientelist factions; rule in their own interest and at the expense of other and more general interests; and their effective near-monopoly over the control of governing positions.

Mosca and Weber also present arguments dealing with the consequences of the presence of clientelist factions for the survival of political regimes. Arguing for the growing predominance of professional politicians, Weber sets out a future of democratic rule characterized by either the predominance of machine-based Caesaristic leaders or the leaderless rule of party bureaucrats:

> However, there is only the choice between leadership democracy with a "machine" and leaderless democracy, namely, the rule of professional politicians, without a calling. . . .[66]

Weber's analysis, based on the specific example of Gladstone's usurpation of Joseph Chamberlain's electoral machine is flawed. Almost all recent studies deny the empirical association of machines and demagogic leaders. Rather, machine-based groups are also associated with Weber's "leaderless democracy."

As noted above, Mosca argues that political clienteles will perpetuate their own rule and will occupy governing positions. This in turn would lead to a situation in which the rulers are estranged from the ruled and, given Mosca's earlier analyses, to the conditions for revolution. The logic of democratic rule, which fosters the predominance of those who further their personal interests at the expense of the collective interests, will lead to their increasing control of the governing positions and with that to revolution.

Mosca's arguments are especially significant because they counter Gramsci's descriptions of Italian politics as well as Marx's analysis of the dynamic of democratic politics. In chapter 3, I will elaborate on Mosca's depiction of Italian social and political conditions at the turn of the last century. Here, I will conclude by specifying Mosca's critique of Marx's answer to Hume's problem. Not only will the party be reduced to the interests of its leaders, but so will the state that is controlled by the party. The communist system will not produce a society where "the strong, who will always be on top, will be less overbearing"; where "the weak, who will always be on the bottom will be less overborne."[67] "Communist and collectivist societies would beyond any doubt be managed by officials. Let us assume . . . they would be elected exclusively by universal suffrage . . . [But] we know that the selection of candidates is itself almost always the work of organized minorities who specialize by taste or vocation in politics and electioneering, or else the work of caucuses and committees whose interests are often at variance with the interests of the majority."[68]

> All the lying, all the baseness, all the violence, all the fraud
> that we see in political life at the present are used in intrigues
> to win votes, in order to get ahead in public office or simply
> in order to make money fast by unscrupulous means. Under a
> collectivist system everything of that sort would be aimed at
> controlling the administration of the collective enterprise.
> There would be one goal for the greedy, the shrewd and the
> violent. . . . Under collectivism, everyone will have to
> kowtow to the men in government. They alone can dispense
> favor, bread, the joy or sorrow of life.[69]

Marx's analysis and hopes to the contrary notwithstanding,
argues Mosca, it is not possible to establish a form of rule that
governs in the collective interest. Particularistic distortions always
prevail. *"No social organization can be based exclusively upon the
sentiment of justice,* and no social organization will ever fail to
leave much to be desired from the standpoint of absolute justice."
[emphasis in original][70]

In all, Mosca's work, added to the implications of economic
analysis, produces many hypotheses dealing with the behavior of
clientelist factions in political competition, policy-making and
their consequences for the persistence of regimes. In the following
chapters, I will show how these and other logically related arguments describe and explain the politics of a clientelist-ridden
regime. The hypotheses to which I will pay particular attention
may be set out formally.

Given the importance of personal loyalty and particularistic
exchanges for the cohesion of political clienteles:

> 1. Political clienteles will act so as to further the political
> career of the leader.
> 2. Political clienteles will act so as to control governing
> positions.
> 3. They will rarely act so as to obtain "collective goods,"
> of value to those who are not members of the group.
> 3a. Those "rare instances" will be occasioned by per-
> ceptions of danger to the faction's survival.

Hypotheses relating to the characteristics of competitive
systems where clientelist factions abound may be suggested:

> 4. Political clienteles are more likely than categoric

factions to succeed in controlling governing positions. The former are less bound by issue preferences. They are less encumbered in choosing political allies.

5. When in competition with political clienteles, categoric factions will adopt the competitive goals of the political clienteles. This follows from the third and fourth propositions. To influence policies, they will find it necessary to occupy governing positions.

6. When in mass elections, clientelist factions will cover their particularistic concerns with universalist claims. Sartori's distinction between visible and invisible politics is crucial here.[71] What they say in public is no guide to the political clienteles' goals.

7. Political clienteles are more likely to coalesce with other political clienteles than with categoric factions. The latter are always a threat to inhibit the particularistic game.

8. Alliances among clientelist factions will be unstable. Each will always be willing to upset the arrangement to improve its own position.

What are the consequences for policies when political clienteles predominate within a regime?

9. Clientelist factions will use their control of governing positions to produce other such posts. The size of the public bureaucracy and those resources controlled by the government will increase markedly. Appointment to those posts will be on political grounds.

10. Most laws and bureaucratic ordinances will aim to provide particularistic benefits to the supporters of the political clienteles. Few laws will seek to restructure the economy or polity. Few will be part of policy packages.

The sources provide some implications for the long-term stability of regimes controlled by political clienteles.

11. Given the unstable governing alliances and the absence of policies dealing with collective issues, the government will be unable to handle societywide problems. This inability, coupled with the alienation of those in the society not part of clientelist factions, will lead to a polity liable to government collapse and revolution. Mosca makes this point quite explicitly.

Each of these hypotheses may be applied to a particular element of a regime: the competition for votes in general elections as well as in forming cabinet coalitions; the structuring of the bureaucracy as well as the content of policies; and the prospects of regime survival. They can, for that matter, be used to analyze the internal structure of a political party as well.

In later chapters, I will specify these hypotheses and show their utility in the analysis of Italian politics. The Christian Democratic party and the regime it has dominated for thirty years abound in clientelist factions. They exist at all levels of the Italian polity. There are political machines and political clienteles that derive from traditional patron-client ties. There are party factions that tie parliamentary deputies to each other to prime ministers and other cabinet officers and to members and heads of the governmental and quasi-governmental bureaucracies and back to local party activists and voters. The pervasive presence of clientelist factions makes Italy particularly suited for the exploration of the hypotheses.

Throughout this chapter, I have juxtaposed Marx's and Mosca's analyses of political competition. Marx's work exemplifies the dominant stream in political sociology. It is a view that attributes primary determinant power to the characteristics of the masses. The central theoretical questions within this framework relate to the patterns of internal division and organization of the masses. With regard to revolution, Marx's "problem," they structure all other phenomena. For Marx, when the proletariat—the revolutionary class of capitalist society—is properly aware and organized, it will overthrow the rule of particularistic personal and class interests and govern in the interests of all. Mosca's analysis not only predicts the ubiquity of personalist distortions of the mode and content of governing but derives that argument from a set of theoretical assumptions counter to that of Marx. The characteristics of the political elite are independent of those of the masses and the activities of the political elite structure those of the masses. My analysis utilizes Mosca's assumptions to show the explanatory utility of his and related hypotheses.

3. Changing Patron-Client Relations in Italy

A recurrent theme in the analysis of Italian social structure is the location of clientelism as a mode of social division and cohesion. In the pre-Republican south, patron-client ties were frequently found; their structural characteristics corresponded to highly valued social institutions such as the church, family, and god-parent relations; they were fostered by complementary cultural norms; and they "infused" the political system.

Scholarly agreement on the presence of clientelism in areas of premodern Italy is matched by disagreement over its fate with the advent of modernization and industrial development first in the north and more recently in the south. Two positions may be contrasted.[1] One response argues that there is an inverse relationship between the incidence of social class formation and clienteles. With the growth of industrialization and bureaucratization, the spread of mass education, and the concomitant changes in cultural norms, social class replaces patron-client ties as the most frequent and highest valued mode of social division and cohesion. In this view, one would expect patron-client ties to be absent in the more industrialized north and to be on the decline in the less developed south.

The opposing view concedes that increases in the level of industrial development and state activity will affect the rise of class-based movements, but it denies that a necessary result is the destruction of patronage as a mode of social grouping. Four outcomes are seen as likely: (1) the spread of patron-client groups into new organizations; (2) changes in the bases of the patron and client positions, from land-related activities to new sources; (3) increases in the functional specificity of particular patron-client arrangements; and (4) individuals using clientelist and class ties. Perhaps the first argument in support of this view was set forth by Pasquale Turiello nearly a century ago:

> It is easier to predict that with the process of time the local clientelistic system (a structure which alone can progress as a result of such institutions in the midst of individual and private interests) will spread from the South to the North,

rather than a collective and objective consciousness to the Southern elective administration.[2]

"Classic" Southern Clientelism

Analysts generally agree that at least until recently southern Italy could be classified a "clientelist" society. The ties of patrons and clients linked persons to one another and, through the church, to God. Outside the family, no other social bonds were perceived as so crucial to existence. To have a patron was to have control over the requirements of economic, and at times physical, survival. To have clients was to assure standing in the community and control over others. Not only were other bases of social division and cohesion unimportant, but they were generally absent. Certainly, religious and ethnic cleavages did not exist. Class distinctions, though pervasive, did not form the bases of collective action. To the contrary, patron-client ties cut across class lines, pitting those in the same strata against one another.

In the southern reaches of pre-Republican Italy, the position of patron was typically associated with that of landowner or "mediator-broker."[3] Landowners provided their clients with land to farm through rental or share cropping arrangements, monetary advances when needed, and tools to work the soil. Where patrons mediated between the local community and the outside world, they controlled access to distant markets and the flow of information to and from Naples and Rome, the society's centers. Clients were typically peasants, a term which covers numerous modes of agricultural toil: small independent proprietors, sharecroppers, tenant-farmers and day laborers. The dependency of the client on the patron varied with each type and was most complete in the case of day laborers, where the patron controlled not simply land for farming but a job where no other means of employment existed. For their part, the clients set aside fixed portions of their produce for the patron and provided services by working the land.

The patron-client ties contained noneconomic elements as well. The patron granted physical protection from marauding robber bands, conspiring neighbors, and a bothersome government, as well as favors to advance the client's personal and family interests.[4] The client repaid with expressions of deference and deeds to protect the patron's good name. He also reported on the patron's enemies and, on occasion, performed illegal acts to advance the patron's fortunes.[5]

The presence of clienteles did not reflect a particular form of land tenure. Contrary to popular assumptions, patterns of land-ownership varied greatly.[6] While in some areas, large estates—*latifondi*—predominated to the general exclusion of other forms of proprietorship, in other sectors, small holdings and sharecropping arrangements prevailed. This last form was typically that of scattered small strips of land rented from different landlords. John MacDonald argues that large estates were most common in Apulia and most of Sicily, and privately owned plots typified the rest of the south as well as sections of Sicily.[7] In all these areas, patron-client relations were the common, and at times the only, mode of extrafamily social grouping.

Similarly, patron-client ties prevailed although social class structure varied. In some areas, the class system was disjunctive. There were three classes—nobility or *signori* (who were typically land-owners), artisans, and peasants—with clear lines of divisions between them. Class endogamy was the rule. Interactions between different strata were rare, with much deference shown to those in the upper layer.[8] In areas with more limited property distinctions, in which most owned some property and in which social mobility was relatively fluid, perceptions of class divisions were less crystallized. As John and Leatrice MacDonald comment: "Certainly one cannot talk about class structure in the deep south except as an unorganized system of vertical ranking, for the main extra-familial relationship was patron-client arrangements cutting across social strata."[9] Again, whatever the form of class structure, clienteles were the primary form of social grouping.

Thus, while patron-client ties were found all over the south and always contained the affective ties of personal loyalty, of major importance were the differences in the bases of the patron and client positions, the material elements of the exchange, and the surrounding economic and social structure. These resulted in different types of clientelism across the region and within each locality as well. In some towns, all patrons were landlords; in others all were mediators; in others, patrons were both; and in still other towns, different kinds of patrons competed with each other. It was not uncommon for the local landlords, government officials, and priest to serve as patrons. That most clients were peasants is clearly related to the condition that most working adults were engaged in agricultural pursuits.

Perhaps the most graphic description of the dependency of the

day laborers or clients on their patrons is Danilo Dolci's depiction
of the recent plight of such workers in Sicily:

> There are at least twenty-five hundred of us in Corleone,
> which is the biggest village in these parts. According to
> custom, we all gather around the lamppost at four every
> morning; it's the market for flesh and blood. There we stand
> waiting, all us men that are for sale, waiting for the half-
> dozen land owners to come by and pick out the four or five
> that each of them wants to hire. . . .

Not only is the daily salary driven down by the competition by
so many for so few positions, but the manner in which the salary
is paid enhances the servile position of the worker. Dolci's respondent goes on, "Sunday is payday. The laborer goes to the owner's
house to get his wages, and quite likely he's gone around to his
club. But he may be home. 'Is Don Turiddu in?' the laborer asks
the servant that opens the door. 'I'll go and see,' she says, and
leaves him standing there. 'There's someone to see you, Don
Turiddu.' she says. 'Who is it?' says the master. 'A laborer, Don
Turiddu,' 'Ask him what his name is,' the master orders. Well, the
servant goes and comes back, and probably the master'll say: 'Oh,
him! Tell him I'm out!' Oftentimes an owner will keep a man
hanging around a whole day. . . ."[10]

In such circumstances, it is not surprising that personalist attitudes toward authority prevail. The members of society seek to
approach those with authority over them on an individual and
affective basis. Those who are able to enter into a regularized
social relationship such as that of the patron-client are indeed
rather fortunate. In this context, individuals when acting politically will not join together with their social peers but will seek to
contact their superordinate directly.

Although most analyses of clientelism stress the person-to-
person nature of the bond, in the Italian south the arrangement
has commonly extended to include family members. The centrality of family ties is a recurrent theme in studies of Italian social
life and it is not surprising, therefore, to find the ties of family
overlapping with those of the clienteles. Banfield uses the "amoral
familism" concept to explain the absence of cooperative activity
in the village of Montegrano in Potenza province: "The hypothesis
is that the Montegranesi act as if they were following this rule:

Maximize the material, short-run advantage of the nuclear family, assume that all others will do likewise." [11] Maraspini places the family at the foundation of the entire social structure: "The family forms not only the basis of the village's social structure; but it acts also as a model or pattern for other important social relationships. . . ." [12]

The most important of the quasi-familial relationships has been that of godparent to godchild: "The godfather [*padrino*] is responsible for the moral and material welfare of his ward, while the latter owes his godfather the same filial affection, respect, and obedience he owes his father." [13] In return for the financial assistance tendered by the padrino, he is granted honor and prestige. The tie, however, is not solely between godfather and godchild but also between the padrino and the parents of the child. "This relationship between the godfather and the child's parents is expressed in the reciprocal terms 'compare,' 'comare.' The relationship involves mutual obligations of friendship, cooperation and assistance." [14]

Given the characteristics of the godparent relationship, it is not surprising that frequently the choice of patron and the godfather for a child overlapped. John and Leatrice MacDonald contend, "Nuclear family households on all the social strata entered into external relations on the basis of short dyadic contracts. A common arrangement was to fuse godparenthood with a patron-client relationship." [15] Thus, if a patronage tie has been a means of stabilizing an essentially economic arrangement, the addition of the ritual and religious formalization of the godparent relationship has further cemented the bond.

The importance of the patron-client tie is further highlighted by the intense and constant personal competition among those who have shared economic and social positions. Examples of this conflict are numerous, and while scholars disagree whether the cause is to be found in the cultural norms or conditions of life, it is an important reason for the absence of intravillage and intraclass cooperation. Lopreato quotes a Calabrian peasant:

> Italy is a stinking place. We are all like cats and dogs, constantly at each other's throats. I don't know why, but you can't even trust the Lord God himself. If you don't look after your own things twenty-four hours a day, people will

spit on you, steal everything you have, and then will say that you did it to them.[16]

Lopreato locates the basis of this view in the precariousness of the peasant economy, the struggle for survival. He writes that the peasant "is constantly on guard against possible impingements on his meager share of the local 'economic pie.' At the same time, he is maneuvering against all but his own dependents to enlarge his share, so as to achieve a higher degree of comfort and security. These views are used to explain such widely diffused maxims in southern Italy as: 'Do not trust even your brother,' 'Friends with all, loyal to no one,' 'Even your best friend is a traitor.' "[17] These and similar attitudes toward conflict and cooperation are reflected in the local folklore and popular games of leisure.[18]

Though, at times there are incidences of cooperative action and perceptions of shared tragedy, they are rarely translated into sustained behavior patterns. Carlo Levi, in his classic *Christ Stopped at Eboli,* describes village life in the mountains of Lucania during the Fascist period: "This passive brotherliness, this sympathy in the original sense of the word, as suffering together, this fatalistic comradely age-old patience, is the deepest feeling the peasants have in common, a bond made by nature rather than religion. They do not and cannot have what is called political awareness. . . ."[19]

The competition between patrons was equally incessant and invidious: "The truth is that the internecine was among the gentry is the same in every village of Lucania. The upper classes have not the means to live with decorum and self-respect."[20] After describing the "poor quality" of the *signori,* Levi concludes, "It is, therefore, a matter of life and death to have the rule in their own hands, to hoist themselves or their relatives and friends into top jobs. This is the root of the endless struggle to obtain power and to keep it from others, a struggle which the narrowness of the surroundings, enforced idleness, and a mixture of personal and political motives render continuous and savage."[21]

Boissevain depicts the world view of members of this society as it still exists in Sicily:

> To an extent, then, every Sicilian feels himself to be isolated in a lawless and hostile world. . . . Not only is he surrounded by enemies and potential enemies, he is also subject to the

authority of an impersonal government whose affairs are administered by bureaucrats, each of whom is trying to derive some personal advantage from his official position or is liable to be maneuvered against him by his enemies. . . . Most resolve these problems by seeking out strategically placed protectors and friends, who, together with kinsmen, make up the personal network of contacts through whom the average Sicilian attempts to protect and advance the fortunes of his family.[22]

Political Clientelism in Its Classic Form

Southern Italy has long been the home of *clientelismo.* There, too, personal fears, cultural expectations, religious, family, and godparent bonds have fostered this form of group. It is not surprising, therefore, to find political clienteles dominating political competition. The work on the pre-Fascist political system by Mosca and Pareto underscores the centrality of patrons and political clienteles at the national and local levels and as the links between the two arenas of government. Two types of political clienteles are located: the local form, in which the bases of patronage are tied to traditional economic resources, and the national political clienteles, in which the patron position rests on the control of government resources.

Between 1876 and 1922, there were thirty-two cabinet changes with an average lifespan for each of eighteen months.[23] The mode of cabinet turnover gave rise to its own descriptive label, *trasformismo,* defined most broadly as the unprincipled change of political allegiance. Its appeal was characterized by Agostino Depretis, transformism's first master. "If anyone wishes to *transform* himself and become progressive by accepting my very modest program, how can I refuse him?"[emphasis in original][24] The chameleonlike character of parliamentary voting was illustrated by Pareto. In the cabinet crises of 1891, the formation of the Crispi government and its replacement after two months by di Rudini's ministry, only 23 of 508 deputies voted consistently for Crispi and against di Rudini, and all but one of Crispi's cabinet voted for the new cabinet.[25]

According to both Mosca and Pareto, the process of cabinet formation, persistence, and collapse was characterized by the structured interaction of candidate-ministers, deputies, and *grandi elettori* (powerful local notables). The task of the prime minister in forming the cabinet was to attract a parliamentary majority by juggling and harmonizing hundreds of different passions, needs, and ambitions: "He must know what each values and desires and appear to give to each what he wants."[26]

The choice of cabinet members reflected the prime minister's need to form and maintain the government in office. Mosca notes that he needed men of consequence in the Chamber who were not unknown in the country and, for some portfolios, had the requisite technical skills. "But these are but a minimal part of the difficulties to be overcome in the choice of partners; for they must also be parliamentary veterans, leaders of parliamentary groups, controlling a contingent of devoted friends who will support the cabinet."[27] The prime minister also had to harmonize their clashing personal rivalries, so that "they are temporarily united by the bonds of the most real and solid interests,"[28] even though they did not share common principles.

The cabinet formed by the tactical alliances of deputies rested on the exchange of material rewards and favors. One consequence was that policies were made with an eye to benefiting the participants—the deputies and especially the grand electors. Another result was the insecurity of parliamentary leaders. Pareto comments, "Now the politician from whom the greatest advantages can be expected attracts the greatest number of deputies, who abandon him without scruple for any other leaders who seem better able to serve their interests; and sometimes they abandon him from mere love of change."[29]

While the success of a minister required meeting the demands of his deputies, in turn the deputies depended on the political support of those who dominated their home districts. As Mosca seeks to demonstrate, the deputies represented not the will of the majority but of an organized minority—particularly the prefect, the grand electors, and local political clubs. The prefect was the chief representative of the national government in the province and controlled the votes of the civil servants and their personal and professional dependents. Frequently, the prefect had so much influence that he could partially redress the power asymmetry between the minister and the deputies: "Where the deputies, given their power to create the minister, always reserve for themselves the right to change him at will, the minister, reacting, creates when and where possible, a number of deputies, who naturally are always interested in sustaining him and protecting his position."[30]

In the electoral contests the grandi elettori were most important. As Mosca describes them:

> The grand electors are those persons who because of their social positions have many dependents, whose votes they can command by mere request. There was a time when many could have been grand electors but were not, and did not interfere with elections. Now, however, since the advantages of having a friend as a deputy are increasingly great and obvious, they, who control a certain number of votes, act so as to insure their particular influence.[31]

The grand elector was the invisible bond and "true irresponsible power of the parliamentary system."[32] His power lay in that many were beholden to him and he was dependent on none. "Above him is the deputy, who is, however, dependent on the grand elector, and above the deputy is the minister who is accountable to the deputy: the grand elector must render account to no one, because the simple voter, whose vote he controls, because of the voter's economic, social and intellectual conditions, is entirely at his mercy."[33]

Who were the grand electors? According to Mosca:

> In the countryside where their power is most extensive, the grand electors are the large landowners and lease-holders. There, especially in southern Italy, where the land is still relatively undivided, frequently a single man or family controls hundreds of votes, and usually has them organized into agricultural or mutual-help societies. In the large cities the grand electors are frequently the lawyers and physicians who have many clients, and capitalists, and in general all those wealthy persons who because of their activities and professions acquire many relationships and a good number of clients and favor-seekers.[34]

The political clubs, which were mainly found in the larger cities, were composed of workers and those without the personal power of the grand electors. Though they apparently organized for non-personal reasons, they too were characterized by the clash of personal desires.[35]

The intense personal competition at the local level is best explored by Mosca's examination of the social and political conditions in his native Sicily:

> The dream of every family of the rural gentry is that one or more of their sons can obtain a university degree, establish himself in a large city, and become a reknowned member of the professional class, a lawyer, physician, or even high government functionary. He who is able in part or whole to live up to these ideals is considered to have succeeded and acquires much prestige and authority among the villagers, who frequently seek to crown his success by sending him to Montecitorio.[36]

Victory in this difficult contest required constant effort not only by the candidate but by those closest to him. Mosca adds, "And in the family, all, men and women, fathers, mothers, brothers and sisters, undergo any privation, in order to push forward the one among them who demonstrates the best characteristics and who when he reaches his position almost always devotes all the opportunities it provides him to advance his brothers and relatives."[37]

This political "demoralization" was not found only in the small towns and cities of the Sicilian interior, but in many other places as well. The difference, Mosca feels, was that it was perhaps "less rare" in Sicily and had therefore developed its own vocabulary in the local dialect. *U currivu* ("competition." in Sicilian) is "the desire to win at all costs, above all so as not to show oneself as less powerful and cunning than one's opponent and sacrificing to that end any other consideration, to begin from one's own personal interests."[38]

The result, argues Mosca, is a mode of government in which everyone from the ministers to the voters sought to push his own private interests without consideration for public concerns. "In order to advance and sustain themselves, all must favor their allies and friends to the detriment of good government, of conscience and justice."[39] The cause was not individual malice or evil as much as the structure of government, and there was no room for the individual unwilling to play the game. To cite Pareto, "He is an outlaw, a man whom everyone can attack. If a lawyer, he has no clients; if an engineer, nobody employs him; if a merchant or tradesman, he is ruined; if a land owner, he is exposed to petty annoyances from prefects and syndics."[40] To return to Mosca: "In many branches of government agencies, it is no longer possible to operate through honest and legal means, it is necessary to act as a *camorrista* [Mafioso] if one is not to fall to an act of *camorra* [Mafia]."[41]

The control of government positions provided the key to an individual's political advancement. Mosca and Pareto agree that buying votes was neither as bad nor as useful as exchanging political support for patronage positions. Indeed, Mosca negatively contrasts Italian patronage with monetary corruption in Britain under Walpole, where each member of parliament was said to have had a price. In the English case, contends Mosca, "the corruption remains circumscribed to members of the House and their principal acolytes."[42] In Italy, corruption infiltrated the entire nation. Pareto lists numerous examples of both forms of corruption in Italy and concludes that "the support of the government, however, is more effective than money; and the most effective form of government interference is, of course, the appointing and removing of officials."[43]

Were there no limits to this "war of all against all"? One constraining factor was the emergence of dominant leaders who were able to coordinate the political contests. The undisputed master of the game of attracting and holding political support was Giovanni Giolitti, who first entered the cabinet in 1889 as minister of the treasury; between 1900–14, he was the most powerful figure in the Italian parliament while holding various cabinet positions, including prime minister. At the base of Giolitti's power was the use of prefects to control elections and ensure the dependence of the elected deputy on the prefect and through him on Giolitti. The result was a large group of *ministeriali,* deputies always willing to vote to become ministers themselves or to support the cabinet ministers. Giolitti's control through the prefects varied from electoral persuasion to fraud and violence. Salomone, citing a contemporary of Giolitti's, writes, "In the North he depended upon the support of the democratic forces, won over by favoritism of all kinds; in the South he depended upon the local oligarchies."[44] The result was cabinet majorities based on Giolitti's personal followers, who remained tied to him at least in part because of the exchange of past and anticipated favors.

A second limit was contained in the informal rules which inhibited the destruction of political opponents:

> The men who govern the country have almost unlimited power to protect and enrich their friends and to ruin their enemies . . . but they do not often take full advantage of their authority. Apart from exceptional cases (as when the Left came into power in 1876), the men who alternately hold and lose authority respect each other's friends and partisans. This is a consequence of that moderation which is a distinct feature in the Italian character. It is also a policy dictated by intelligent self-interest. The minister of today spares the partisans of his predecessor that his own partisans may afterwards be spared by his successor."[45]

Two analyses written fifty-five years apart summarize the extension of clientelism into an all-pervasive mode of conduct. In 1911, the historian Gaetano Salvemini illustrates the presence and ramifications of southern clientelism:

> Accustomed as he is to magnifying the recommendation as the only means of getting ahead in the schools, courts, banks, local government, Rome, the southern petit bourgeois sees life as nothing but a game of protection, a contest of more or less useful influentials, a prevailing of capricious friendship and animosity. For them there exists no objective scale of moral values. Merit consists in having a powerful protector.[46]

And Paul Stirling describes the nature of the southern patron-client relations as they existed some forty years later in the early years of the Italian republic:

> In the *paese* of southern Italy until the late 1940's the local *borghesia* was in an extremely strong position, partly because of its monopoly of education and contacts with the sources of power and authority, partly because the Fascist regime supported them, and partly because population in relation to resources was so intense that the bottom ranks of society were divided by competition for bread and unable to combine against their rulers. The only path was to become a client, as servile as possible, in the hopes of being rewarded with work or with land to rent. Fear kept people submissive, and in this situation a paternalistic client-patron relationship

flourished in which the rulers and owners had to do very little for their supporters—in striking contrast with many much more primitive societies, where offended followers might rebel, or simply walk out and join another chief.[47]

Joined to the other analyses, these descriptions show a society of want, fear, distrust, and the omnipresence of patron-client ties through the early years of the republic. Social bonds typically associated those of different strata; class membership was rarely perceived, and almost never led to sustained social relationships or collective action. At the same time, those engaged in attempts to influence the governments—from avoiding the tax assessor to controlling cabinet ministries—formed personalist alliances that were modeled on and whose members were drawn from the patron-client arrangements.

Changing Forms of Political Clienteles

How have the massive growth in Italian industry, waves of internal migration, and the general political and economic modernization during the post-World War II era affected clientelismo? Have they affected the presence, importance, and content of patron-client ties? A response to these questions requires examining the clashing positions set out at the start of this chapter. Though crucial to the analysis of contemporary Italian political competition, the changes in Italy may be taken as indicative of developments in other clientelist societies. My answers rest on sets of interrelated studies: analyses of clientelism in the south; an examination of differences and similarities in mass attitudes in the "industrial-modern" north and the "developing" south, as well as evidence drawn from fieldwork conducted in the north and south. There is increasing evidence against the position that as industrialization proceeds, clientelism declines. Rather, the intense personal competition and the particularist use of powerful positions have infiltrated the new social and political organizations.

Stirling's study of social values focuses on the conflict between the impartiality expected and required in the new bureaucratic organizations and the traditional personal morality still found in southern Italy. He argues that most rural communities in southern Italy have been "typically closed" to the world and have consisted of "a society with an intense network of many stranded ties. No one is a complete stranger to anyone else, almost every act toward anyone else takes place within an established network of relations which controls conduct. . . . Thus duties to others are not general duties, but duties to specific people in specific relationships."[48] In such situations, "to refuse a request was to end a friendship."

> If anyone has or thinks he has a lien of any kind on someone in a position to grant him a favor he considers it his natural moral right to use this lien. Persistence of attitudes like this leads to the constant use and importance of the *raccomandazione,* the support of a person with sufficient importance to obtain what is wanted. However, when others use this very same method it is labelled as *imbroglio,* intrigue, or corruption, which in turn is criminal.[49]

As Stirling points out, success is not perceived as a function of the individual's qualifications: "The way to success is by acquiring efficient protectors by *raccomandazione* or *imbroglio.* If one fails it is not oneself, but the system which is to blame for leaving one out."[50]

Observers also agree that although the patron-client tie has changed from a multifaceted arrangement to one tailored to specific tasks, it has not disappeared. Commenting on the changes in Sicilian patronage, Boissevain notes:

> The present-day Sicilian normally has more than one patron, and works through the one he deems most useful in a given situation. But should two patrons come into direct competition, he must choose one to the exclusion of the other. However, as social relations become increasingly specialized, and the Sicilian moves out of relatively isolated community to deal with increasingly diverse decision makers—thus requiring functionally specific patrons—the danger of an encounter between two patrons operating in the same social field diminishes.[51]

Weingrod's argument parallels that of Boissevain and suggests the one I offer. He notes the basic change between the traditional and current forms of clientelism in Sardinia:

> Rather than a single line of authority, there now exist multiple lines of competing systems. As is obvious, these lines focus around the political parties: since state activities are so numerous and of such import, and since the parties are so

closely associated with the state, it follows naturally that the parties have become major lines of contact and communication.[52]

There is also general agreement on the change in the form but not the disappearance of political clienteles. Though traditional notables formerly could translate other resources into political power, influence over government resources—whether through access to the central government's development projects, control of local offices through electoral victories, or both—has increasingly become the primary basis of the patron position. Joseph LaPalombara cites a member of the bureaucracy who "notes that the *Cassa per il Mezzogiorno* [fund for the South] has become a gigantic patronage organization which employs people and awards development contracts strictly on the basis of political consideration."[53] A second source contends that the land reform projects "have become essentially instruments of local patronage. Land is awarded, loans are made, credit is received, fertilizer is distributed, and contracts are awarded on a fairly strict basis of loyalty to the Christian Democratic Party."[54]

Sidney Tarrow details one element of the new southern clientelism that has replaced the old *clientelismo* of the notable and lawyer with the patronage of the mass political party, particularly of the Christian Democrats. Tarrow relates the traditional clientele system to the granting of favors by the patron in return for electoral support. In its place, Tarrow argues, is coming "the judicious manipulation of blocs of votes through the allocation of economic development projects from the state. The old techniques are being linked on a grand scale to government fostered modern economic development."[55]

An essential element in the new clientelism is that the development projects supply large numbers of positions. They have replaced the earlier attempts at mass patronage, the exchange of votes for food and money. In the words of a Christian Democrat (DC) activist:

> I remember the elections of 1958; there were no political beliefs then. The only convictions were the packages of macaroni, sugar, flour, milk, etc. Moral convictions were of no use. The packages arrived and the packages convinced.[56]

As Mosca and Pareto note, money is much less effective a tool of

patronage than positions. The political clienteles in the Italian
south depend more frequently and substantially on the control of
employment opportunities.

> I use all the means at my disposal. . . . I am not engaged in
> the politics of talk. . . . Here we produce only facts . . . be-
> cause he who must favor someone must do so with all his
> ability and sincerity . . . to find him a position, a job . . . and
> these persons are grateful to the party and the politician . . .
> and vote for us.[57]

The clients frequently amount to as many as half the employed.
They not only provide votes for the Christian Democratic party
but also preference votes for particular party leaders.

Perhaps the most striking argument for the persistence of the
competitive norms and practices associated with clientelism and
their location in the north as well as the Italian south may be
found in the impressionistic picture developed by Luigi Barzini.[58]
After describing the wiles necessary for sheer survival, Barzini
details the characteristics and tactics needed for competitive
success. These, he suggests, would certainly lead the practitioner
to important places of power in any other society. "If a man has a
modest ambition and wants to improve his lot, he has no alternative. He knows he must not count merely on his worth and talents;
he must compete in a game without rules; the man who wins is the
best man exclusively in the art of inventing new ways to paralyze
and destroy his opponents. . . . "[59]

Barzini lists two rather "deceptively obvious rules." The first is
to choose the right companions: "In order to succeed a young
man must not only join a large and powerful group but also, once
in, worm his way to the top. In order to reach the top he must
develop an entourage of his own. He must succeed in joining and
then influencing a smaller group of his own."[60]

However, acting alone or with peers does not bring success.
Thus Barzini suggests, "Rule Two (perhaps the most important
rule of all): choose the right protector. All inner cliques are
usually dominated by a few influential men, sometimes by one
leader. . . . Any young man who wants to excel must attach himself to the proper mentor, become his aide-de-camp, and use him
for his own purposes."[61]

These two general rules are then combined with rather specific instructions:

> He must be around as much as possible, to begin with. He must be seen. He must be available. This is one of the reasons why the waiting-rooms of powerful men are always crowded with people offering their services and asking for favours, sometimes merely waiting for hours in order to speak to the leader for a few minutes, walk a few steps with him, offer him a match or a cigarette, hold his coat, do whatever will attract his attention and put them in a favorable light. . . . A few favoured ones follow him in the street, anywhere he goes, or on longer trips when he travels. Such hangers-on are still known as *clienti,* in the south, from the Latin term used to describe them in the old Roman days, *clientes,* people who offer their services and demand aid, protection, and advice.[62]

Such practices, Barzini notes, are quite common in the south. What though of the more industrialized areas? "The practice is not as visible nor as picturesque in the more modern centres. Nevertheless, the great men of business, finance, industry, and science in the north are just as surrounded by *clienti,* though in a discrete way."[63]

The evidence indicating the persistence of southern clientelismo may be complemented—though not with the same scholarly agreement—with support for the case that patronage and its associated cultural norms are present in the Italian north. The north-south dichotomy frequently found in the analysis of Italian political behavior exaggerates the differences between the two areas and the similarities within the north. For many political attitudes and patterns of behavior, these differences do not warrant the view that the north and south are contrasting political cultures.

It is by no means true that developments in northern Italy conform to the characteristics of the ideal type of industrial society and its class relations. The norms of the upper classes, for example, are not those which are predicted by the ideal type of industrial society. Schneider notes, "In Marx's sense they never became true bourgeoisie. . . . Like the intermediaries, their 'vested interests' continued to reside as much in their positions at the peaks of various clienteles as in their relationship to the means of production."[64] Certain attitudes and policies of the northern industrialists parallel those of the southern landowners. La-Palombara comments:

> In popular Italian parlance, both are referred to as *padrone,* and the social distance of the rural, semifeudal South can be quickly and readily transferred to the industrial plants. In many instances management's attitude toward labor is at best condescending; the factory is viewed as personal, inviolable property; trade unionists are considered social upstarts and dangerous revolutionaries; and a rigid discipline over workers is upheld as the sanest and most efficacious means of conducting industrial enterprise.[65]

Field studies in central and northern Italy directly corroborate the view that clientelism is found and is of major importance throughout Italian society. Silverman's study of patronage in a village in the Umbrian hills stresses the importance of the mediator as well as landlord bases of the patron role and the overlap between the patron-client tie and the *mezzadria* mode of agricultural organization.[66] Between the 1860s and 1945, she contends, the patrons were a small group of local signori—twelve landed families to be exact—who controlled the links to the national society. These patrons provided their clients with economic aid, personal favors, legal help, protection, assistance in emergencies, as well as such perquisites associated with the mezzadria relationship as a farm and necessary provisions, fixed capital, half the working capital, technical direction, all capital advances and loans, and a margin of protection during crises. The clients extended, in addition to the legal requirements of the contract, the choice of the produce and housework for their patrons; in addition, they did not cheat the patrons and spoke well of them in public. Here too, notes Silverman, the patron-client tie linked families, not only individuals.

Silverman's picture of patron-client ties in this village evidences no significant differences between the clientelism described in the south. However, her description is limited to the years before the establishment of the republic and the concomitant opening of the village which ended the mediator position. Indeed, Silverman contends that although patronage *was* present, it is no more.[67] Weingrod criticizes Silverman's equation of patron and mediator because it precludes locating clienteles in other than remote vil-lages.[68] The patron as landlord-mediator may be on the decline, but in the north as well as in the south, there is no reason to assume that patronage is not linked to other bases.

Additional similarities of structure in northern clienteles are suggested by comparing Bailey's study of Losa, a village in Pied-mont,[69] and Lopreato's description of Stefanconi, in Catanzaro province.[70] In both cases, the signori are those with wealth, education, personal dignity, and the ability to derive respect and overt acts of deference from the others. Bailey notes three main elements: wealth, particularly when combined with generosity; high levels of education and sophistication; and *autorità,* the right to be treated with respect. Lopreato describes the signori of Stefanconi at the turn of the century: "refined, intelligent, beauti-ful, superior, leisurely, learned. Their wealth, their education, and their newly acquired tastes and customs combined to present a strong stimulus for emulation. . . . Further, the signori behaved so as to deepen the chasm between them and the rest of the people. . . ."[71] Sixty years later, the signori of Stefanconi, though now in two groups, and those of Losa all share the very same characteristics.

Losa's social structure parallels that of southern villages on other dimensions as well. The signori are frequently called on to provide the services of patrons for their *debitori* clients. Bailey cites examples and concludes with a description of clientelism that underlines the similarities between the south and the north:

> In short, a *signore* is someone who has more resources, more skills and more connections than I have and is willing to use them on my behalf. I could not return the favor by doing him a similar service, nor could I pay him in cash; instead I pay him in deference and various small quasi-menial services. This transaction between us is what marks him out as a *signore.*[72]

Finally, and again as in southern villages, a new form of signore-patron, whose positions are linked to the control of resources beyond the confines of the village, has emerged in the last two decades. These new signori do not guard the village against the outside world, but rather control its entry into the national community.

In a final parallel description of southern and northern villages, Wade's analysis of the norms and behavior patterns "Colombaio," a central hill village, reproduces Banfield's classic description of Montegrano:[73]

> Two propositions about resource allocation explain much of the social life in Colombaio:
> (1) The behaviour of those *outside the family* is believed to be motivated by the desire to achieve their own advantage.
> (2) The world is seen as stratified, with responsibilities divided.[74]

The effect of the first proposition, which is openly stated in Colombaio, is to increase distrust and decrease cooperation in extrafamilial relationship. "The second premise defines certain kinds of action as the business of certain categories of people. In particular, it defines 'public action' as the business of high-status people."[75]

As in Montegrano, one upper-class Colombaio man was willing to engage in action for the public good and was castigated for it. As in Montegrano:

> (1) Authority-holders in voluntary organizations are believed to take the positions in order to follow their own advantage, whether in money terms or prestige.
> (2) The running of voluntary organizations is the responsibility of those elected to do so.[76]

No one else is expected to take part.

Wade's Colombaio is not an exact copy of Banfield's Montegrano. A number of voluntary associations in Colombaio compete in the annual festival; its Communist party has an ongoing political organization based on patronage, while the other parties are active during election campaigns; and the government (and the Christian Democrats) are found in the local development agency. However, many of the norms and behavior patterns of Montegrano also occur in this village in the western hills of central Italy. Fieldwork in Italian villages generally depicts strong similarities in local social and political structures. In the north and center as well as the south, the norms and behavior patterns associated with clientelism pervade society. Even their differences may result more from the timing of the relevant studies than from other factors. It is very likely that in the mid-1970s Montegrano and Colombaio were exact copies of each other.

Field studies of villages are only one indication of the wide-spread presence of clienteles. By themselves, they do not provide sufficient evidence. The villages are too easily seen as outposts of a way of life now increasingly uncommon in an ever more industrialized and urban society. Survey responses provide an additional means of indicating the presence of clienteles. Contrary to frequently voiced arguments, the values associated with patron-client ties—distrust of others, highly competitive behavior patterns, personalist norms—and clienteles themselves are present throughout Italy. They do not vary significantly by the areas' levels of industrial growth. Where differences are present, they cluster together individuals in the industrial north and rural south more frequently than they divide them. Finally, particularly in clienteles within formal political activities, there is no clear link between level of social and economic development and the presence of clientelist factions.

The Almond and Verba survey data show that in 1959 Italians generally agreed that it is best not to trust others.[77] Responses varied slightly by region. Eighty-four percent of those in the north, 85 percent of those in the south, and 91 percent of the respondents on the islands contended that "one cannot be too careful" in trusting others, while 65 percent of those in the center agree to that statement. The responses to the proposition that "people will take advantage of you" give evidence of a similar breakdown: 77 percent of the north, 49 percent of those in the center, 73 percent of the southerners, and 90 percent in the islands agreed.

A slightly different breakdown occurred in responses to the statement that "people are generally cooperative by nature." Here the responses given in the north and south were rather similar; those in the center and on the islands were also close: 62 percent of the northerners and 63 percent of the southerners agreed with the statement as did 35 percent of those from the center and 37 percent of the islanders. The regional breakdowns of responses to the statement "no one cares about you" show that 62 percent of the northerners, 49 percent of those in the center, 68 percent of the southerners, and 59 percent of the islanders concurred.

In "general political awareness," the pattern of responses shown in general "interpersonal" attitudes and behavior persists. Almond and Verba sought patterns of political awareness by inquiring about the frequencies and ways individuals occupy themselves with national and local government and political activities as members of organizations and as observers. (see table 3.1).

Table 3.1 portrays both the overall lack of attention to politics and the tendency for southerners to be somewhat more interested in political events. When the claimed ability to understand both national and local issues is compared, once again the residents of the south evidenced a claim for greater comprehension. Twenty-seven percent in the north, 18 percent in the center, 35 percent of the southerners, and 23 percent of those on the islands claimed either to understand "very well" or "moderately well" the issues facing the country as a whole. The ability to understand local issues rose in all four areas, with greater increases in the south and

Table 3.1. Attention Given Government and Political Affairs

	North	Center	South	Islands	Total
Regularly	55 (12%)	11 (6%)	33 (15%)	7 (6%)	106 (11%)
Time-to-Time	118 (25%)	50 (26%)	50 (22%)	34 (31%)	252 (25%)
Never	290 (62%)	122 (64%)	138 (62%)	69 (62%)	619 (62%)
Other	4 (1%)	7 (4%)	2 (1%)	0 (0%)	13 (1%)
Don't Know	2 (1%)	1 (1%)	0 (0%)	0 (0%)	3 (0%)
No Answer	1 (0%)	0 (0%)	0 (0%)	1 (1%)	2 (0%)
Total	470 (100%)	191 (100%)	223 (100%)	111 (100%)	995 (100%)

Source: Gabriel A. Almond and Sidney Verba, "Five Nation Study," made available by Inter-University Consortium for Political Research.
Note: Percentages are rounded.

on the islands. Thus 36 percent in the north, 23 percent in the center, 50 percent in the south, and 50 percent on the islands claimed either a very good or moderately good comprehension of local issues.

Once again, the regional differences in patterns of political action and perceived political effectiveness were rather slight and were not as predicted by the "dual polity" model. In response to the question about the kind of action they would take to change a bad local law, a large majority of all the regions responded with either "Don't Know," "No Answer," or that they would do "Nothing." The regional breakdowns on a bad local law were as follows: 85 percent in the north, 91 percent in the center, 88 percent in the south, and 87 percent on the islands. The number of responses falling in these three categories increased with respect to a bad national law in all areas but the north. There was a general increase in the do-nothing category from the local to the national levels. In the north, responses went from 9 percent to 17 percent; in the center, from 9 percent to 15 percent; in the south from 12 percent to 18 percent; and on the islands, from 15 to 25 percent. On the local level, the only responses which 3 percent or more of the respondents said that they would do were (1) the individual directly contacting political leaders in the north (4 percent), south (4 percent), and on the islands (4 percent); and (2) the individual directly contacting administrators in the north (4 percent), south (3 percent) and on the islands (4 percent); and (3) the use of "informal, unorganized groups" in the north (3 percent). To effect a change in a bad national law the only response to score 3 percent or more was the individual directly contacting political leaders in the south (4 percent).

Attempts to tap the respondents' perceptions of their political effectiveness generally evoked similar responses. Three percent of those in the center—as opposed to 8 percent in the north, 7 percent of the southerners, and 7 percent of the islanders—said that it was "very likely" that they *could* change a bad local regulation. The pattern shifts somewhat in perceived ability to change a bad national law: 3 percent of those in the north and south, in contrast to none of the respondents in the center or islands, said it was "very likely" that they would be successful.

While Italians generally felt unable to change bad laws and rarely attempted to do so, there were some differences in the methods they said would *ideally* be most successful. Table 3.2 presents the regional breakdown on this variable.

The data reveal a tendency for northerners to favor "informal groups," followed by "writing to government officials," "using personal and family contacts," and "working through political parties." Those in the center offered the same four, however, with less emphasis on personal contacts and more on "working through political parties." Southerners and islanders placed an even greater reliance on the use of political parties. They differed in the degree to which they rank "personal and family contacts" and the use of

Table 3.2. Most Effective Method of Influencing the Government

	North	*Center*	*South*	*Islands*	*Total*
None	29 (6%)	10 (5%)	6 (3%)	10 (9%)	55 (6%)
Personal and Family Connections	61 (13%)	15 (8%)	18 (8%)	22 (19%)	116 (12%)
Writing Government Officials	62 (13%)	23 (12%)	38 (17%)	13 (12%)	136 (14%)
Forming a Group	78 (17%)	24 (13%)	23 (10%)	8 (7%)	133 (16%)
Working through a Political Party	53 (11%)	26 (14%)	52 (23%)	30 (27%)	161 (16%)
Protest Demonstrations	37 (8%)	11 (6%)	11 (5%)	4 (4%)	63 (6%)
Other	9 (2%)	3 (2%)	4 (2%)	3 (3%)	19 (2%)
Don't Know	141 (30%)	79 (41%)	71 (32%)	21 (19%)	312 (31%)
Total	470 (100%)	191 (100%)	223 (100%)	111 (100%)	995 (100%)

Source: Gabriel A. Almond and Sidney Verba, "Five Nation Study," made available by Inter-University Consortium for Political Research.
Note: Percentages are rounded.

"informal groups"—southerners favored the former and islanders the latter. It is generally assumed that the "least effective methods" are "organizing of protest demonstrations" and "writing to government officials."

Again, though most Italians generally did not belong to voluntary organizations of any type, the existing differences did not follow the pattern of economic differences. Seventy percent of those interviewed belonged to no such organization at all. However, 35 percent in the south belonged to at least one such association, as did 32 percent of the northerners, 30 percent of the islanders, and 18 percent of those in the center. A similar pattern exists in organizations that deal with "governmental, political, or public" affairs. Of those who claimed membership in such organizations, 9 percent lived in the south, 6 percent in the north, 3 percent in the center, and 3 percent on the islands.

Italians, in general, perceived that the government had little effect on their lives and believed that the effect the government did have was not positive. This, however, was less so in the south. Thirty-six percent of the southerners, 23 percent of the northerners, 14 percent of those in the center, and 7 percent of those on the islands responded that the national government affected their lives. Sixty-one percent of those in the south felt that the national government tended to improve their lives as opposed to 49 percent in the north, 40 percent in the center, and 51 percent of the islanders. Similar answers were given in response to questions about local government and its effects.

In addition, the responses concerning the perceived "fairness" of the bureaucracy in its relations with the individual reveal similar patterns in the north, south, and islands, but responses differed in the center. Thus, for example, 36 percent of the northerners, 45 percent of those in the south and 39 percent of those living on the islands—as opposed to 18 percent of those in the center—stated that a government official would give their views "serious consideration in the handling of a given question." In addition, 33 percent in the center, 57 percent in the north, 57 percent in the south, and 62 percent on the islands agreed that the government would give them "equal treatment."

The data reported by Almond and Verba lend support to neither the conception of a dual polity nor to the proposition that political attitudes and behavior as evidenced by the Italians interviewed may be explained as a function of economic differences. Both northern and southern political attitudes and stated patterns seem to be rather far removed from the politics typically associated with bureaucratic-industrial societies.

Surveys taken by Samuel H. Barnes and Giacomo Sani in 1968 and 1972 also depict northern and southern Italians with many shared political views.[78] The differences found relate primarily to the frequency of use of preference votes. Though nearly half of those born in the north and residing there reported casting preferences votes in the 1968 and 1972 elections, slightly more than 75 percent of those born and living in the south did so in the two elections. In both years, Italians, no matter where they were born or living, generally agreed that politics is too complicated; that the government doesn't worry about them; that it wastes funds; and that workers are disadvantaged. Similarly, most thought there was no need for a divorce law and had no interest in politics. With the same north-south similarities, Italians shared views on the church and the desirability of their country being independent of the United States. These north-south similarities are also found in the answers to questions asked only in 1968 or 1972. The only areas in addition to the use of preference votes to elicit clear north-south differences were that those living in the south in 1968 were more likely to claim to know their representative's name and to know him personally. Furthermore, even these differences must be seen in context. True, a smaller portion of northerners made preference choices than did southerners, still the former did so in substantial numbers. A 1964 survey reported by Allum compares motives for the use of preference votes and does not reinforce notions of major north-south differences:

> "I follow the advice of my party or faction:" north—21%, south—21%.
> "I prefer someone from my political faction (*Corrente*):" north—8%, south—3%.
> "I know the candidate I choose:" north—32%, south—23%.
> "I choose a candidate who has or can be useful to me" or
> "I've been told or heard he was good:" north—39%, south—59%.[79]

In sum, it is not that there are no differences between regions; rather, throughout Italy many use preference votes. That more do so in the southern areas and are openly rewarded with highly visible patronage projects certainly does not indicate the absence of clientelist arrangements in the north. The primary issue, therefore, is not whether there are north-south differences, because they are found on some dimensions but not on others,[80] but that the use of preference votes (along with the survey and field studies) indicates the persistent presence of clientelist arrangements throughout Italy. A more detailed look at election results corroborates the varied use of preference vote by geographical region (and level of industrialization) but also by party and within each party by political as well as socioeconomic determinants.

Table 3.3 reports the use of preference votes by party and geographic area of Italy for the 1958 national elections.[81] It provides the range in the percentage of voters who indicated their preferred candidates on the party lists. In a recent article, Franco Cazzola updates these patterns for three parties—the Christian Democrats (DC), Socialists, and Social Democrats.[82] His data complement the preceding picture and also indicate slight gains in the use of preference votes by DC voters, to almost 40 percent in the 1972 elections, and major gains among Socialist and Social Democrat voters. In 1972, 29 percent of the Socialist voters and 22 percent of the Social Democrat supporters cast preference votes. Like the 1958 election data, the 1968 and 1972 returns for these three parties show a greater tendency for preference votes to be cast in the south and islands than the north and center, and also that more than a fourth of the Christian Democrat electors in the north and center made preference choices compared to more than half the party's voters in the south and islands. Taken together, the data indicate an increase, not a decline, in the use of preference votes—further support for the contention that clientelism has not yet seen its demise in Italy.

The data surveyed in table 3.3 as well as in Cazzola's analysis point to the importance of examining for clientelism not only in the different Italian economic zones but also in the different political parties. Christian Democrat voters are so given to the use of preference votes that their totals in several northern and central election districts outdistance the other parties both in those areas and in the Mezzogiorno. In 1958, DC voters in Perugia and Pisa made preference choices more frequently than did Socialist voters in all but two of the southern election districts and Communist

Table 3.3. Percentage Use of Preference Votes in 1958 Election
(Range by Election District)

	Total Electorate	Christian Democrats	Communists	Socialists	Social Democrats	Republicans	Liberals
North	14-22	14-31	9-20	6-13	8-20	9-19	11-25
Center	16-30	16-38	16-32	8-16	8-16	11-33	14-27
South	35-51	46-60	22-43	21-45	20-33	10-33	30-46
Islands	42-51	51-60	39-51	33-43	24-32	22-32	32-50
Total	30	37	26	17	15	21	28

Source: Adapted from Giovanni Schepis, "Analisis statistica dei risultati," in *Elezioni e comportamento politico in Italia*, Alberto Spreafico and Joseph LaPalombara, eds. (n.p., Edizioni di communità 1963). Derived from table 26, which is located between pp. 398 and 399.

voters in half those districts. While the 1968 and 1972 totals are not as dramatic, the pattern of Christian Democrat supporters casting far more preference votes than voters in the other parties persists.

Cazzola's analysis provides important data on the place of preference votes within the Christian Democrat party. Most important, he shows a high rank-order correlation between a region's percentage membership in the party and the number of preference votes cast for the DC: the greater the proportion enrolled as party members, the more frequent the use of preference votes.[83] He also demonstrates slight correlations between the use of preference votes and the numbers voting Christian Democrat and the extent of local faction conflict and the use of preference votes.[84]

It is necessary to understand how DC activists use preference votes to interpret these data. From the perspectives of the patron, the ability to accumulate votes indicates personal political power. In contests for the control of party and government positions, the relative strength of the competitors is measured in large part by the amount of preference votes obtained in party and government elections. They show the size of personal followings.

The allocation of votes in party contests is tied to the size of the local membership in the party, hence the high correlation between proportion enrolled in the DC and the use of preference votes. When DC activists are engaged in national party contests, there will be large numbers on the party membership lists and casting preference votes. The size of the preference vote is tied less to the presence of local faction conflict than to the presence of local leaders with national ambitions as well as the willingness of the electorate to make preference choices. Perhaps because of the prolonged presence of patron-client ties throughout the south, southern voters more readily make these selections.

Clearly, the key to the relative accumulation of preference votes is the presence of leaders with national political ambitions. Almost all election constituencies in which the DC attracts very high preference votes have national faction leaders. In 1972, in all four northern districts with relatively high use of preference votes, national faction leaders were present: Genoa, 30.9 percent—Taviani; Trento, 37.8 percent—Piccoli; Verona and Vicenza, 36.2 percent—Rumor and Bisaglia; Cuneo, 33.8 percent—Sarti. In the center, this rule applies in Ancona, 39.0 percent—Forlani, but not

Perugia, 47.2 percent. The rule holds in the south and islands: Rome, 48.4 percent—Andreotti; L'Aquila, 60.9 percent—Natali and Gaspari; Campobasso, 51.5 percent—Bosco; Naples, 51.5 percent—Gava; Benevento, 66.8 percent—DeMita; Bari, 57.7 percent—Moro; Potenza, 64.6 percent—Colombo; Catanzaro, 61 percent—Pucci; and in Sicily, approximately 57 percent—Gioia, Ruffini, Gullotti, and Lima.[85]

Many areas, particularly, but not exclusively in the south, rank low in local faction conflict, have faction leaders present, and rank high in the use of preference votes. Potenza, for example, is lowest in local faction conflict and second in the use of preference votes; Vicenza (with Verona), is sixteenth in the use of preference votes but twenty-sixth from the top (of a total of thirty) in local factional conflict; and Milan, high in local conflict, ranked tenth, and low, twenty-sixth, in the use of preference votes.[86]

Stated most generally, field studies of villages and national surveys show the widespread presence of the beliefs, fears, and behavior patterns of clientelism. Italians, particularly those in the south and in small towns and villages, evidence the norms of clientelism and are frequently tied in patron-client relations. Using preference votes as indicators, political clienteles occur throughout the peninsula, if also more frequently in its southern reaches. The Italian evidence supports the view the clientelist factions find their source in the social bonds and values of the society. The strength of their presence in the north raises questions about the simple, if generally accepted, association between high levels of industrialization and the absence (or even low levels of) political clienteles. The more frequent use of preference votes by southerners should not obscure the fact that as many as half the northerners surveyed in 1968 and 1972 reported casting preference votes.

The distribution of political clienteles bears elaboration. By comparing different areas of the country for the location of clientelist factions, one is only testing part of the argument. The general contention is about political changes resulting from social and economic alterations. Is there evidence of declines in the use of preference votes? Only Barnes and Sani give an indication of such a drop. They show a very slight decline by those born and living in the north in casting preference votes between 1968 and 1972. Their evidence does not indicate anything like the amount expected by the argument from modernization. When this is combined with the still very high levels of preference voting, some increases, even in the north, especially by socialist voters, and the outpouring of such ballots in Turin and Milan in the 1976 elections, it would seem that there is no inverse relationship between industrialization and political clienteles. As Pasquale Turiello first stated, the practices and norms of clientelism have been able to infiltrate the "rational" organizations of modern society.[87]

Increases in preference voting among Christian Democratic and Socialist voters raises a critical issue. It supports the explanation of clientelist factions with *political* factors. The requirements of success within the parties and the availability of government patronage emerge as very strong determinants of the variations in the strength of political clienteles. The most explicit support for this comes from the Socialist party. Its entry into the national government was followed by marked increases in preference balloting throughout its electorate. The most obvious support comes from the Christian Democrats, who have long dominated Italian government. One element of this argument shifts the analysis to the political activists, not the voters. Because the size of a candidate's preference vote is an accepted measure of political strength, those engaged in contests within the parties, especially the Christian Democrats, strive to gather such supporters and employ their campaign workers to that end. Within the DC, the greater the national ambitions of local leaders, the greater the number of preference votes cast.

Thus, if Italy abounds in the norms and practices of clientelism, it also contains the specific political factors said to explain the presence of political clienteles. Although there appears to be a slight indirect link between level of industrialization and the presence of clientelist factions, I have not been able to isolate the affects of cultural and political factors. To do so, I will have to shift to the analysis of those within the political elite.

4. The Christian Democratic Party

The presence of political clienteles may be explained by their access to government resources as well as their links to patron-client ties in the society. In Italy, the availability of massive amounts of government resources parallels the presence of clientelism in the social structure. Whether its start is dated from the advent of the republic or from U.S. Marshall Plan aid, certainly by the mid-1950s clientelist factions controlled enormous numbers of positions, inside and outside the government. The rules of political competition have abetted the political clienteles. Much patronage can be controlled through elected positions and through posts appointed by elected officers. In addition, because elections may be called at any time and especially because governing councils have no defined period in office, political maneuvering is constant. One reason that Christian Democratic voters are much more likely to cast preference votes is that throughout much of Italy as well as in national politics, it has been the governing party. Its leaders have been most likely to be patrons of political clienteles. Although there are clientelist factions in other parties and not all the party factions within the DC are political clienteles, in number and importance their home is within that party. It provides the key to controlling government resources.

The Christian Democratic party, the focus for this analysis of clientelist factions, has gathered the most votes, parliamentary seats, and cabinet portfolios. Its "doctrines, ideas, methods, its style" have structured all political events. "Public opinion believes [it] to be dominant. . . . Even the enemies of the dominant party, even citizens who refuse to give it their vote, acknowledge its superior status and its influence; they deplore it but admit it."[1] In the more colorful phrase of Italian politics, the Christian Democrats hold the keys to the *stanza dei bottoni*—the control room.

Historical Background

Although Arian and Barnes have used the predominance of the DC—and the Israeli Labour party—to construct the "dominant party system" concept, the Christian Democrats' control of Italian politics is a phenomenon of the recent past, stemming from the end of World War II.[2] In the immediate postwar period, three large parties emerged—the Party of Christian Democracy, the Socialists (PSI), and the Communists (PCI). In the 1946 elections to the Constituent Assembly, the DC gathered 35 percent of the votes to a combined PSI and PCI total of 38 percent.[3] The Christian Democrats' predecessor, the *Partito Popolare Italiano* (PPI), was formed only at the end of the pre-Fascist period. That party, like the DC after it, reflected the social and ideological complexities of Italian Catholics.

Two major factors determined the activities of Catholic political groups from the unification of Italy until the establishment of the Popular party in 1919.[4] The first was the "Roman question," the conflicting temporal claims of the church and the kingdom of Italy for traditional church property and the decision of Pius IX, in 1870 to retire as a "prisoner" behind the walls of the Vatican rather than to recognize the liberal state. The position of the church authorities led to the papal *non expedit*, in 1874, which prohibited Italian Catholics from participating in political life. The second was the formation, by the early 1890s of political groups of Catholic inspiration, "conciliarists" who sought a political understanding with the government. The removal of the papal ban, in 1904, and the Gentiloni pact, in 1913, doomed the Vatican "intransigents," who had sought the full restoration of the church's temporal powers.

The conciliarists burgeoning Christian Democrat movement was itself divided into competing groups. One group of left Christian Democrats was led by Don Luigi Sturzo, the future leader of the Popular party. Don Sturzo argued that full Catholic participation in the government was "both natural and necessary." The means of this participation was to be a political party of democratic policies independent of the church, but with relatively close ties to the "White" (that is, Catholic) labor movements in industry and agriculture. The Catholic conservative groups were primarily composed of individuals representing large landowners. While the left enunciated ideas combining corporatism and social democracy, the right was strongly attracted to the new forces of Italian nationalism.

The divisions were reflected in the Catholic political groups' attitudes toward World War I. Though most Catholic deputies supported prime minister Salandra's decision to enter the war, they followed two conflicting policies. Webster writes, "Meda and the Clerico-Moderates upheld the successive war governments of 1915-1919 and publicly stood by the Government during the dark days of 1917, while Sturzo and the rest of the central giunta of Catholic Action . . . were far more reserved in their attitudes."[5]

The Popular party, formed at the end of the war on January 1, 1919, played an important role in postwar Italian politics and in the eventual formation of the DC in 1943. It rejected the revolutionism of the Socialists while affirming the necessity of a radical change away from the liberal state. It presented itself as a full-fledged alternative to both the Socialists and the government.

As a struggling third force in an increasingly polarized society, the Popular party gathered 20.5 percent of the vote in the 1919 parliamentary elections and 100 of the 529 seats. Two years later, in an election in which the Socialists' percentage of the vote declined from 34 to 29 percent, the PPI held fast at 20 percent and 107 of the 526 seats. It received strong support in many rural areas of the north and center, especially in the Veneto and the Marches. However, it made almost no inroads in the south.[6]

During the violent conflicts of 1919-21, the PPI assumed an ambiguous position. Had it chosen to support the government it would certainly have supplied a strong and perhaps a sufficiently powerful prop to ensure the survival of liberal Italy. Had it chosen to ally itself with the Socialists, a new and much more radical government would have formed. It did neither. Its presence blocked the coming to power of the Socialists and the spread of socialism among the masses. Webster quotes Pietro Nenni: "The truth is that without this so-called black Bolshevism in 1919 no dikes would have been found to hold in the Socialist tide."[7]

The existence of the PPI was brief. Don Sturzo had been able to receive Vatican approval for the party by presenting it as a means of keeping the vast majority of the Catholics loyal to the social teachings of the church, while permitting the Vatican a free hand in Italian politics. The unresolved issue of the Roman question was fatal to the party. In the PPI's attempts to deal with more urgent and pressing social issues it chose to ignore this problem, thereby incurring the enmity of many important Catholics.

The coming to power of Mussolini and the election of a new pope brought to the fore the policy divisions between the PPI and the Vatican. The first sacrifice to the Vatican's increasingly direct political activities was Don Sturzo himself. In July 1923, Sturzo resigned as head of the PPI and was replaced by Alcide De Gasperi.

The growing political activity of church leaders and the rise of the Clerico-Fascists weakened the importance of the PPI within the society in general and within the Catholic political movement in particular. By the election of 1924, the two Catholic political groups, the PPI and the Clerico-Fascists, were backing different voting lists.

The end of the PPI coincided with the demise of the other organized nonfascist political parties. During the period of the Aventine opposition, the Vatican attacked the nonconfessional, and, therefore, independent status of the Popular party, which crushed both the party as such and De Gasperi's budding attempt to establish a nonfascist centrist government with the participation of the PPI. Mussolini's assumption of dictatorial powers in January 1925 and the subsequent attack on the opposition parties put the finishing touches on the end of the first Catholic political party in Italy. Two years later, at the end of 1926, the life of the party officially came to an end.

The Partito Poplare Italiano, which began as an attempt to bring the Catholics into the life of the Italian polity as a democratic force of the center was defeated by the goals and policies of the Vatican and the Fascists. The party had succeeded in reaching a large portion of the Catholics, but not in organizing them. Its dependence on the church for organizational strength and for authority led to its failure. Mussolini sealed its doom.

During the Fascist period several groups divided the Catholic political movement. At the highest levels, where direct interaction with the government occurred, church leaders were most active. By securing a special place for the church within Italy with the Lateran Pact and the Concordat, the Vatican regularized its position within the Italian polity. Much of the history of church-state relations under fascism was marked by the church's attempts to secure areas of freedom for itself and its associated institutions within Italy. Thus Catholic Action (the church's various lay organizations) and its subsidiaries were permitted to organize and engage in activities, and the Catholic University Youth Federation (FUCI) proved a fertile source for future DC leaders.

Two groups within the Italian Catholic movement had particularly close ties to the Fascist government. The politically dominant Clerico-Fascists, by dint of their institutional and family positions, served as mediators between the church and the government. The Catholic University of Milan, under the direction of its rector, Father Gemelli, also had very close links to the regime.[8]

There were also a number of Catholic groups acting directly and indirectly against the government. A small cluster of ex-Popolari, like Don Sturzo, Donati, and Ferrari, lived in exile and worked in ooposition to the regime, while actively preparing for the post-Fascist era. Others, such as De Gasperi, found a haven behind the walls of the Vatican. De Gasperi used this period to formulate his plans for a great mass Catholic party which would join together with parties of the center-left and the center-right to govern Italy. FUCI, the Catholic "integralists" who formed around La Pira and the Milanese Guelph movement, provided other sources of non-fascist future activists. Out of FUCI came such leaders as Moro, Gonella, and Andreotti, and the *Base* faction finds much of its historic roots in the other two groups.

The formation of the Christian Democratic party in 1943 reflected these diverse sources. Foremost among these groups was one led by De Gasperi and other former Popolari such as Mario Scelba. De Gasperi, the last leader of the PPI and the first head of the DC, was its dominant political figure for the next ten years. Other founders of the DC were those too young to have been active in PPI or from areas in which the Popolari had made no inroads, particularly the south. Many of those from the north who helped in founding the DC had been active in the antifascist resistance movement.[9] In the southern parts of Italy, many of the leaders of the new DC entered the party from collateral associations, such as the various branches of Italian Catholic Action.

The highly organized factions that marked the party from the middle half of the 1950s onward were blocked during the early years. First, De Gasperi's personal dominance allowed him to defeat the challenges of the left wing factions. Second, until the first national elections in 1948 the relative political power of the DC was unclear, and all its groups devoted themselves to fighting the common enemy—the PCI and the PSI. Third, the weak party organization offered no political prizes and did not challenge the power of local leaders. De Gasperi's death and Fanfani's rise to national party dominance furthered the party's institutionalization as a separate political force. Fanfani's efforts at party-building succeeded in making the DC less dependent on church-related voluntary associations and furthered the power of his allies within the party at the expense of traditional old notables. His efforts to limit the power of local leaders resulted in bitter opposition and personal defeat. Meeting at the Convent Domus Marie, many of his original followers sought to maintain their own personal bases of power within a strong party. They formed the *Dorotei* and removed Fanfani from office.

The final element crucial to the history of the current faction structure was the formation of the center-left governing coalition with Socialist (PSI) participation. This decision exacerbated left-right divisions within the party and also led to splits within the Dorotei itself.

This overview of the Italian Catholic political movement has emphasized two crucial factors: the recurrent divisiveness within the movement, and its success.

The DC in National Politics

Elections

The place of the Christian Democratic party in parliamentary elections has been clear and consistent. While the Italian party system has frequently been used to exemplify the classic problem of the multiparty system—many and deeply divided parties with the resultant frequently collapsing cabinets—patterns of electoral stability have been hidden by surface flux.[10]

During the first ten years of the republic, a two-bloc electoral pattern existed: the governing coalition of the center, composed of the DC and one or more of the Republicans (PRI), Liberals (PLI), and the Italian Social Democratic party (PSDI), arranged against the left opposition. The first cluster controlled 64 percent and 54 percent and the Marxist opposition held 32 percent and 37 percent of the seats in the first two chambers. The development of the center-left coalition formula in the early 1960s partially changed the picture. No longer was there a united Marxist-inspired opposition on the left, nor was there a cohesive center bloc. The PSI's decision to lend parliamentary support to the government expanded the government's majority to well beyond 60 percent.

By the mid-1960s, a new pattern of groupings within parliament had solidified. The government forces now included the DC, the PSI, the PSDI, and the PRI. The opposition on the left was composed of the Communists and the Italian Socialist Party of Proletarian Unity (PSIUP), established in 1964. On the right were the divided forces of the PLI, the Neo-Fascists (MSI), and the rapidly declining Monarchists. This pattern lasted through the 1975 elections, which were followed by the eventual collapse of the center-left alliance. Several patterns in Italian voting stand out during the first twenty five years. The first is the large bloc of votes that has gone to the parties of the traditional left: the PCI, PSIUP, PSI, PSDI, and PRI. The proportion of the electorate voting for these parties has varied from 44 percent in the election for the Constitutional Assembly of 1946 to 40.6, 41.5, 42.9, 46.6, 47.9, 46 and 49 percent in the legislative elections of 1948, 1953, 1958, 1963, 1968, 1972 and 1976.

The various positions taken by the different Socialist parties limit the utility of this classification. If the Republicans, the Social Democrats, and the Socialists after 1963 are excluded from the left, then it is possible to speak of a "radical" left composed of the remaining parties. Thus, excluding the 1968 elections, the radical left of the PCI and the PSI show a rather shallow bowllike curve starting with a high of 39.6 percent in 1946 to a low of 35.4 percent in 1953 and a rise to 39.1 percent in 1963. If the 1968, 1972, and 1976 elections are included and only the PCI and the PSIUP are classified as the radical left, then this group accounts for 31.4, 29.1, and 34 percent of the total. The PCI has come to dominate the traditional left electorate. In 1946 it garnered 18.9 percent of the national votes; thirty years later, its percentage had risen to 34.4. The increasing deradicalization of the Socialists, however, led to a diminution of the forces of the radical left, so that the vote percentage of this group was approximately the same in the elections of 1948 and 1968. In the former, the PCI and the PSI accounted for 31 percent; in 1968, and PCI and the PSIUP gathered 31.5 percent. The 1976 results were the first to show a significant growth of the radical left.

The Christian Democratic party has accounted for the largest share of the remaining votes in each election, a plurality of more than 35 percent of the votes. For the last five national elections, it received a mean of 39.5 percent, varying between 38.3 and 42.2 percent. Only in the 1948 election did it come close to gathering a majority of the votes, when it amassed 48.5 percent. Because the issues and pressures of the 1948 election campaign make it atypical, its exclusion from the survey points to a rather steady vote for the DC at approximately 40 percent.

Excluding the 1948 election results also points to an interesting relationship between the power of the DC and the Italian Liberal party. Both parties have competed for a rather constant 45 percent of the electorate. A comparison of the electoral results of both parties between 1946 and 1953 shows a DC gain of 4.9 percent and a PLI drop of 3.8 percent. In 1958, the DC gathered 42.3 percent, as compared to 3.5 percent for the PLI—a combined percentage of 45.8 percent. In the 1963 elections, the DC dropped 4 points to 38.3 percent and the PLI gained 3.5 to 7 percent, a total of 45.3 percent; in 1968, the DC rose 1.8 percent to 39.1 percent, and the PLI fell 1.2 percent to 5.8 percent, amounting to 44.9 percent, and in 1972 they combined to 43 percent. Again the 1976 results, a combined total of 40 percent, are the first signs of change.

Patterns of electoral stability during much of this period are reinforced by examining national and local comparisons between elections. For the DC the correlations have been high and increasing over time: The Carlo Cattaneo researchers report the results for the following years: 1946-48 (.798), 1948-53 (.813), 1953-58 (.854), 1958-63 (.909).[11] Giacomo Sani notes similarly high correlations of voting percentages for the DC in ninety provinces between 1946-72 (.836). Parallel correlations are found for the other voting blocs. For example, Sani finds a .894 correlation for the Communist vote across ninety provinces between 1946-72.[12] Barnes and Sani have also demonstrated that the aggregate patterns do not result from individual voter changed across party lines that cancel out movements in opposite directions. Rather, individual voters tend to choose the same party in election after election. "Of respondents who voted in 1968 and 1972, 86% claimed to have voted for the same party both times. The figure was 93% for both the DC and the PCI."[13]

Thus, analyses of aggregate and survey data point to the marked stability of Italian electoral behavior up until the 1976 national elections. Increasingly in this competition, the DC and the PCI are the primary contestants. The former occupies the point of reference for the nonleft voter. Within the electorate's left bloc, the

Communist party has grown in size. Sani and Barnes also note that the shifts which have occurred through the 1972 elections have been linked to the smaller parties and are most pronounced among those with weak party loyalties.[14] Through the 1972 elections they could find no long-term sources of electoral change.[15]

These trends are emphasized by the results of the 1976 election, which was characterized by much apparent change. The Christian Democrats and the Communists emerged even more clearly as the dominant parties. The smaller parties, the Social Democrats, Liberals, and Neo-Fascists, but now the Socialists as well, were the major electoral losers. In addition, much of the electoral change appears to have come from the choices of the many young and new voters with weak party loyalties.

Parliament

The electoral stability has produced a similar pattern in the structure of control over parliamentary seats. Table 4.1 displays the relative parliamentary strength of the political parties. The size differential between the largest and smallest parties has been relatively constant. In addition, while there has been some flux in the relative position of each of the small parties, the positions and relative sizes of the three large parties have remained constant. Since the election to the first legislature in 1948, the Christian Democratic party has controlled the largest bloc in the Chamber of Deputies. This bloc has been almost twice as large as the Communist contingent and three times as large as that of the two socialist parties—that is, the PSI and the PSDI. The Socialists, in turn, have been fifteen times as large as the smallest party. Changes in the relative positions of all parties have been minimal.

Of perhaps greater significance is that alliances among a subset of the political parties to provide parliamentary support for the cabinets have persisted over relatively long periods. Until 1963, all cabinets were based on the support of two or more of the center parties and between 1963 and 1972 all cabinets received the support of the parties of the center-left. Each of these parliamentary alliances, known as the coalition formula, has provided ample parliamentary majorities. In the two legislatures of the first center-left coalition formula, the DC, the two socialist and the Republican parties controlled parliamentary majorities of 82 and 58 seats. These parliamentary alliances of the parties have not only

Table 4.1. Party Strength in the Chamber of Deputies

	Legislature I (1948-53)		Legislature II (1953-58)		Legislature III (1958-63)		Legislature IV (1963-68)		Legislature V (1968-72)		Legislature VI (1972-76)		Legislature VII (1976-)	
	N	%	N	%	N	%	N	%	N	%	N	%	N	%
Communists (PCI)	131[a]	23	143	24	140	24	166	26	171	27	179	28	227	36
Social Proletarians (PSIUP)									23	4				
Socialists (PSI)	52[a]	9	75	13	84	14	87	14	61[c]	10	61	10	57	9
Social Democrats (PSDI)	33	6	19	3	22	4	33	6	30[c]	4	29	5	15	2
Republicans (PRI)	9	2	5	1	6	1	6	1	9	1	15	2	14	2
Christian Democrats (DC)	305	53	262	44	273	47	260	41	265	42	266	42	263	42
Liberals (PLI)	19	3	14	2	17	3	39	6	31	5	20	3	5	1
Monarchists (PDIUM)	14	2	40	7	11 / 14	2[b] / 3[b]	8	1	6	1				
Neo-Facists (MSI)	6	1	29	5	15	3	27	4	24	4	56	9	35	5
Others	5	1	3	1	5	1	4	1	10	2	4	1	14[d]	2
Total	574	100	590	100	587	99	630	100	630	100	630	100	630	99

Sources: Adapted from Raphael Zariski, *Italy: The Politics of Uneven Development* (Hinsdale, Ill.: Dryden, 1972) p. 157; and *Corriere della Sera* (June 23, 1976), p. 1.

a. In the 1948 elections, the PCI and PSI presented a united list.
b. There were two Monarchist parties in this election.
c. Before the 1968 elections the two Socialist parties merged to form the Unified Socialist Party. The alliance lasted one year.
d. Includes a number of small left-wing parties.

been openly established and formalized but have persisted even as the cabinets dependent on them have not. Between 1963 and 1972 the center-left coalition remained intact, though there were eight cabinet changes.

Patterns of parliamentary competition have been stable not only in the distribution of seats and the formation of parliamentary alliances but also in the role of the Christian Democratic party. Within the parties of the coalition formula, the DC has always controlled the vast majority of the parliamentary seats. (see table 4.2) During the fourth legislature (1963-68), the DC held 260 of the coalition parties' 384 seats in the Chamber of Deputies; and in the fifth legislature, (1968-72) they made up 265 of the 365 parliamentary members of the center-left parties.

The Christian Democratic party has been able to translate its power within the coalition alliance into dominance over the cabinet. All presidents of the Italian Council of Ministers (prime ministers) have been Christian Democrats. Indeed, the pool of potential prime ministers has been filled solely by members of that party.

Table 4.2 reveals the dominant position of the DC in Italian cabinets. Approximately 80 percent of all cabinet members have been Christian Democrats, and about 70 percent of all ministers appointed in coalition cabinets have been DC members. In addition, for approximately seven of the twenty-eight years between May 1948 and June 1976, Italy was governed by *monocolore* cabinets composed solely of members of the Christian Democrat party. During the entire 1948-76 period, 665 senior-level cabinet positions were distributed at the formation of cabinets. Of these, 255 positions were given out to single-party cabinets, and therefore, went solely to Christian Democrats. Four hundred and twenty cabinet positions were distributed at the formation of coalition cabinets; somewhat more than two-thirds of them went to members of the DC. During the first span of the center-left coalition formula, the distribution of cabinet portfolios to the other parties was equally constant. Thus, between 1963 and 1972, there were six coalition cabinets and three monocolore cabinets. Within the coalition cabinets, the most frequent distribution of cabinet positions was the following: DC, 16, PSI, 6, PSDI, 3, and PRI, 1. The only deviation from this pattern occurred after the merger and subsequent split of the Socialists and

Table 4.2. Distribution of Cabinet Positions
by Party (Legislatures I-VI)

	I	II	III	IV	V	VI	Total
Number of cabinets formed	3	6	5	4	6	4	28
Number of coalition cabinets formed	3	3	2	3	3	3	17
Number of cabinet positions distributed	64	125	119	102	155	100	665
Number of coalition cabinet positions distributed	64	67	48	78	81	72	410
Cabinet position distribution by party							
Monocolore cabinets							
DC		58	71	24	74	28	255
Coalition cabinets							
DC	46	51	40	48	50	45	280
PSI				18	18	6	42
PSDI	5	9	6	9	10	10	49
PRI	8	7	2	3	3	7	30
PLI	3					4	7
Independents	2						2

Sources: Adapted from *Italy: News and Notes* (Rome: Presidency of the Council of Ministers, 1971), nos. 4-5, pp. 295-325; ibid., 1973, nos. 4-5, pp. 253-56; ibid., 1974, nos. 5-6, pp. 392-95; ibid., 1975, no. 1, pp. 9-11.
Note: Includes positions distributed only at the formation of cabinets.

the addition of one new cabinet position (a minister without portfolio) in 1969.

In addition, cabinet dissolutions and formations did not result in the wholesale shift of members out of and into cabinets. Rather, the same persons frequently returned to occupy offices, and at times the very same ones, in cabinet after cabinet. The eight collapses during 1963–72 resulted in the formation of five new interparty cabinets. A total of 133 senior positions were distributed at the formation of cabinets. Of these, 18 were filled by individuals who had never before served at that level of government. Nine of the 18 entered with the first Rumor government, after the 1968 elections.

Contests for the control of cabinet positions have no seasons. They may occur at any time, last as long as it takes to form a coalition or temporary arrangement, and recur at any time. There are no formal limits on the politicization of these contests. Similarly, the control of positions in the government and quasi-public bureaucracy has become highly politicized. The DC's successes in all spheres of political competition have given the party enormous amounts of government resources—the food for the presence and growth of clientelist factions.

The DC and the Control of the Bureaucracy

Christian Democrat dominance of the Italian government extends beyond positions controlled directly or indirectly through electoral competition. Its governmental vocation is equally well demonstrated by its control over the bureaucracy and the quasi-governmental agencies and corporations that dot the Italian economy.

LaPalombara has developed the *parentela* concept to describe the pattern of DC control over access to and decisions within the administrative agencies: "*parentela* involves a relatively close and integral relationship between certain associational interest groups, on the one hand, and the Christian Democratic Party (D.C.) on the other.[16] It is a tie between those of the same political family (*parente*). It permits those interest groups and individuals associated with the DC to intervene directly with the governmental bureaucracy.

LaPalombara cites the response of an official of the Ministry of the Treasury: "The only groups that count in Italian public administration, as long as the Christian Democrats hold governmental power, are the Catholic groups. The Catholics, because they have direct access to the ministers, are likely to get anything they wish from the ministries. Other groups, such as left-wing parties and trade unions, are not as fortunate. They are compelled to come to the ministry hat in hand."[17] This somewhat exaggerated portrayal highlights the crucial importance of the DC in gaining direct access to the bureaucracy. The presence of the Socialists in the governing coalitions since 1963 changed this picture. The DC no longer had a veritable monopoly. It had to make room, but not much, for its new partner.

Not a small part of the party's dominance rests on its ability and willingness to use its political power within the bureaucracy. "The Christian Democratic Party . . . is in a very strong position to corrupt the bureaucracy because those bureaucrats who do not cooperate with the party—and therefore with the groups that have power within it—have little hope in general of making a career."[18] Central to this political power is the control, where possible, of appointments to strategic decision-making positions. LaPalombara reports that political considerations color appointments to the State Accounting Office and many other such bodies.

> In the final analysis, the powerful Minister of the Treasury must ask the State Accounting Officer whether there are funds available to do something the Minister wishes to do. If he wants to do so, the latter is in a strategic position to make life difficult and uncomfortable for anyone in the bureaucracy. Because of the strategic nature of this position, the respondent says that no one who is in any way unacceptable to the dominant party is ever likely to be appointed to it.[19]

On resigning as head of the Bank of Italy, a position he held for a decade, Guido Carli issued a summary statement:

> Our political forces are not interested in how well the banking system works, the policies it proposes or carries out. They merely want to get their own henchmen into the system and keep out those of rival power groups. . . . I've fought this tendency all along, not always with success.[20]

While the DC has been able to exert is presence within the state agencies, its power is perhaps most obvious and easily seen within the branches of the public corporations. The Italian political economy is filled with public and quasi-public corporations, almost 60,000 of them, established during the last fifty years. Begun as attempts to salvage failing banks and business enterprises during the depression, they now occupy a predominate portion of the economy. Their activities range from the control of investment funds to social security and workmen's compensation, from shipbuilding to Cine-Città, the film-making corporation, from Alfa-Romeo and Alitalia to AGIP, the Italian gas and oil company, to the lion's share of the banking and credit industry. Here, as in the state agencies, access to the decision-making positions is primarily in the hands of the Christian Democrat party. Of greater importance the reverse is also true; the DC has greater access to such positions as well as career appointments and promotions below.

Giuseppe Tamburrano has documented the extent of DC dominance.[21] At the end of the 1960s, all presidents and vice-presidents of the IRI (the industrial reconstruction agency) were Christian Democrats, as were thirteen of its eighteen other top administratives. In the ENI, the hydrocarbon trust, all leading officials, except its vice-president, who were not technocrats were associated with the DC. In other public corporations all but two, both technocrats, of the ten top officials, were associated with the party.

At the lower levels of these organizations, the pattern of Christian Democrat dominance remains. Tamburrano reports that while the ENI and the EFIM (an agency to aid manufacturing firms) have a relatively high percentage of technocrats, this is not the case in the other public corporations. Of the twenty-six branches of EAGAT (autonomous government agencies that run thermal plants), eleven presidents were Christian Democrats, five were Socialists, and one was a member of the PSDI; of the five top figures in the Cinema corporation, four were Christian Democrats. In all, argues Tamburrano, the control of financial resources and crucial decision-making power rests with Demochristians.[22] Even more recent analyses sustain Tamburrano's findings. In 1976, the DC had exclusive or majority control in nineteen of the twenty-four associations of the IRI, had equal power in three, and was in the minority or absent in only two. Areas controlled by Demochristians included the vast holdings of Finmare, Finsider, Finmeccanica, and the national highway corporation among many others.[23]

Christian Democrat control is equally apparent in the detailing of the heads of government associated welfare and social insurance associations. At the end of the 1960s, eleven of the seventeen appointed presidents were Demochristians; the other positions were split between the Socialist and Social Democratic parties, and four of their five elected presidents were Christian Democrats.[24] Table 4.3 reports the number of positions controlled by DC and other political parties in Italian banking.

However, this picture exaggerates the image of the party as a united actor. Rather, given the complexity and autonomy of the vast reaches of the bureaucracy, control of particular agencies can

Table 4.3. Party Control of Banking Positions (1969-71)

	Christian Democrats	Socialists	Liberals	Social Democrats	Republicans	Bank of Italy	Technocrats
Major national banks							
President	11	2	1	1		2	1
Vice-president	4	4	1			2	2
Director-general	3				2	2	9
Regional savings institutions							
President	21	1		2			
Vice-president	10	4		10	1		
Interbank associations							
President	4						
Vice-president	4						
Regional agrarian credit							
President	7						
Vice-president	6					1	
Real estate credit							
President	8						
Vice-president	1	1		1			
Medium-term credit							
President	5			1			
Vice-president	5						1

Sources: Adapted from Giuseppe Tamburrano, *L'Iceberg Democristiano* (Milan: Sugarco, 1974), p. 117; and *L'Espresso* (May 2, 1971), financial supplement, p. 5.

be isolated from the others and serve as the bases of power for individual DC leaders, and with them their factions.

Like the state administration, the public corporations extend to all levels of Italian society. They are important sources of employment, investment credit, and DC party patronage. Reports prior to the 1976 elections emphasized these areas as bastions of DC power at the local level. In Catanzaro, the only city to show an increase for the Christian Democrats in the 1975 regional elections, 28,000 of the 60,000 employed worked for government corporations. In neighboring Matera, half the workers were in the public employ; 700 worked for Ferrosud (the railroad corporation) in an area with few trains. Where no jobs were available, government and quasi-government assistance agencies were used. In Calabria, 260,000 people were receiving various forms of pensions.[25] This mass patronage was primarily meant to affect the 1976 elections, but was not the only form of clientelism. Just before the election the head of the IRI, Petrilli, sought to maintain the Demochristians' lock on the 1,600 positions in his holding corporation's 180 administrative councils.[26]

The positions in the state administration and public corporations are crucial to the DC power over local areas and to the development of local political clienteles. Tamburanno cites Orazio Erdas's analysis of the Christian Democrat power in Sardinia which is generally descriptive of areas of DC dominance.

> The reality is that the DC control 90% of the key decision-making positions; it is assured of the key assessor positions; it is in a dominating position in the communes and the provinces; it has its men in all the *enti* that constitute the power structure, from industrial to agricultural credit; from tourism to artisan work; from industry to handicraft; from health to insurance; from the mines to the banks. . . .[27]

The control of patronage resources from the national level is but a portion of the party's local level strength.

The DC and Local Governments

Christian Democrat control of decision-making positions at the local level is also fostered by its predominance in local elections and possession of seats in local governments. Tables 4.4 and 4.5

survey DC control of positions in communal and provincial administrations during the 1956-72 period. They not only indicate DC power but also the sheer number of people in the Italian government affiliated with the Christian Democrat party. As at the national level, the DC has been especially successful at transforming local electoral pluralities into cabinet majorities.

The pattern of provincial coalitions during the *centro-sinistra* (center-left) period is shown in table 4.4. Sixty-three of the 89 provinces with party governments were controlled by the DC in coalition with other political parties. The *centro-sinistra* coalition formula, the suggested strategy by the national party headquarters of the national coalition, ruled in 59 provinces. In 13 provinces the Christian Democrats ruled alone. Thus the DC was the dominant force in the ruling majority in 76 of the 89 provinces (85 percent). A survey of the relative power of the parties indicates that in 46 of the 61 provinces where the DC and the PSI coalesced, the Socialists were crucial to the coalition.

The Christian Democrats, the PCI, and the PSI have also held dominant roles in the provincial councils. Together the three parties made up 85 percent of the total of 2,680 provincial council seats. The DC occupied 1,100 (41 percent), the PSI 451 (17 percent), and the Communists 678 (26 percent). Given the nature of the governing coalitions, it is not surprising that the DC and the

Table 4.4. Provincial Administrations (1966-69)

Coalition Partners	Number of Provinces
Center-left	59
DC alone or with local party	13
Center	2
PCI	2
PCI-PSIUP	6
PCI-PSI	1
Left	4
DC-PSI-PRI-PSIUP	1
DC-PLI-PRI-PSI	1
Commissions	4
Total	93

Source: Data provided by internal sources of Christian Democratic Office, Enti Locali (local governments).

PSI held 85 percent of the *Assessori* (local commissioners) and presidential positions—a 65 percent Christian Democrat and 20 percent Socialist split. All the *Assessori* and presidential positions held by members of the PCI were in the Red Belt—that is, Emilia, Tuscany, and Umbria.

Of the 89 presidents of provincial councils during 1966–69, 86 were from the three largest parties. Two provincial presidents were members of regional and local parties, and one position was vacant. Seventy of the 86 were members of the DC; 6 were Socialists and 10 were Communists. With one exception, all the provinces with PCI and PSI presidents were located in Red Belt regions. In every other province, except Bolzano with its Peoples party of the South Tyrol president, the president was a Christian Democrat.

The predominance of the DC, PSI, and the PCI increases in communal-level governments. After the 1964 elections, there were 3,580 members of communal councils in the provincial capital cities of Italy. Of these, 45 percent were Christian Democrats, 20 percent were Socialists, and 22 percent were members of the PCI. The other parties divided the remaining 13 percent of the seats.

In communes with populations of less than 5,000, the proportional representation system is replaced by a system of election based on majority rule. The Italian multiparty system almost becomes a two-party system in these rural communes. Usually only two lists—or at most three—are presented. Although the official figures do not present breakdowns by political party affiliation, all but a very few lists are probably linked to the Christian Democratic and Communist parties.

Table 4.5 estimates the number of local government positions occupied by members of the Christian Democratic party. Except for central Italy's Red Belt, the DC has been able to dominate the positions and policies of local Italian government. The 1975 regional election results were the first breaks with this pattern. As on the national level, DC control of governing positions is used to capture the resources and jobs attached to local agencies.

Electoral Sources

Christian Democrat control of governing positions rests on its ability to attract and hold the largest fraction of Italian voters. In election after election, at the local as well as national levels, the

Table 4.5. Local Government Positions Controlled by DC

	1951-52	1956	1960	1963	1964	1969	1970	1971	1973-74
Communal mayors				3,037				3,529	5,020
Communal mayors in provincial capitals						57			69
Communal assessors				8,380					22,152
Communal council leaders		7,726[b]	8,338[b]	1,048				802	
Communal councilors		3,700[c]	3,200[c]	21,858	17,828[d]		17,522[a]	21,316	
Communal councilors in provincial capitals		1,226	1,338		1,432[a]		1,427[a]		
Provincial presidents				73		66	70		
Provincial assessors				231			371	313	
Provincial councilors	986[a]	1,086[a]	982[a]		1,100				

Sources: Adapted from *Italy: News and Notes* (Rome: Presidency of the Council of Ministers, 1964), no. 6, p. 498; ibid., 1970, nos. 4-5, p. 409; G. Schepis, "Le Elezioni Amministrative Del 6 Novembre 1960," in A. Spreafico and J. LaPalombara, *Elezioni e Comportamento Politico in Italia* (Edizioni di Communità, 1963), pp. 951-63; *Elezioni Amministrative Del 22 Novembre 1964* (Rome: Istituto Centrale di Statistica, 1967); Jacques Nobecourt, *Italia al Vivo* (Milan: Etas Kompass, 1971), p. 47; Giuseppe Tamburanno, *L'Iceberg Democristiano* (Milan: Sugarco, 1974), p. 108; and sources in the DC Office of Organization.

Note: The figures show DC control of approximately 50 to 60 percent of local government positions and are best treated as estimates.

a. Excludes Sicily.
b. Only communes with populations greater than 10,000.
c. Sicily.
d. Only communes with populations greater than 5,000.

DC has amassed approximately 40 percent of the vote, nearly 12 million Italians. (Whether the regional elections of 1975 and national election of 1976 portend major shifts is discussed later in chapter 7.) Although patronage ties are crucially important bases for the participation of party activists, and these links do pull in voters, most of those voting for the DC do so for reasons other than their direct personal link to those controlling political resources.

Studies of aggregate data by the Carlo Cattaneo Institute and Mattei Dogan, as well as the survey analyses of Gianfranco Poggi, build a picture of the DC vote sources.[28] The Cattaneo studies argue for the presence of two voting blocs in Italy: a left that has come to be dominated by the Communists and a center-right, controlled by the DC. They demonstrate that DC voting correlates negatively with increases in industrialization, literacy, the spread of education to the middle school level, and commune population. The Christian Democrats attract most of their electoral supporters from generally sparsely populated rural areas, where education generally ends before the middle school, and where illiteracy was common in 1963.[29] Within the northeast, northwest, center, south, Sicily, and Sardinia, these correlations break down somewhat, especially in the three areas south of Rome. In the White areas (where the numbers of practicing Catholics has been high), there is no definable positive or negative correlation with degree of industrialization. There is a positive correlation between increased middle school education and voting for the DC in the industrial northwest.[30]

In the 1963 election several variables correlated positively with voting for the DC: membership in the Christian Democratic party (.496), percentage of void ballots (.359), membership in CISL (the Catholic labor union) (.312), and membership in ACLI (the worker association in Catholic Action) (.293). In 1953 the variables were somewhat different: direct cultivators (.448), completion of elementary school (.368), membership in ACLI (.359), membership in the DC (.324), percentage of women working in industry (.275), and percentage of population working in industry (.253). In both 1953 and 1963 there were negative correlations with several variables. Many of them, such as percentage of population who are PCI members (.668), were connected to the traditional left activities and organizations. The differences lead to the conclusion, however, that between 1953 and 1963, the DC increasingly became removed from the traditional left and its electoral sources.[31]

Mattei Dogan's analysis of the 1958 election also relies on social class distinctions and aggregate data. He depicts the DC's ability to draw from all social categories, especially from small-plot and middle-class farmers. Only among agricultural workers and tenant-farmers was the DC unable to gather at least one-fourth of the agricultural category vote.[32]

In a society in which almost everyone is at least nominally Catholic and in which large numbers practice that faith, it is not at all surprising that religious practice is a powerful determinant of electoral choice. Early survey work reported by Gianfranco Poggi clearly shows that the higher the score on an index of clericalism, the more likely is the individual to vote Christian Democrat, no matter the social class.[33] The most elaborate analysis, however, of the relationship between social cleavages and DC voting sources is by Samuel Barnes.[34]

Barnes shows the strong association between religious ties and DC voting. The party does particularly well among active Catholics (both in how they vote and their portion of the entire DC electorate). At the same time, the Christian Democrats have the widest social appeal of all Italian parties. Only those who do not regularly attend church and who have links to the Marxist trade unions and those workers and peasants with no church or trade union ties (together 15 percent of the population) are poorly represented among DC voters. The party draws better than its share of the population among those active in the church, especially among the middle class, but also from the workers. It attracts more votes than any other party among all categories, except those with links to the Marxist trade union or without any organizational ties. Last, the DC does better in Marxist areas of the population than do Communists and Socialists in Catholic areas.[35]

How much of the DC's vote comes for reasons associated with patronage and political clienteles? It is difficult to give a precise answer. As I noted, 30 to 40 percent of DC voters cast preference votes. Turning these figures around, they say that between six and eight of every ten who vote for the Christian Democrats do so for other than patronage reasons. First, the DC's position in mass politics—its success at the polls—has depended on much more than jobs exchanged for votes. This rather obvious point needs to be underlined, lest I be accused of claiming that all facets of political competition are linked to political clienteles. The second is to specify the place and role of clientelist arrangements within the party that link the remaining DC voters, those ties to clientelist factions to activists within the party. In turn, the third point, to do this requires entering the DC itself.

The Party's Formal Organization

Unlike the caucus-based political parties found in the United States, the Christian Democratic party stands as a mass party peopled by active members, nationally organized to extend through the Italian polity. It is not only active in Italian politics but is part of the international Christian Democratic movement. In Italy, as elsewhere, it was organized by Catholic leaders, lay and clerical, who saw in it a vehicle for promoting Catholic interests and combating that other international political movement, marxism. One consequence, as Duverger and Zariski have observed, is that the formal organization of the Christian Democratic party reproduces in all but name the formal organization of socialist parties.[36]

The geographic divisions of the DC follow the administrative lines of Italy—national, regional, provincial, and communal—and also contain the "party" units, zone and section.[37] The division of functional responsibility is the same at each level of the party organization: an assembly or congress, a governing committee and directorate, and an administrative unit, the secretariat.

The national level of the party is composed of six structures: the Party Congress, the National Council, the Political Secretariat, the Central Directorate, and the Parliamentary Groups, one in the Senate and one in the Chamber of Deputies. The most important of these, according to the party statutes, is the National Congress, which must meet once every two years. It "decides upon the general policy directions and elects the National Council" and is the formal ruling body of the DC.[38] The council, directorate and Secretariat differ in the ways which they assume the responsibilities of the National Congress when the latter is not in session.

The party statutes define the National Council as the organ that "is subordinated to the National Congress and within the policy line fixed by the Congress is the maximum decision-making body of the party. It guides and controls the activity of the party in all fields."[39] The council is composed of 120 members elected at the National Congress (60 from the Christian Democrat members of the parliament and 60 nonparliamentarians), the presidents of the DC groups in the Chamber and the Senate, and other DC government and party leaders; included in the latter are the national delegates of the "collateral movements"—the women's movement, the youth movement, the veterans' group, and the party-affiliated sports association. In addition, organizations who participate "on the national level in an activity inspired by Christian-Social principles" have consulting votes. Such organizations include the Catholic-inspired labor union, the Italian Confederation of Workers' Unions (CISL), the peasant association, *Coltivatori Diretti,* and the various branches of Italian Catholic Action.

The party statutes recognize the unwieldy size of the National Council by delegating much of its power and authority to the Central Directorate and the Secretariat. The Central Directorate is defined in the constitution as the body that "enacts the policies of the party according to the directions fixed by the National Council."[40] It has approximately thirty-five members, of which twenty-seven are elected by the National Council. The other eight are members by virtue of past or present position in the governing bodies of the party or the national government. Some or all of Christian Democrat cabinet ministers of senior and junior rank may also be invited to participate and have a consulting vote in directorate meetings.

A simple majority of the members of the National Council is sufficient to elect the two most important official party leaders: the political secretary[41] and the administrative secretary. The other members of the Secretariat, also known as the executive group, are chosen by the Central Directorate. The executive group is composed of the political secretary, the vice-secretaries, the administrative secretary and the directors of the party offices: organization, SPES (publicity and propaganda), local government, and planning.

The members of the executive group control the daily activities of the party. According to the party rules, "The political secretary . . . represents the party, takes heed of the policy decisions that are made by the Central Directorate, maintains contact with the government, with the parliamentary groups and with the other political and social bodies, and promotes and coordinates the political policy and organizational activities of the party."[42]

During national government crises, the Central Directorate, with the agreement of the directorates of the parliamentary groups, is responsible for adopting party positions that best resolve the crisis. The National Council is convened within thirty days after the solution of the crisis to deliberate on the work of the directorate and the parliamentary groups.

In its role as a parliamentary party, the DC is composed of two parliamentary groups, one in each national house. All Christian Democrat members of parliament are required by party statute to belong to one of these bodies: "The parliamentary groups and each of their members, for all relevant political questions, must adhere to the general directions fixed by the Congress and to the directions of the National Council and the Central Directorate through which the directions of the Congress are interpreted and applied."[43]

Membership in the DC, which exceeds 1.5 million, is open to those over the age of eighteen who are of "uncensorable" moral and political conduct. Accepting a membership card implies accepting party policy, discipline, and agreement with the statute's view of the member as a dedicated activist.

As in Socialist and Communist parties, leaders are elected from below. Delegates to the National Congress are chosen at regional congresses by representatives elected at provincial congresses. These, in turn, are chosen at section meetings. Officeholders are elected at meetings of the relevant party unit. In all cases, proportional representation by faction is the electoral rule. Unlike Marxist parties, however, party functionaries are not permitted to be elected to office, which both limits the power of the functionaries within the party and makes it difficult for individuals of little outside sources of income to become party leaders.[44]

A section in the party statutes lists individual members' roles in determining party policy and prohibits the existence of factions:

> The members contribute to the determination of the party's planning and policy orientation in a manner that does not contrast with its moral and political unity. Decisions of the competent bodies must be accepted while bearing in mind the absolute respect of the individuality of all members.

It is not permissible to construct within the party organized groups or factions.[45]

As is evident from the concerns of this volume, the provision is ignored in practice.

DC Party Members

In the image of a mass party, the DC boasts well over 1.5 million members. Reflecting the earlier geographic spread of the Popular party and the general distribution of voluntary organizations, the DC's initial years were marked by a predominance of members from areas north of Rome.[46] The period through 1953 saw a massive and successful DC effort (as well as one by the PCI) to increase its numbers in the Mezzogiorno. By 1953, party membership, which in 1945 was placed at 537,582, had grown to 1,621,620, with most of the new members coming from the southern reaches of Italy.[47] In 1946, 34.7 percent of the DC party members lived in the northwest and 19.6 percent in the northeast, while 22.6 percent lived in the south and 7 percent on the islands of Sicily and Sardinia. The remaining 17.1 percent were to be found in the center.

Seventeen years later, in 1963, the south and the islands combined to account for 58 percent of the membership, 41.9 percent in the south and 16.5 percent on the islands, while 17.5 percent were in the northwest and 11.2 percent in the northeast. In 1963 party membership in the center declined to 12.9 percent.[48] However, almost all these changes occurred between 1946 and 1953. By the latter year, the location of party members was rather similar to that of 1963 (northwest, 16.9 percent; northeast, 13.1 percent; center, 11.3 percent; south, 43.5 percent; and the islands, 15.2 percent). Between 1953 and 1963, changes in residence of party members varied only slightly by region.[49]

It is a proud claim of DC leaders as well as a point of general observation that the party draws members as well as voters from all Italian social classes. Table 4.6 and 4.7 report the sectors of employment by occupation between 1963 and 1972.

Just as one must not overstate the patronage sources of votes, one must bear in mind that this is a mass party more in name than in fact. The reality of party membership is a far cry from this impressive array of numbers, geographical, spread and balanced

Table 4.6. Christian Democratic Members:
Sectors of Economy and Selected Occupations
(percentages)

Sector	1963	1964	1965	1966	1967	1968	1969	1970	1971
Agriculture	19.51	18.73	18.049	17.005	16.78	16.085	16.218	15.375	15.275
(direct cultivators)	(11.44)	(11.81)	(11.749)	(11.236)	(11.303)	(11.087)	(11.103)	(10.611)	(10.670)
Industry	20.99	19.35	18.671	18.254	18.51	18.43	17.467	17.9	17.461
(blue-collar workers)	(17.06)	(15.98)	(15.082)	(14.480)	(14.89)	(14.55)	(13.971)	(13.973)	(13.59)
Commerce and tourism	5.37	5.79	6.033	6.509	6.51	6.652	6.358	6.294	6.115
Banking and insurance	.35	.57	.626	.686	.62	.664	.594	.684	.668
Artisans	5.67	5.47	5.497	5.674	5.55	5.637	5.097	4.998	4.893
Professions	2.37	1.88	1.820	1.838	1.81	1.918	1.851	1.879	1.842
Public activity	11.67	12.49	12.987	13.149	13.52	13.543	12.922	12.809	12.715
Students	2.74	2.75	3.039	3.359	3.45	3.959	4.750	4.823	5.014
Retirees	5.58	6.16	6.809	7.515	7.85	8.253	7.365	7.231	7.019
Housewives	25.60	25.20	24.864	24.464	23.91	23.275	25.056	24.624	24.842
Others	.55	1.61	1.605	1.547	1.42	1.584	2.285	3.385	4.106
Total	100	100	100	100	100	100	100	100	100

Source: Data provided from internal sources of Office of Organization, Christian Democratic Party.
Note: Because of reporting inaccuracies, percentages do not always sum correctly.

Table 4.7. Christian Democratic Members:
Sectors of Economy and Selected Occupations
(numbers)

Sector	1963	1964	1965	1966	1967	1968	1969	1970	1971
Agriculture	314,553	305,964	282,713	270,757	259,000	272,855	273,307	267,346	277,281
(direct cultivators)	184,560								
Industry	338,516	315,894	292,464	290,625	248,500	312,653	293,708	311,269	316,841
(blue-collar workers)	(275,153)	(260,923)	(236,244)	(230,550)	(238,472)	(246,800)	(234,911)	(242,984)	(256,625)
Commerce and tourism	86,563	94,538	94,499	103,626	102,000	112,834	106,925	109,446	110,950
Banking and insurance	5,648	9,207	9,805	10,928	8,500	11,264	10,467	11,905	12,119
Artisans	91,446	89,357	86,110	90,339	84,500	95,635	85,723	86,918	88,782
Professions	38,288	30,633	28,515	29,262	26,500	32,547	31,125	32,666	33,424
Public activity	188,093	204,009	203,430	209,350	214,000	229,752	217,272	222,753	230,729
Students	44,198	44,893	47,602	53,476	5,000	67,156	49,871	83,875	90,990
Retirees	89,953	100,556	106,653	119,646	123,000	139,996	123,849	125,746	127,370
Housewives	412,960	411,586	389,485	389,497	468,000	394,845	421,297	428,206	451,690
Others	2,512	26,366	25,138	24,628	21,000	26,865	38,430	58,863	74,502

Totals: 1963 = 1,612,730; 1964 = 1,633,003; 1965 = 1,566,428; 1966 = 1,592,134; 1967 = 1,600,000; 1968 = 1,796,002;
1969 = 1,681,404; 1970 = 1,738,996; 1971 = 1,814,578

Source: Data provided from internal sources of Office of Organization, Christian Democratic Party.
Note: Because of reporting inaccuracies, numbers do not always sum correctly.

representation of social classes. Active participation in the party
meetings and even in electoral campaigns is the preserve of a very
small portion of formal members. Most important, those who give
their time and energy to the DC do so not out of the ideological
commitment that typifies members of mass parties but rather for
the particularist reasons of machine politics, a contention supported by interviews with party leaders and members as well as the
characteristics of party leaders.

In response to a question concerning the place of members in
the party's decision-making, one national party leader offered the
following analysis:

> Here we must speak on the manner in which the parties are
> formed here in Italy, in particular, the mode in which the DC
> is formed. The members as such count very little. Very
> frequently they do not really exist, because their names are
> placed on the party lists without their knowledge. Often, the
> names are simply taken from the phone book. Members are
> therefore not interested and do not even know that they are
> party members. It is done even here in Torino, but less
> frequently than in the south. . . . In the areas around Rome,
> many people do not know that they are members of the
> party or many listed are dead, but continued as members. I
> know a professor who is a member in three party sections.
> He is from a *paese* in Canavese, Perosa, and is a
> member there. He was married in Torino where he joined a
> section controlled by right-wing factions. He moved to a
> residential area on the outskirts of Torino, where he joined
> the local section. He is, therefore, a member in each of three
> places. He does not know this, and votes only in his current
> place of residence where he votes for the left. In the other
> sections, there are others who vote for him and cast his ballot
> for the right. And it is done like this even for the dead.
>
> Now, this has always been a maneuver of the right and it
> occurs even here in Torino. . . . I went to a meeting of one of
> the sections here, one with 1,100 members. Of the 1,100,
> each year 400 change; in two years 800 change. Almost all
> are southern immigrants. They are all promised lodgings. Of
> those, 60, 70, or 80 do get lodgings, jobs, etc. The others no
> longer remain as members and others are sought to replace

them. Those who no longer remain as members almost always vote Communist.

This tale of membership padding is frequently repeated in descriptions of the DC. It reflects a party composed of professional activists in which large membership totals are useful in external and internal political conflicts.

Large portions of the listed membership are public employees and housewives. If party membership cards and DC activity are crucial to entry into and success within the public and quasi-public agencies, it is not surprising that public employees (and perhaps their wives) account for approximately one-third of party members.

Support for the view that most are party members in name only comes from other interview materials. The same respondent continued:

> Thus, the members practically count for very little. Who is it that counts among the masses? It is the "intermediate strata." Who are they? Those who are above all interested in the control of the majority, because that provides the control of the distribution of governing positions. This is true also at the communal level, which also controls the communal administration and positions appointed by that administration. The commune distributes, for example, all the positions for the public corporations, like the president of the Tram and Autobus Company of Torino, which employs 5,000 workers as well as the other public corporations, here, in Torino, twenty to thirty of them. The DC places approximately thirty members on each corporation—I am not certain of the exact number. Then, there are the public health corporations and other agencies which provide similar opportunities. These are present in Torino and in small communes as well. They are very important.
>
> This "intermediate strata" of the party, I would say, is interested essentially in those questions of power—and in truth the policy debate is almost completely missing. It is maintained by the left where there are centers of intellectuals or labor leaders, but for the rest there is no debate. So we see that the regroupings of the majority are regroupings in the

names of men. That is to say, there is no center and right,
there are the friends of Fanfani, Taviani, Moro, Piccoli,
Colombo. These are very large clienteles of very powerful
men. Emilio Colombo, the minister of the treasury, names
men to many powerful positions—heads of banks, savings
institutions, credit agencies—and from these forms groups of
power.

Asked whether there are enough possibilities for party members
to influence national leaders, he responded that there should be
more opportunities

but fewer members! If we were to have a nonfalsified accounting of members we would find 300-500,000 members,
no more! That is to say, we would have the 100,000 who
count plus those who every so often want to interest themselves. There are now at least 1 million members who have no
political interest and join for other reasons: the requirements
of labor, hunger, and poverty.

Another national party leader agreed with this description of 1
million too many members. "Yes, I too believe so. They are
members in name only. I do not know if the percentages are
correct, but I agree—perhaps even more. Thirty percent are active,
no more. However, when there are important, dramatic decisions
to be made, then participation is greater, but only then."[50]

This description of a large but inactive party membership was
echoed in interviews in the provinces of Vicenza, Potenza, and
Milan. One Vicentine leader argued: "The life of the party should
be influenced by the sections, but they are not at all active. The
provincial committee does not reflect the sections and consequently it does what it likes without feeling responsible to the
sections. It has been my experience that after the election
campaigns the sections close down or barely exist. The maximum
number that participate in the activities of the party, for example,
the selection of delegates to the party congresses, approaches 30
percent."

A Vicentine party leader pointed to the key distinction among
party members:

Members may be divided into two categories: those who
count and those who do not count. With those who count,

> the secretaries of the zones, the leaders, etc., are very friendly. . . . With the others, they do not ask their opinion, do not interest themselves, etc. They are more cold.

Another local leader described the members as follows:

> Our rank-and-file is difficult. It is always a rather small group on the local level that concern themselves and decide on the issues. It is the secretary of the section and the majority head, the two most important individuals who, in general, influence the judgment of the others in determining policy. Therefore, more often than not the rank-and-file reflect what is heard on a higher level. While it should be the case that the rank-and-file make suggestions.

The organization of the DC in the province of Potenza supports this general description. Though the formal organization indicated the presence of 113 sections, its outline reflected the rules more than the practice. I was unable to validate the general claim to 10,000–20,000 Christian Democrats in the province. The dearth of data was attributed by the chief functionary to the fact that full-scale organization of the DC in the province has been only recent. Many names that I selected were of dead people. Whether there were as many as 10,000 party members is considerably less significant than the number that took part in party activities. Discussions with leaders and my observation of section meetings make it clear that the number of activists was as few as 1,000. In addition, some party leaders thought that the rank-and-file attachments to the ideals, goals, and institution of the Christian Democratic party were weak. One leader told me that in the event of violence the PCI and MSI could each gather 400 or 500 youthful supporters. He doubted that the DC could amass more than a handful.

While the DC organization in the province of Milan occupies an impressive office building with a full complement of such organizational attributes as a well-organized bureaucratic staff, a weekly newspaper, frequent assembly meetings, and a computerized list of members' names, during my fieldwork it too suffered from infrequent member participation. Rarely did more than 20 to 30 percent of the 60,000 Milanese Christian Democrats engage in party activities; those who did most frequently attended section meetings, voted for congressional delegates, and sought favors from party leaders. In the words of one member of the party directorate:

> I believe that it is rare for the members to be active. They must be solicited to act, to contact the party leaders. Usually, member-initiated direct contacts with leaders occur when the members are concerned over particular local issues or at moments of difficulty or crises. . . . This is usually quite rare. Most of the time, rank-and-file attitudes and desires must be sought out by the leaders, who call on the members to ask for their positions.

Interviews of Milanese leaders and other party officials and followers confirmed this general lack of interest in party activities.

The rank-and-file members in the three provinces that I talked to described the influence and participation of the general membership in much the same terms. For the most part, they noted that they were not active but felt they should be more involved in party decision-making and general activities. They too disagreed whether more influence channels were needed or whether existing channels should be used more. Personal contacts and organized groups of members and leaders were the usual means of influence.

Except for those who claimed to have personal contacts in the provincial leadership, they all agreed that it was extremely difficult and, therefore, rare for them to have any influence in the party's decision-making process. Few interactions between party superordinates and subordinates occurred; many rank-and-file members perceived a considerable gap between party leaders and the rest of the members. In addition, several maintained that it was important for the party to end the divisions between the leaders and the rank-and-file, as well as those within the leadership. Several contended that there was a need for a more highly organized political party, even if it meant that the rank-and-file were to be subservient to the leadership.

With many inactive rank-and-file members and very many others who do not know that they are party members, who are the DC activists? The relatively high proportion of public officials and employees among the published categories of membership provides the clue. They are political professionals. Participation in party activities, from campaigning to officeholding, is typically associated with the control of political resources and jobs. Put simply, those who take part owe their professional and occupational success to their DC association.

Tables 4.8, 4.9, and 4.10 survey the characteristics of party leaders and underline the frequent association of officeholding in the DC and employment in government and quasi-government occupations. This pattern is present throughout the country but is most pronounced at the national level where there is no formal ban on the simultaneous control by a person of elected state and party offices.

The 39 members of the Central Directorate in January 1969 exemplify this picture of extraordinary overlap between the control of party and government offices. Only three were not

Table 4.8. DC National Council

1964	Elected	Nonelected
Incumbents	91	34
Returners	1	4
New	28	22
	120	60

1967	Elected	Nonelected
Incumbents	91	23
Returners	7	10
New	22	38
	120	71

1969	Elected	
Incumbents	82	
Returners	10	
New	28	
	120	

1973	Elected	
Incumbents	71	
Returners	22	
New	27	
	120	

Sources: Adapted from *I Congressi della DC,* supplement to *Il Popolo,* June 23, 1969; and *Il Popolo,* June 11, 1973.

Notes: Limitations of data: includes only 1960-73, which makes the "Returners" artificially low. Figures for 1969 and 1973 do not show nonelected members, which makes data for 1973 artificially slanted against finding incumbents. Thus, if anything, the data overstate the amount of turnover.

Table 4.9. DC Leaders in Party and Government Positions (percentages)

In party (N = 769)	Section secretary	Communal secretary	Provincial committee	Regional committee
	24.1	8.3	69.8	31.5

(N = 588)	One position	Two positions	Three positions	Four positions
	44.4	39.6	12.9	3.1

In government	Communal counselor	Communal assessor	Mayor	Provincial counselor	Provincial assessor	Provincial president	Regional deputy	Member of regional executive
(N = 779)	48.9	17.8	22.6	17.5	7.7	6.3	3.0	2.3

Source: Franca Cervellati Cantelli et al., *L'Organizzazione Partitica del PCI e della DC* (Bologna: Il Mulino, 1968), pp. 503-04.

Table 4.10. DC Leaders Who Have Worked or Held Positions in Various Sectors

Sector	N	%
Welfare, Assistance Institutions	792	34.3
Municipal Corps	792	3.2
Banks and Credit Agencies	792	12.4
Public Corps	792	8.8

Source: Franca Cervellati Cantelli et al., *L'Organizzazione Partitica del PCI e della DC* (Bologna: Il Mulino, 1968), p. 506.

members of parliament. Of the remaining thirty-six, nine were in the Senate and the rest in the Chamber of Deputies. Four had been presidents of the Council of Ministers and ten were in the cabinet, among them Rumor, the prime minister. During various stages of their careers, these men had controlled well over 200 positions in the national and local governments. They had reached and controlled the highest levels of Italian political power.

The professional character of DC activists is shown not only by their control of government positions but also because the "ladder of success" within the party is filled by these professionals. Access to the highest levels of the party is typically preceded by control of lower party offices and it is also increasingly closed to new entrants.

The DC in Mass Politics

Two threads are interwoven in this analysis of the Christian Democratic party. One is the party's place in the world of elections. The other deals with its activities in the contests which control government resources. Since the end of World War II, the DC has been the governing party of Italy. Until the 1976 election, its predominance was assured of itself, and it was recognized by all. To underline its electoral accomplishments, during those thirty years, it reduced to relative insignificance all other non-Marxist political organizations. At the same time, it developed from scratch a party organization able to compete with the well-oiled machinery of the Communist and Socialist parties. It has been supported by the largest and most diverse segments of the Italian populace—religious and nonreligious, rich and poor, urban and rural. It has, in short, been extraordinarily successful in mass political competition.

My analytic focus reaches into the contests within the party and government. It moves away from the realm of the voters. To analyze politics within the political elite, the electoral and organizational successes of the party must be considered to find factors that explain the presence of political clienteles—the availability of enormous amounts of government resources, few formal limits on contests for those resources, and the professional nature of party activists. In addition and as important, it highlights what is missing from my analysis. Examining the arena of competition within the political elite emphasizes but one side of DC politics—the care and feeding of political friends and the consequences of those actions— and ignores many of its successes. Most important, I do not deal with how it has drawn so many voters and members who are not concerned with its control of the pork barrel. I omit this for the purposes of my analysis. To delve more deeply into these topics takes me far afield and dilutes the clarity of the argument.

Stated most simply, the smoothest and safest road to political power in Italy is through the Christian Democratic party. The party is led and manned by individuals who control governing positions and who are employed by official and quasi-official bodies. It is a party composed of political professionals. Competition for the control of authoritative positions, in the party and government, occurs through its party factions, and most of them are political clienteles. As one party leader told me, "To be in Demochristian politics is to join a faction."

5. Factions in the Christian Democratic Party

The factions in the Italian Christian Democratic party violate two sorts of rules. The first is the section of the party statutes that proscribes factions. The second is a behavioral expectation. Over the years of the Italian republic, the number of political parties running candidates for parliament has never dipped below seven and it has almost always been as many as nine. If the political formations outside the parties, from the church's Civic Associations of the 1950s to various radical groups, are also counted, the number of actively competing political associations in Italy moves well beyond fifty. It would seem that political activists could find their demands met in any of the already existing political associations. Why then have there been seven to eight factions within the Christian Democratic Party? If they do not exhaust the number of possible positions on any given issue, surely the addition of the fifteen or so party factions (to count also those within the socialist parties) takes the issue beyond exhaustion. Put simply, there appear to be more political groups than issue positions.

The first objection to the presence of party factions founders on the unwarranted assumption that legal statutes determine behavior. Here, as in many other instances where there are neither sanctions levied against violators nor much legitimacy attached to the institutions, behavior as often as not ignores the rules.

The second objection is of equally limited power here. As Sartori argues, the logic of this argument applies solely to political groups tied by issue agreement in opposition to other such political associations. It is precisely the absence of issues as the bases of the cohesion of these factions that precludes the utility of this argument. In the analysis of party factions, Sartori's distinction between "visible" and "invisible" politics is most useful. While faction politics is the realm of invisible politics, it occurs in Italy in a political system in which visible (that is, publicly stated) claims are frequently tied to ideological pronouncements. Hence, the visible statements of faction leaders and followers must be couched in those same terms, even if, as frequently happens, what pass for the faction's principles change. It is necessary to

distinguish the tactical requirements of competition from the
bases of cohesion. Still, I do not contend that faction members
share no policy concerns. Indeed, demonstrations of loyalty to the
patron require agreement with his positions in visible politics. I
claim that issues do not keep the factions together. Hence, the
number of potential issue positions does not affect the number of
factions.[1]

The link between the two spheres of political competition is
obvious. Demands and claims are not only made in backrooms but
on the pages of newspapers and at public occasions. In addition,
faction leaders see themselves not only as horse-traders but also as
statesmen. They spare no efforts to frame their competitive
positions with principled arguments in their speeches at party
congresses and at section meetings, and in their frequently published collections of essays and addresses.[2] Furthermore, several
factions are associated with established and consistent positions on
several important issues. For twenty years, the *Fanfaniani* (the
followers of Amintore Fanfani, formally known as the *Nuove
Cronache* faction) have been viewed as especially interested in
institutionalizing the DC as a force independent of the Catholic
church and its collateral associations. Certainly, the two left-wing
factions, the Base and the Forze Nuove, have consistently ad-
vocated positions that have set them apart from the other factions
and from each other, and that are tied to well-developed political
ideologies. Still, with the exception of the left factions (and not all
elements of the Base), the DC factions are "groups of power," a
phrase used by Christian Democratic leaders themselves. One indication of the limited importance of principled issues to these
factions is that many have frequently shifted their positions on
general issues of party and government policy. The Fanfaniani
have followed their leader's trips to and from the ends of the DC's
political spectrum, variously being labeled and labeling themselves
"left" and "right." To a somewhat lesser extent, the *Morotei* and
the followers of Taviani and Sullo have done the same. All have
seemed at different times to be acting to provide the votes for a
new winning party coalition, and to have adapted their principles
accordingly.

The factions are groups of power, because their members are
tied by mutual interest, advantage, and personal loyalty, and

arranged in hierarchical order. They exchange unequal goods and services, typically government-related resources and votes; they are tied by patron-client chains; and they succeed in controlling government positions. Each faction operates in the spheres of national and local as well as in elective and appointive politics.

It is clear from the visible claims of the DC activists—from the faction headquarters, press agencies, formal organizations, not to mention their lists of candidates in party elections, as well as the observations of newsmen and scholars—that there are factions in the DC. My purpose is rather to develop the differences between the factions and to demonstrate that most are political clienteles.

Recent Faction History

The persistence of the factions and their relative strength at the various National Party Congresses between 1954 and 1973 is shown in table 5.1. Until the Naples Congress in 1954, De Gasperi and his "centrist" followers dominated the party, if not to the exclusion of other factions, at least to make it unnecessary to detail their size. The rise of the Iniziativa Democratica, in that year, led by Fanfani and Taviani marks the turning point in faction history. The Fanfani secretariat initiated at the Naples Congress dates the effective end of party control of the older leaders and the inauguration of the attempt to establish the DC as a bona fide political institution. The successes of the Fanfani group structure the subsequent goals and modes of competition within the party.

That Fanfani and his supporters have controlled the party since 1954 is most readily shown by noting that four of the factions at the 1969 Congress and five of the factions at the 1973 Congress derive from the Iniziativa Democratica. The faction split when the Dorotei formed in 1959 and ousted Fanfani from the position of party secretary; it split again when Taviani seceded from the Dorotei in 1966 and again when Moro and his followers dropped out in 1968; and finally once more when Rumor and Piccoli separated from Colombo and Andreotti in 1969. The last division ended a period of Dorotei predominance, in which they controlled the position of party secretary and most of the positions in the Secretariat. The shift in the party majority in 1969 returned Forlani, a follower of Fanfani, to the head of the party. In 1973,

Table 5.1. Factions in the DC National Council

Faction	1954	1956	1959	1964	1967	1969	1973
Centrismo Popolare-Forze Libere	2	6	7	14	8^b	4	
Notabili		3	3				
De Gasperiani	8						
Primavera	3	10	4				
Iniziativa Democratica	52	76					20^c
Dorotei			79	56	50^b	46	35^c
Fanfaniani			39	26	20^b	18	24
Morotei						16	10
Tavianei					14	12	7^c
Nuova Sinistra						2	
Base	8	10	9	12^a	14^a	11^a	12^a
Forze Nuove	3	3	3	12^a	14^a	11^a	12^a

Sources: Adapted from Gianfranco Pasquino, "Le Radici del Frazionismo e Il Voto di Preferenze," *Rivista Italiana di Scienza Politica,* vol. 2, no. 2 (1972), p. 357; *I Congressi della D.C.* (*Il Popolo,* special supplement to the edition of June 27, 1969); *Il Popolo,* July 2, 1969 and June 11, 1973.

Note: The sources omit the faction divisions of the 1962 Party Congress. In 1961, four members of the Council were Tambroniani.

    a. The Base and Forze Nuove presented a combined list of candidates.

    b. These factions presented a combined list of candidates.

    c. In 1970, the Dorotei split into the Rumor-Piccoli and Colombo-Andreotti factions. The larger, Rumor-Piccoli, joined with the Tavianei to present a common list of candidates.

Fanfani himself assumed the position once again. The selection of Zaccagnini to replace Fanfani in 1975 marks the first clear repudiation of this generation of party leaders.

    Standing outside the descendants of the Iniziativa Democratica are two groups of factions that share little except minority status during most of this period. One group, perhaps best considered right-wing, has controlled a small and declining segment of the party. The other, drawing on the left-wing sources of the Catholic trade union movement and political and intellectual support, has occupied a somewhat larger and much more solid bloc within the National Council. The alliance between the Base and Forze Nuove and the Morotei begun in 1969 has added much to the left's power and is the basis for Zaccagnini's present party majority.

The analytic literature on DC party factions contains both scholarly agreement and bitter dispute.[3] There is a consensus that the same factions, often the same individuals, have controlled the party since the early 1950s. Observers also agree that the early 1960s marked an increase in the number of factions and the intensity of their conflict. In addition, by the late 1960s all the factions had administrative headquarters and staffs, study groups, news agencies, and regularly scheduled formal meetings of their leaders. Analysts divide over the genesis of the factions and the determinants of the recent changes.

Three issues are of primary importance: the sheer number of factions; the increase over the years in the number of factions; and the upturn in the volatility of faction conflict. Attempts to relate any of these to sustained policy divisions within the party or to the party's electoral sources—in terms of social class or region—can be only partially successful. Neither the bases of membership nor the formation of party factions after the end of the 1950s may be tied to these phenomena. Both observers and participants agree that ideological divisions alone would produce no more than three factions and could not account for the increase in their number or the intensity of their conflict in recent years. Most recent analyses focus on the importance of the continuous control of government patronage and the mode of interfaction competition as primary causal factors for each problem.

Lombardo associates factional growth with the changes in the mode of competition for cabinet positions that followed the center-left alliance. Once the party leaders agreed that the Socialist tie was irreversible, Lombardo argues, those seeking to control cabinet positions required the tactical support of other factions in the PSI and PSDI, as well as in the DC. Also, the only way for the minority factions in the DC to influence their party leaders was through the factions of the other parties. The shift in the mode of competition for cabinet ministries increased the importance of the factions and brought about their fragmentation and the rise in the intensity of their battles.[4]

Sartori links the growth in the number of "factions of convenience" to changes in the internal party rules. These factions, primarily concerned with the control of party and government positions, grew with the introduction of proportional representation as the decision rule governing party contests.[5] Others share this description of the growth of clientelist factions within the party, if not the explanations offered by Sartori and Lombardo. Passigli contends the presence of clientelist factions preceded the use of proportional representation,[6] and Pasquino demonstrates that there were nine party factions even before the center-left agreement with the Socialists and the establishment of proportional representation.[7] In Pasquino's argument, as Lombardo's, proportional representation was installed to assure a threatened and weakened majority faction access to governing positions.[8]

The different responses derive from contrasting theoretical starting points. Sartori commences with the individual political actors and sees proportional representation as facilitating those seeking governing positions. Lombardo develops a similar argument, using the modes of competition for cabinet positions. Once in power, both argue, the competitive pattern persists as it denies the need for policy consequences and keeps from power those with more general concerns. The contrasting position in this literature held by Passigli and Pasquino draws on the presence of patron-client arrangements in the society and party prior to the installation of proportional representation and the center-left coalition formula. All agree that each of those factors has exacerbated internal conflict.

The growth in the number and importance of clientelist factions coincided with (1) the institutionalization of the party; (2) a marked increase in the number of economic positions controlled by the government (and the party); (3) the use of proportional representation as a decision rule in party contests, and (4) the center-left governing coalition. As I noted in chapter 3, their presence also occurs in a society long characterized by the norms and practice of clientelism. As such, it is impossible to determine whether the political clienteles formed to take advantage of the new opportunities or whether the opportunities themselves provided the means for the institutionalization of clienteles whose sources are elsewhere, whether in cabinet competition or the lower levels of the party and society. That is to say, in Italy both sets of explanatory variables are present. Thus the resolution of the theoretical conflict awaits tests of the arguments where it is possible to isolate the relevant phenomena.

Types of Factions

With numerous transient and persistent factions, how does one distinguish among them? One way is to classify according to policy differences. Analyses of ideology underscore the distinction between left and nonleft factions, and between the Base and the Forze Nuove.

One regional leader of the Fanfaniani told me:

> The most important preoccupation of the left is the relationships with other parties, with the forces of the democratic left in Italy. The Fanfaniani are preoccupied with the contents of the party programs. The Dorotei are concerned above all with the control and use of power for themselves and the maintenance of the social equilibrium.

The Forze Nuove leader cited in chapter 4 bears repeating:

> I would say that the intermediate level of the party [the party activists] are essentially interested in questions of power and, in truth, the policy debate is almost completely missing. It is maintained alive only by the left. . . . So that we see that the regroupments of the majority are regroupments in the names of men. That is to say, there is no center and right; there are the "friends" of Fanfani, Taviani, Moro, Piccoli, Colombo. . . .

He went on to associate the differences between the Base and his own faction with their respective social sources:

> The Base derives from the ethico-social roots of Christianity, from the liberal Catholics of the Risorgimento and the post-Risorgimento. We have roots in the social left—the workers' movements, the unions, ACLI, and the like. They are closer to the "cultural" liberals and radicals. Thus, it is a very real difference. We find it very hard to join the majority in which there is not real change in the structure and distribution of economic power and with it political power. While the impression that one has of the Base, as with all intellectual groups, is that they "play the game more easily."

A Base leader drew different conclusions from a similar description of the two factions:

> We derive from the Catholic movement's political tradition. Therefore, we operate at the general level, striving to work for the interests of the entire party. The Forze Nuove is drawn from the unions, the ACLI, from particular social sources, and therefore tends to represent, in a vivid manner, a part of the party, a particular interest, and tends above all to give prevalence to economic/social problems. On the other hand, we emphasize institutional policies, foreign policy issues, and the party's relations with other political forces.
> We have quite different fundamental thoughts and traditions, even if current needs force us to work together to renew the party and battle the other factions.

Another Base leader who has frequently occupied cabinet positions echoed these analyses.

> The sindacalisti [the unionists, i.e., the Forze Nuove] have a religious mission: they seek to get the rich to be good. This is derived from our religion, but it has no place in politics. We strive to work with the other forces of the left, the Socialists and, if you want, the Communists, to bring about reform and democracy. Reform must be done in Italy with the consent of the left, because the others do not care for reform.

These differences between the Base and the Forze Nuove seen so clearly in Rome frequently become obscured at the local levels of the party. In Vicenza and Milan, both factions were present but were not easily distinguishable. A Vicentine leader of the Forze Nuove first surveyed the faction differences as tied to their respective social and cultural sources and therefore to particular and general policy interests. He then added: "I am a member of the Forze Nuove faction because of its left-wing policies. I have never been a union member. I am a lawyer, and, from my point of view, there is not a very strong difference between the factions. Very often there are differences of persons. There are differences based on personal desires." In Milan, the policy differences between all the factions were related primarily to national problems. One Milanese leader of the Dorotei noted: "There are differences not in relation to Milan, but over the national party program, especially over relations with the Communists at the national level." Another echoed this association between local factions and national concerns:

I would say that the national situation has its counterparts and results on the provincial and communal levels. Because of their organizations, the factions have a provincial-level presence as well. There are differences over attitudes and positions. We are more of an interclass nature than the left. They have, perhaps, a more limited view. Locally, there are issues, for example, the recent demonstrations against NATO. We differ from the Base who seek a more independent foreign policy.

Interfaction policy differences frequently stem from national issues as reflected by the unity of the left in Vicenza:

I am a member of the "left" faction. I would say that I was one of the first of the left in the party in Vicenza, before the birth of the [national] Base faction of Granelli, DeMita, and Galloni which was formed in the early "centrist" period. Thus the left faction was formed early here in the city. I would say about 1953-54. We pressed for the "center-left" against the policy of 1953 which had us working with the bourgeois party, the Liberals, on the national level.

We formed the left here in Vicenza, as, in the words of Giovanni Gronchi, to return the party to its origins. . . . In those years, 1953, 1954, and 1955, the left was considered—I would not say like Communists—but with much disfavor. We of the Vicentine left are united. We have never agreed with all that is done in Rome by the left factions, either the Base or the Forze Nuove. We are truly united. When the Forze Nuove was formed on the national level we continued together. . . .

The distinction between the united Vicentine left and the other factions also characterizes the others as political clienteles. One young left faction leader in Vicenza contended:

We by tradition are not fully associated with the national factions, because we are in a very difficult position in the party. Here, there is a majority group of the Dorotei; against them are all of the groupings of the party left—the Base, the Forze Nuove and the youth. . . . We have not split into different components but seek to present a united left in the province and in the region as a whole. And for the most part, we are successful. . . .

There are significant differences between the left-wing and

the Dorotei and the rest of the right-wing. I would say, for example, that the Fanfaniani in Vicenza do not exist. They have chosen to align themselves with the Dorotei and to form a single list of candidates for party office. Thus, even if they call themselves Fanfaniani, they are really a group within the Dorotei. The same applies to the members of the right-wing of the party, the followers of Scelba or Scalfaro. They are in actuality members of the Dorotei. . . . There is then a clear distinction between the left and the rest in Vicenza and this split has lasted at least eight to ten years (since the late 1950s).

Now the clear difference between the two positions is that we of the left have always attempted to establish a very clear policy line for the Vicentine party. The DC controls all of the 122 communes in the province. This is the only province in all of Italy where this is true. . . . We should therefore strive to make this a model of Christian Democrat administration for the entire country—as the Communists have done in Emilia—Romagna. Sadly, we have not done so. This great large majority . . . has limited itself to a leadership which seeks only the servicing of power. . . .

A Dorotei leader provided a different perspective on the personalist components of faction differences and battles. After outlining the general agreement among party and faction activists over the principles of Catholicism, he described the differences within the majority Dorotei:

There are battles within the group—battles based on personality and on method. . . . We do not have a democratic mass base which discusses the ideas. Most of these issues and ideas are based on clienteles and are predetermined ideas and ways of looking at things presented to the masses at the Congresses, where the results are predetermined. The leaders— already selected—are chosen on personalist grounds. There are some within the Dorotei who are trying to change this system. . . .

If a nonleft faction is not tied by shared issue and policy preference, how then does it cohere? The key is the attachment to the political patron. One Vicentine activist contended that

Groups are formed around men. When a leader dies it is hard to say what will happen to the followers. It is not a matter of having opinions and ideas in forming and belonging to a faction. It's a matter of having confidence in a certain person. If the groups were based on ideas then it would be possible for the groups to survive. But this is not the case. The only ideals that the members of the factions have to believe in are those that are publicized by the leaders.

Another leader, generally less critical in his comments, repeated the view that there were no policy differences between the nonleft factions: "The policy diversity is not real and substantial but formal. It is a diversity of alignment rather than content."

Two other faction activists stressed the discrepancies between the claim that the factions reflect issue differences and the reality that they do little more than compete for power: "Theoretically, from an ideal point of view, they should be factions of opinion, expressions of different political views, the products of social and cultural differences. They are that but, in reality and in most cases, they are *'gruppi di potere'* [power groups] acting to defend and enlarge their influence." Another strikingly similar view:

In theoretical and perhaps ideal terms the factions are opinion groups, offering ideas which are promoted by a democratic process. This would be less dangerous than what we have now. Initially, the factions were opinion groups, which served to make the DC a vibrant party. In more recent years, groups concerned with power united around particular men. . . . Rather than fight for ideals, they fight for positions. These groups are now well delineated. They fight for positions, and thus their differences are not ideological but tactical ones tied to the competition. It's hard to find any real differences between the nonleftists. . . .

The dominance of the leaders within the factions is further underlined in the next comment, by another Vicentine activist:

There are a few leaders. They meet often; they reason among themselves and decide what is best to do to keep power. . . . The leaders decide; the others must follow. The leaders, of course, must try to interpret public opinion, but what is

decided must be accepted. Those on the national level have a
greater possibility to synthesize, to mediate and have a
greater view and range. There are many groups within the
party and they must get together to rule the party. . . .
Because the factions revolve around individuals, no single
group has enough to control the party.

A Vincentine faction member described the internal structure
of the nonleft factions:

I would say that theoretically each faction ought to have
similar types of members throughout all of Italy. However, in
all frankness, it seems to me that there are divisions within
the factions and that certain members of one faction are
closer to certain leaders within their faction than they are to
other leaders. For example, those who follow Colombo are
closer to him than they are to Rumor or to Piccoli. This
should be condemned because they are based on personalist
followings. I believe that there ought to be agreements or
disagreements based on the problems rather than on the
personalities involved.

These comments drawn from local-level fieldwork were echoed
and emphasized by national faction leaders. A leader of another
faction summarized the link between the internal structure of the
factions and the patterns of internal party competition:

According to me the conflicts should be resolved on the basis
of internal discussions of the group [that is, the directorate]
regarding the general interests of the party, and not on the
basis, as is often the case, of the interests of the leaders. Our
party is divided into groups, and because of this a group
leader has a determining influence.

These descriptions chosen from my initial fieldwork interviews
in 1968 and 1969 were echoed during my discussions with faction
leaders in 1972. One long-time faction leader and cabinet minister
laid to rest any notions of ideology and policy as bases of faction
cohesion:

Did you think that there were philosophical or ideological
bases for these groups? Given the policy differences in the
party, there ought to be three groupings: a "left" (with

perhaps two parts); a "center"; and a "right." That there are now nine factions is caused by the presence of proportional representation.

Similarly:

The number of factions has now grown to nine. This is due to personal power games within the party. When a new faction forms, such as the Tavianei, or the Morotei, it must justify itself in ideological terms, but this is artificial. The factions are power groups.

Another faction leader characterized the general picture:

The factions have no internal constitution. They are informal, and are groupings of political leaders. Within the Tavianei and the Morotei, they are devoted followers of the leader and the faction members always obey the decisions. Within the Fanfaniani, the same applies, but there has been a shift of power to Forlani.

Some general features of the party factions emerge from these statements. Most of them are not bound by agreed political principles or policy issues; most are tied to particular political patrons. With regard to policy, even philosophical differences, at best a left and nonleft division may be distinguished. To call those in the latter cluster centrists or rightists is to place them on a political spectrum, not to analyze their policies. Within the left, there are also divisions which affect their behavior within the party and government. This is not so for the others. What is crucial to each of them, what keeps them tied, is attachment to the faction leader or leaders. Adding these factors to the professional character of party activists noted in chapter 4, another feature emerges. The factions are instruments of elite politics. They do not engage the passions of most of the party members, but of those active within the party.

At the same time, the various links and levels within each faction should be underlined. Although each is a united contestant in the arena of national politics, the ties between members throughout the country may be weak. In some instances, national divisions are not reproduced in local politics. In others, although there are competing local factions, they all claim fealty to the same national patron. In still others, local factions are tied to different national factions. Each clientelist faction is composed of chains of local factions. Each is led by a leader or alliance of leaders. Central to all of them is the choice of leader and how he retains his power. He is a political patron.

The Structure of Clientelist Factions

There is a recurring formula to the accumulation of local political power, the first step to faction leadership. The prime ingredient is the exchange of governing positions for support in party and governmental electoral contests. In the system of proportional representation that rules Italian elections, political power is best indicated by the size of the candidate's preference vote. Given the patterns noted in chapter 4, it is not surprising that the control of public works positions provides major sources of local patronage and underpins the leader's local power base. Numerous sources have described the Cassa per il Mezzogiorno (the Development Fund for the South) as a major fount of patronage for southern politicians. In particular, *auto-strada* (highway) construction has provided numerous jobs and contracts to be dispensed in return for political support, as well as visible evidence of the leader's power. This method has been used by Andreotti (the Avezzano-Sora highway), by DeMita (the Avellino-Volturara-Lioni autostrada) and by Natali (the highway in Gran Sasso).[9] Perhaps the most famous example of the correlation between political power and highway construction is the auto-strada connecting Bolzano, Vicenza, and Rovigo, the home provinces of Piccoli, Rumor, and Bisaglia.[10] As in other polities, the construction of post offices is also a major source of patronage power, and Gaspari (Chieti province) and Bosco (Caserta province) appear to have made particular use of such sources.[11]

Chapter 4 showed that the DC controls most of the positions in the government and quasi-governmental institutions of Italy. This control has been turned into sources of personal and factional power as much and perhaps more than party power. Giuseppe Tamburrano reports a series of studies detailing the accumulation of personal power by DC faction leaders:

> According to the Corriere della Sera (study by Gian Paolo Pansa) Gullotti controls almost all the Demochristian communal and provincial assessors; he has men in the Banca del

> Sud, the harbor corporation, the Consortium for industrial growth . . .

as well as a host of other organizations in Messina, including the consortia for the Messina-Palermo and Messina-Catania highways. "It is unnecessary to say that Gullotti also controls the party's and government's elected positions. In addition, he is also at the center of the relations between all the categories of the local bourgeoisie. . . ."[12] Tamburrano argues that the extent of Gullotti's power in Messina is replicated by other leaders in other parts of Italy. Gioia is described as being equally well connected and powerful in Palermo; a major part of his power rests with the control of the Banca di Sicilia. Lima's power in Sicily also stems from his control of governing positions.[13] However, the location of these political clienteles in Sicily should not be used to argue that machine factions are to be found only in southern Italy. Tamburrano and others cite evidence of political clienteles throughout Italy.

The links between the national and local levels in the patron-client chains are nicely illustrated in the following description of the Neopolitan party organization:

> The party section and the new Headquarters in Via Marconi are a coming and going of jacks of all trades who smile or who have the small official's frown; when one of them passes among the groups of small clients who are habitually to be found on a weekday waiting for an errand to be rewarded with a *raccomandazione* or an entry pass to one of the VIPs, a name is whispered. . . . It is not the name of the person who is passing, but the name of the notable to whom the small official, the jack of all trades, the section secretary, is tied in one way or another. Behind the severe look of a secretary, there is the memory of a minister, or a "dynamic" under-secretary.[14]

Local prominence requires the support of a national leader, for it is through national contacts that a budding patron can first obtain the control of local branches of national institutions. Local leaders are provided with the exclusive rights to particular organizations controlled by national leaders; in return, they must support the patron. This is the first link in the chain that ties local and national leaders.

The rise to regional and national power requires patronage sources at each of those levels of government. Thus, a frequent pattern has been for the move to national leadership to follow extended periods at subcabinet and cabinet positions—for example, Gava (Naples), Bisaglia (Rovigo), and DeMita (Avellino) dominate the political life of their provinces; they gather massive preference votes in party and election contests (in the 1972 parliamentary elections DeMita gathered 127,000 such votes and Gava, 96,000; in the 1969 Party Congress, Gava and Bisaglia placed eighth and fifth, respectively); they control party appointments and elections; and they have effective sway over local party politics.

The political ascendancy of each has depended on the control of public offices, and each moved to regional and national prominence after serving in cabinets and gaining access to national sources of patronage. While the Gava clan has recently lost regional power (to a group supported by DeMita), Bisaglia and his followers have scored victories in DC contests in the northeast, even at the expense of Piccoli and Rumor. In the spring and summer of 1975, Bisaglia succeeded in replacing Rumor as co-leader of the national Dorotei.

Gava, Bisaglia, and DeMita not only exemplify the mode of rising within the party, but they also evidence the pervasiveness of this pattern within the party in the north (Bisaglia) as well as the south (Gava), in the nonleft factions (Bisaglia and Gava), and in the left factions (DeMita). The latter, a national Base leader, has defeated Gava's forces in regional party elections in Campania. DeMita's political base combines a clientelist organization: personal contacts, the exchange of raccomandazioni and jobs for political support with policy statements supporting development and modernization in the south and a left-wing position at the national level. Like other patrons in their areas, he maintains absolute control of politics in Avellino. Tamburrano cites a study by Manlio Rossi Doria which argues that in the province of Avellino all the presidents and a majority of the administrative councils and councilors and those on the governmental and quasi-governmental agencies are controlled by the DC. This is true of the local development agency, the chamber of commerce, the consortium for technical instruction, and the hospital administrations as well as a host of other institutions in Avellino, Ariano, and Solofra.[15]

Finally, to make it to the pinnacle of power, to be consistently named to key cabinet positions, and particularly to become prime minister, one must have access to national level patronage positions. No small part of Fanfani's amazing staying power at the highest level of Italian politics derives from his control of numerous and key positions in the state-owned Italian radio and television system. Other prominent national leaders have access to similar, if not as many, positions. Thus, Rumor also controls important positions in RAI-TV, as did Moro until his death, and IRI; Colombo, when the minister of the treasury, controlled numerous offices in the world of banking and finance. The importance of these offices to national level power is well underscored by the bitter fighting between Piccoli and Zaccagnini in 1975 over control of RAI-TV offices for the DC.[16]

Fanfani's place at the very top of the Italian political pyramid for over twenty years has also rested on the support of many local level powers, as well as his sources at the national level and in his home region, Tuscany. Gioia's power in Palermo, Bosco's dominance in Caserta, and Natali's power in Chieti are but part of the clientele chain that has tied Fanfani to national political dominance. The effects of the disastrous regional elections in June 1975 have begun to unravel the clientele and to weaken Fanfani's power. The defection of Gian Aldo Arnaud with part of the faction has provided a picture of the Fanfaniani as it existed through much of this period. Table 5.2 describes the faction's internal organization. Because the evidence emerged only after Arnaud's splitting the faction, the table emphasizes the number of those who left Fanfani and does not provide sufficient detail on Forlani's following. Still, it underlines the checkerboard character of the distribution of faction members and the predominance of single leaders in their home areas.

Thus, the factions are "groups of power," not only because their primary goal is to control political offices, but also because of the relationship between faction members and leaders. Each nonleft faction is organized around a leader or an alliance of leaders. Each patron is supported by two sets of followers. The first set, located in his home province (Fanfani-Arezzo, Moro-Bari,

Table 5.2. The Fanfaniani
(1968-74)

Chief	Area	Cabinet	Parliament	DC National Council
Fanfani	Tuscany	x	x	x
Primary leader				
Forlani	Marche	x	x	x
Secondary leaders				
Arnaud	Turin	x	x	x
Bosco	Campania	x	x	x
Butini	Florence			
D'Arezzo	Tuscany	x	x	x
Malfatti	Umbria	x	x	x
Gioia	Sicily	x	x	x
Sullo	Avellino	x	x	x
Vincelli	Calabria	x	x	x
Martinelli	Como	x	x	x
Tertiary leaders				
Cannarella	Bergamo-Brescia			
Prandini	Bergamo-Brescia			x
Rampa	Bergamo-Brescia	x	x	x
Moria	Parma			x
Ercini	Umbria			x
Radi	Umbria	x	x	a
Ciaffi	Marche			b
Terzoni	Marche			
Santonasto	Campania		x	x
Perugini	Calabria			x
Becciu	Sardinia		x	

Source: Adapted from *Panorama,* October 2, 1975.
Note: Omitted are such Fanfaniani as Bernabei and Principi who control public agencies.
     a. Regional president.
     b. Regional party secretary.

Taviani-Genoa, Rumor-Vicenza, Piccoli-Trento, Andreotti-Lazio, and Colombo-Potenza) contains his local political clients, the party activists, and the mass-level supporters organized to supply preference votes. The second set is made up of the political clienteles of other patrons also active in national politics who have tied themselves as clients to the national leader. One consequence of this internal structure is that the geographic spread of each faction is directly tied to the personal sources of each faction leader and of the other leaders aligned with him. Tables 5.3 and 5.4 outline the structure of the factions during the height of the center-left period.

The political bases of Colombo and Rumor more fully describe the national-local links of the clientelist factions in Potenza and Vicenza. Each has been a DC party leader since the late 1940s and each has served as prime minister. In addition, Rumor, one of the founders of the Dorotei faction, was party secretary between 1963 and 1969 and has occupied numerous key cabinet positions. Colombo has controlled cabinet positions which determine economic policy.

Colombo has been the dominant power in his native province of Potenza and region of Basilicata. No other political leader in the area has equal stature, and until recently all DC political activists were members of this faction. Several factors indicate his controlling position. He has maintained very high preference votes in party and national elections. In 1968, 66.7 percent of those voting for the Christian Democratic party in his district cast preference votes for him, thereby setting a percentage record of preference votes received by a candidate in Italy. In 1972, he increased those votes, gathering more than 117,000 personal ballots. At the DC National Party Congress in June 1969, he received the third largest number of preference votes. Furthermore, his control of the party organization in the region is best summarized by noting that during Moro's tenure as DC general secretary, the only region to which he was never invited to speak was Basilicata.

A leader of one of the national factions described to me Colombo's rise to political power:

> Colombo is an above-average man from the south who became vice-president of GIAC [the youth branch of Italian Catholic Action] at the end of the war in an area in which the Popular party had had no followers. Where the PPI had followers in 1945 and earlier the political leadership class of the DC was formed by the former members of the Popolari— that is, those who were forty to fifty years of age—who were

Table 5.3. Factions as Patron-Client Chains
(Geographic Spread 1968–74)

	Morotei	Tavianei	Fanfaniani	Rumor-Piccoli	Colombo-Andreotti
Chief (area)	Moro (Bari-Puglia)	Taviani (Genoa)	Fanfani (Arezzo-Tuscany)	Rumor Piccoli (Vicenza) (Trento)	Colombo Andreotti (Basilicata) (Lazio)
Primary leader (area)		Gaspari (Chieti)	Forlani (Pesaro-Ancona)	Bisaglia (Rovigo)	
Secondary leaders (area)	Gui (Padova) Kessler (Trento) Belci (Trieste)	Sarti (Cuneo)	Natali (Chieti) Gioia (Sicily) Bosco (Caserta) Arnaud (Turin) Butini (Florence)	V. Russo (Foggia) Gullotti (Messina) Ruffini (Palermo) Pucci (Catanzaro) Gava (Naples) Ferrari-Aggradi (Emilia)	Lima (Palermo) Evangelisti (Rome) Signorello (Rome)

Table 5.4. Sources of Votes for Faction Deputies in Italian Geographic Zones (percentages)

Zone[a]	Forze Nuove		Base		Morotei		Tavianei		Fanfaniani		Rumor Piccoli		Colombo-Andreotti		Forze Libere	
	1968	1972	1968	1972	1968	1972	1968	1972	1968	1972	1968	1972	1968	1972	1968	1972
I	29.2	20.6	31.6	32.7	8.3	6.1	40.9	36.4	14.4	8.6	13.2	14.1	12.9	16.7	15.8	50.0
II	20.8	22.2	15.7	10.7	30.5	33.3	4.5	9.0	11.4	11.4	37.7	32.1	6.4	3.3	10.5	10.5
III	25.0	18.5	10.5	7.1	13.9	15.1	4.5	4.5	31.4	36.2	13.2	14.1	12.9	10.0	15.8	16.7
IV	8.3	7.5	36.8	46.5	39.0	36.4	45.6	45.6[b]	31.4	31.4	24.5	26.9	51.7	53.3	26.3	8.3
V	16.7	22.2	5.4	3.6	8.3	9.1	4.5	4.5	11.4	11.4	11.4	12.8	16.1	16.7	31.6	25.0

Source: Franco Cazzola, "Partiti, Correnti e voto de Preferenza," in *Un Sistema Politico alla Prova*, Mario Caciagli and Alberto Spreafico, eds. (Bologna: Il Mulino, 1975), p. 134.

a. Zone I: the industrial northwest; Zone II: the "White" northeast; Zone III: the "Red" center; Zone IV: the south; Zone V: the islands.

b. This corrects an apparent typographical error.

young or not so young—and those who were sixty years old
who had been leaders of the PPI, like De Gasperi, Piccione,
Spataro, and Scelba, who had been Sturzo's secretary. While
in those zones in which the PPI had no structure as in almost
all of southern Italy—the Popolari were strong in the north
and in parts of Sicily, but that was all—the GIAC members
formed the party. Colombo who found himself with
practically no one in front of him at twenty-six years of age
was elected a deputy.

Colombo's control of the DC persists even though new political
forces control the party in Potenza. During my initial fieldwork in
1969, the majority faction was composed of young men who
proclaimed their desire to bring about fundamental change within
Potenza and the entire region. This transition was greatly resented
by older party leaders who felt that their rightful position to
control the party had been stolen. One such leader, a mayor of a
commune, argued, "It is the third generation which is in the
minority and wrongly so. The second generation passed on the
power to those of the fourth generation to save themselves and in
the process cut off those in their forties from their rightful
positions."

This new political group of men in their late twenties and early
thirties with university degrees is best typified by their leader,
Angelo Sanza, the provincial secretary between 1968 and 1972
who was elected to Parliament in 1972. When first elected, he was
the youngest secretary in the DC. Sanza joined the party in 1958,
and at eighteen, when he became a member of the Youth
Movement, was elected the provincial delegate, and then rapidly
rose to national leadership position. After receiving his degree in
economics at the University of Rome, he rejected a faculty
position at the university to return to Potenza. The reasons that
several young party leaders decided to leave the more developed
areas of Italy where they were educated and to return to Potenza
have colored much of their political activities.

In our talks, the new political leaders described themselves and
how they saw their tasks:

It must be made precise that we are a group of quite
homogeneous persons, young, twenty-five to thirty years of
age. Thus we are different than the rest of the party. In the

past, in Potenza, they were not homogeneous. They were of all ages and all ideologies and relied much more on individuals actions and leadership. They were more restrictive in making decisions.

Decisions in a modernizing society such as Basilicata cannot be made solely at the top. The people in our region have suffered hundreds of years of misery and have a sense of fear, a lack of confidence, in the political leaders. Many political leaders have exploited them in the past.

I believe that it is our task to gain the confidence of the people by this new type of political leadership and to criticize and condemn that which they feel is wrong. Even though the DC has received such a large vote the people still have no confidence in it.

Another leader echoed this theme:

We are a poor region and in the past people would seek party positions for economic or prestige reasons. The new leaders are young and care more about "popular" issues.

Colombo's dominance is further exemplified by his ties with local party activists. Not only were they all members of his faction, but they all agreed that he could control local party decisions whenever he so desired. One party leader told me that that Colombo intervened on a local issue perhaps only once a year. When he did, the provincial secretary had no real power. In addition, the secretary was an observer for Colombo. He kept Colombo informed on local issues and relayed the national patron's wishes to the party in Potenza. For those in the majority faction, national-Potenza relations (really Colombo-Potenza relations) were excellent: "The situation in Potenza is exceptional, as the provincial and national majorities are the same. Thus, national decisions are completely accepted in Potenza and we do not try to influence the national leaders." Another leader added:

Our relations with the national level of the party are excellent, because our provincial secretary was a leader of the youth movement in Rome and he knows many people and we have Colombo in the Direzione Centrale. We cannot influence the national party leaders.

Two other leaders provided somewhat exaggerated views of the virtues and costs of Colombo's dominance:

> We have no factions. We are all of the Impegno Democratico [Dorotei]. . . . There is no majority or minority caused by different interpretations of the party statutes or by the division into party factions. The splits that we have are local. We are all united in the ideology of the DC, particularly that of the Impegno Democratico and of our leader, Emilio Colombo. . . . Our situation is unique.

Another and contrary view:

> The control of the party is in Colombo's hands. He is tied to the local leaders and the deputies through the personal ties of clientelism. They are his satellites.

The minority group in in Potenza in 1969 was composed of two factions, the largest of which had recently been the majority faction and was headed by the former provincial secretary. The collegial characteristics of the new majority clearly did not apply to this faction. According to one party leader, "In the past the provincial secretary expressed his position and it prevailed. The problem was never examined collegially. Therefore, the conclusion of one man was brought before the provincial committee where it was ratified." The new majority faction differed from this in the relatively more equal relations among its members and their greater concern with the modernization of the area.

The elaborate policy goals of the majority faction notwithstanding, they, too, were all members of the Colombo clientele and had very close relations with him. They adapted their policy desires to the pattern of political competition which had been successful in their area for generations. They neither joined the class-based political parties nor the principle-based political groups within the DC. Rather, they adapted the policy demands of a broad strata to the only successful tactics of political competition. Even as they assumed a great policy focus, they maintained the competitive style of the political clientele and joined themselves to Colombo.

Colombo is the dominant political figure in Potenza. He has a veto power over all decisions taken in the party and is consulted on all important issues. To succeed in political competition within the DC in Potenza necessitates receiving Colombo's support. The fate of the "third generation" indicates this best.

The party factions in Vicenza are not subgroups of a single dominant faction as in Potenza but have definite links to competing national factions.[17] The majority group in the provincial organization of the party is composed of adherents to two national factions, the Rumor-Piccoli and the Fanfaniani. The minority group is composed of members of a united faction of the two national left factions and a group with local Vicentine historial roots which has consistently sought to draw together all the left groups into one organization.

During my fieldwork in 1969 and 1972, the division within the Rumor clientele later reflected in Bisaglia's rise in 1976 was clear. A split had developed over two issues: the question of what would be done after Rumor retired from politics, and the desire by some to initiate social policies in the province. When I first studied the province, the power of the two groups of Rumor's followers was evenly divided. Thus, five meetings of the provincial committee were needed to elect the provincial secretary. Acting as a residual category, the Fanfaniani faction attracted those who would not join with Rumor or the left faction.

The members of other national factions made Rumor's dominance in his province different from Colombo's in Potenza. However, all members of the Dorotei were followers of Rumor and they controlled the provincial party organization. All my informants agreed that Rumor hardly ever cared about the daily issues of the provincial party. His perceived desires were, however, a focal point for decision-making. Even when local leaders did not know what he wanted, they claimed that their position reflected his. As in Potenza, the resident national leader had the right to veto any decision and was consulted on all major decisions.

Rumor's predominance may be shown in his ability to gather preference votes in governmental and party elections. In the 1972 parliamentary vote, he received 266,710 preference votes, nearly 100,000 more than in 1969, a figure that placed him second (to Andreotti) among DC leaders. In addition, he also received the second largest number of preference votes at the 1969 Party Congress.

While Rumor has held important national sources of patronage, he has also maintained control of positions in Vicenza and the

Veneto. Thus, even after losing some power to Bisaglia, he controlled the presidencies and key offices in the Bank of Verona, Vicenza, and Belluno, their chambers of commerce, hospitals, highway agencies, and municipal and welfare offices, as well as local water works and the company that bottles the local sparkling water, not to mention the "Pi-Ru-Bi" highway.[18]

In 1969, a local DC leader elaborated at length on the dominant position of Rumor:

> There are two groups of Dorotei here in Vicenza. One group which has been in power for twenty years occupies all the important positions in the Commercial House and similar organizations in the province. Then there is another group, which I would call the Maoists because its members come from the province. It seeks to destroy the power of the first group within the Dorotei faction. Rumor is between and above both these groups. His power is quite consolidated. Local leaders cannot act against his wishes. His position is of the highest order, one which encompasses all the others. It is a position of intelligence, in which the party is for him as the church is for a bishop. It is his life. He is an activist of the first order. Rumor's rise to power was based not on his great knowledge of economics or sociology. He has little of that. His area of expertise is literature. He does not have a great image such as did De Gasperi. He has a mediocre one as he is a mediocre product of the post-De Gasperi DC.

A Vicentine leader of the Fanfaniani described Rumor's power in provincial politics:

> In Vicenza we have the current president of the Council of Ministers [Rumor]. The Majority group is very close to Rumor—a "Rumorian" expression. However, at the last Congress autonomous positions were set up within the majority. And Rumor, perhaps due to his national position, has remained a bit above these positions, and, therefore, there was some confusion over the selection of the new provincial secretary. . . . However, let us say that in reality the presence of Rumor has certainly a heavy relevance. . . . We must understand what Rumor wants. Certainly on problems of educational policy, union policy, or economic

policy he does not interfere much. Rather, he informs us of his needs in the particular situation.

Another view of the power of Rumor was set forth by a left faction leader. He noted that

The provincial secretary is actually an honorary position inasmuch as the DC in Vicenza is controlled by others. The national leaders of the party have always provided each and every choice to the party. For fifteen years, we have had on a grand level Friend Mariano Rumor, first as vice-secretary of the party, then as a minister, then as party secretary, and now as president of the Council of Ministers. He is the man with the most power within the party in Vicenza. Who commands. Who decides. Who orders. It is our Friend Mariano Rumor.

In response to my attempt to specify Rumor's areas of control, he continued:

All the aspects, particularly the eminently political aspects—that is, on local elections, the communal council, the provincial committee, the National Delegates, the election of mayors, the selection of candidates for elections of all types. All. . . . He who has power over these is Rumor. It is enough to state that in the election for provincial secretary (when we had to have five meetings to elect one) that the last provincial secretary was in constant telephone contact with Rumor.

Another left-wing faction leader gave a somewhat more balanced view of Rumor's presence in the Vicentine party:

Rumor has much prestige and power in the party given to him by his sergeants, his political followers, his political sons. However, this should be modified to say that on national issues and contests they follow him completely and on specifically local issues he gives them much freedom and he supports them in turn. Thus, the provincial secretary must always be conditioned by Rumor's desires. The secretary can never make a decision by himself. This is certain. He must always have it cleared by Rumor. . . .

One of Rumor's followers drew the same picture:

> As I said previously there are certain very important men in the party whose opinions are always sought. For example, a provincial secretary can never go against a national leader. . . . Concerning Vicenza, however, we must understand that there must be an accepted premise, in this Rumor is special. He allows much liberty and independence to the local decision-making bodies so that we do not feel any limits on our freedom. We, on the other hand, must not place him in difficulty on a national or international level.

One such embarrassment occurred in 1963 when the united left faction and the Fanfaniani allied to supplant the Dorotei and gain provincial power. Their tenure in office lasted six months. The discrepancy between a left-wing majority in Vicenza and Rumor's position as DC general secretary at the head of a Dorotei-controlled alliance caused the national leadership to unseat the local group.

Most of those interviewed in Vicenza agreed that Rumor has exceptional power over and concern for the province. In particular, he could dominate local party decisions if he chose to. The Vicentine leaders could not influence the decisions of the national party. One local leader, a member of the Dorotei, did not agree with this picture. He argued, "There is a great deal of independence between the two levels of the party. Even though the president of the Council of Ministers comes from Vicenza, the national leaders in Rome grant us a great deal of independence. . . . Rumor is our friend. He is an expression of Vicenza on the national level. We esteem him and we respect him." Another Dorotei activist conveyed a similar view of Rumor's place: "I would say that our possibility to influence Rome is at a high point now. There, we have our prime minister, Rumor, as a national leader from Vicenza. There is no need to interest him, because he knows very well what our problems are."

While the presence of competing factions with national ties characterizes the DC in Vicenza, the number of positions controlled by the Rumor faction gave it absolute control over all party decisions. The few compromises between the two local groupings were favors granted to the minority rather than negotiated agreements. A left-wing faction leader described one such compromise:

Compromises can happen, and a typical example would be on the selection of the makeup of the electoral lists of the party. At the last national elections (1968), we were given the option of naming either two men for the Chamber of Deputies or one senator. They told us you could have either one senator or two deputies but not both. We decided to have one senator and chose the man already backed by CISL.

The majority's dominance meant that real decision-making in the Vicentine Christian Democratic party took place in the majority caucus, which gathered before each meeting. This not only describes the majority's power but it also outlines a position normatively valued by many. One majority faction leader argued:

I would say that solutions are always reached, because we are able to find a majority. Therefore, for me, at least for me, the majority must resolve the problem and the minority must adhere. The question of minority-majority relations is of great importance because the definition of democracy rests on this issue.

The majority is always right, i.e., correct in governing. The role of the minority is to point out to the majority that is erring. If the majority does not agree that it is mistaken, then it has the right—not just the right but the duty of the majority—to go ahead. If it does not do so then the democracy is immobile.

The chains of patrons and clients that tie ministers in Rome and political activists and voters in Potenza and Vicenza have direct counterparts in other areas of Italy. To cite Antonio Gava, son of the senator and minster, and with his father the two dominant DC leaders in Naples:

When one talks of the DC in Rome, one talks of Andreotti, when one talks of Lucania, one talks of Colombo, and so on for Apulia with Moro, for Tuscany with Fanfani, for the Veneto with Rumor, for Trento with Piccoli. I don't see what is the difference between these situations and ours, that of Gava in Naples.[19]

All these political clienteles are characterized by the use of political power to control economic positions, which, in turn, are used to expand further the group's political power. This form of political clientele stands in marked contrast to earlier forms in Italy, examples of which are frequently found in other societies: the use of economic power as a means to political power. The clientelismo described by Mosca and Pareto and located in rural Italy differ in a crucial respect from the DC party factions. Current examples of the use of economic power as a means to political power, such as the Calleri grouping in Torino, stand apart from the DC factions. Indeed, Caleri's efforts at accumulating political power have included his attempt to bulid cross-party clienteles.[20]

If, as I have argued, so many of the Christian Democratic party factions are political clienteles and depend for their survival on the control of governing positions, what will happen if and when the DC falls from power? For the period of the Italian republic, answers to this question could not be examined against the flow of events. With several shifts of local governing coalitions that followed the 1975 regional elections and with the increasing, if still low, probability of the DC falling from national power, this question takes on political as well as theoretical importance. One consequence has been to lay bare the clientelist character of the DC factions. In the 95 elections for provincial party congresses that preceded the 1976 Party Congress, 484 faction lists were presented, with a particularly high portion coming from the south. Paolo Cabras, a Forze Nuove leader analyzes this struggle:

> It is a phenomenon that has its sources in the clientelist leadership of the party. Especially now, that the local power centers are declining, the various *clientes* fear that they will be abandoned by their leaders and seek to emerge, to show in some way if not their power at least their presence.[21]

To reach the regional congress, an aspirant had to control 25 votes, an amount easily obtained by any zonal secretary, argues Cabras. But to get to the National Congress, he needed 500 votes and that was where the local leaders destroyed each other. In Cabras's view, the regional congresses remained "places to be seen, to meet those who count."

6. DC Factions and Policy-Making

If most DC factions are political clienteles, what happens when they contest for governing positions? I argued earlier that they will engage in political competition with specific goals and tactics. Generally, they seek to control governing positions and the easily divisible resources, particularly jobs, attached to those positions; they seek to further the career of the patron-leader, as he seeks more and better positions; and they will aid those who are not faction members only when their own survival is at stake.

Factions and DC Party Rule

The formal rules of the party invest the Party Congress, National Council, and Central Directorate with primary policy-making duties. Much of the actual decision-making occurs within the majority bloc of the Central Directorate and the Secretariat, but less because of the unwieldy size of the formal institutions and more because of sharply divided party factions. Indeed, factions are the key units in the party's decision-making process. Because they compete to control the relevant positions, they constrain the behavior of those in power.

The Party Secretary's authority and ability to initiate action derive primarily from his position in the majority. As the recognized leader of a solid bloc, like Fanfani in the mid-1950s, he has wide latitude of action. When supported by a weak and divided majority, like almost all secretaries since, his powers are narrowly limited. One party leader described the situation as it existed under Piccoli:

> The Secretary must consult with certain party leaders—namely, the heads of the factions that form his majority. Currently, Piccoli is the political secretary based upon a majority of the Dorotei, who have as leaders Piccoli, Rumor, Colombo and Andreotti; the Fanfaniani, led by Fanfani; and the Tavianei, led by Taviani. These faction leaders have no institutional authority. All or almost all are members of the Central Directorate; one is president of the Council of Ministers; one is head of the party's parliamentary group, but

137

even if they were not, they would still have power in the party.

The alliance of factions into majority and minority groups is central to the competition. During most of the past twenty years, the majority has been composed of all or almost all the clientelist factions, and the Base and Forze Nuove, later joined by the Morotei, have formed the minority. In recent years, however, the faction alliances have changed several times.

Factions in the Central Directorate

During my initial fieldwork in 1968 and 1969 the Central Directorate met at least once every three weeks, when it made major party decisions. While all respondents agreed that the directorate's decisions were made in a collegial manner, some insisted that its actions merely ratified decisions made elsewhere. There were two general limitations on the Central Directorate's ability to act as a collegial body. The first and most important were the faction alliances, particularly the majority and minority groups. The second was the size of the group. A party leader maintained:

> Because the Central Directorate has forty members it has become very difficult for it to act as a decision-making body. In fact, the Central Directorate has become a place of conflict between the majority and the minority, where the majority presents its decisions which are practically already completed.
>
> The decisions of the majority are reached based on the confidence placed in and the independent latitude of the political secretary and the Executive Group. The latter, though in the formal party statutes conceived as an executive body and a working group and not as a decision-making body, has, however, been transformed in practice to a policy-making body. It is composed of the political secretary, the members of the Secretariat, the secretary of administration, and the presidents of the DC parliamentary groups. Only members of the majority are in this executive group. Therefore, there is an appearance of collegiality, but then there is a quite personal process, with some controls.

There was general agreement that directors of the secretariat's offices could and usually did act on their own to decide issues which fell within their spheres of authority. When there were conflicts within this group, the party secretary acted as mediator. However, when issues related to factional or majority-minority interests, consultations among those of the same grouping always took place. Thus, while all stated that mutual aid and assistance should be extended to all members of the directorate, in practice, help was offered only to political allies, and close working relationships applied only among those of the same faction. The support of one's friends extended even to instances of error and mismanagement. A left-wing faction leader complained:

> It would be best that when an individual erred frequently, he had to pay for it. Instead, there is, in effect, a species of general amnesty, especially if it occurs within the majority, which has its own solidarity for other reasons. It should be that when a leader has his own program to realize, one criticizes it; one substitutes other thoughts, and one changes it without bringing a split in the solidarity of the majority. Sadly, this does not happen often.

The strong cohesion of the clientelist factions and their allegiance to the majority bloc allowed them to monopolize party policy-making. Another left-wing faction leader contended that within the directorate, "There exist no disagreements, because there is a pre-constituted majority. When there are disagreements the majority in the Central Directorate is changed." A member of the majority echoed this view of the policy-making process: "Normally, when disagreements revolve around majority-minority differences, they are almost always resolved by a vote, the outcome of which is always known in advance."

Party leaders faced highly divisive issues in a limited number of ways. All agreed that some items had been tabled to avoid a split. For the most part, however, agreements within the majority were sought. The manner of reaching the agreement depended on the issue and the time available. In the infrequent divisions over policy in which time was not a factor, the issues persisted through long periods of maneuvering during which each faction sought to obtain as much as possible. Differences about patronage items were usually settled quickly and almost always within the majority. When differences within the majority could not be resolved, the majority changed.

Disagreements within the directorate were rarely resolved on a noncompetitive basis, in which generous and equal concessions were granted to all. When asked to evaluate on a formal scale the relations within the directorate, the members placed themselves just below "competitive"—that is, relations marked by hostility, in which each usually seeks to aid his own interests and often attempts to hinder the activities of others; when members work together it is with much tension.

Not surprisingly, most members of the majority bloc were content with the mode of governance, while not one of the minority group was. A left-wing leader stated, "There should be a substantial acceptance of the democratic method, in which there is a function for the minority. It is wrong that the minority should always say 'no' and the majority 'yes.' The opinions of the minority should be taken into account."

Factions in Provincial Party Politics

The presence of faction majorities cohesive enough to impose their policy views on the minority factions and to monopolize governing positions describes local-level party organizations as well, although this pattern varies somewhat among the three provinces I studied. In general, distinctions were made between areas which pertained to the individual offices of the secretariat and those for which all members of the provincial committee or directorate were to meet and decide. In all cases, however, the control of positions and the content of policy required membership in the party majority.

In Vicenza, the deep split between the majority, composed of clientelist groups, and the left-wing minority limited the collegiality of decision-making. The majority controlled 75 percent of the seats on the provincial committee, which negated the need for compromise and even for consultations between the two blocs.

A leader of the Vicentine minority described the local pattern of decision-making.

> It depends on the interests of the groups in the majority. Even when an official errs and he does so in the interests of

the majority, they sustain him. This, I feel, is very bad and very serious. One must have the courage to condemn someone even if he is part of the same group.

There are certain decisions which are discussed in the provincial committee with which the minority does agree. When an issue arises with which the minority does not agree, then there may or may not be a discussion, but in any event a vote is taken and the decision always goes to the majority. If the minority says no or proposes another plan, then sometimes the majority accepts it, but this is most infrequent. In general, however, they reject it through a vote.

A majority leader echoed his description:

I will say that the policy line is not an issue of factional warfare. The policy line is always that of the majority. The battle occurs at the congress. At times, the majority follows the minority but the majority can do whatever it chooses. Normally, the most important decisions are taken by the majority group.

Were there then no areas of compromise which alleviated the control of the party by the majority factions? A Doroteo set out the core of the issue. "I would say that compromises occur when the two opposing forces are approximately equal in power. However, when there is an ample majority in favor of a proposal and a minority against it, there is no reason and no need to compromise. The majority prevails." Compromises within the majority depended on the issue areas. The same party leader continued:

If the discussion is on the level of personal positions and local boards then a compromise is made by one side agreeing to sacrifice in this case and to be rewarded with a position in the next case. When, however, the issue is one of a party project or policy, then the compromises are difficult to reach, and the issue is resolved by the majority outvoting the minority. At times this is true within the majority as well.

The majority's monopoly over patronage positions was attested to by all respondents. One member of the Dorotei noted, "Those issues which regard the selection of members for local boards remain in the area of the majority. It is not the case that the majority and the minority are so close that members of the minority can be placed in these positions. . . . In general, I would say that the majority group seeks to maintain its members in the positions that are available." This view of the competitive process is underscored by the majority's perception of the minority. One Dorotei leader noted, "There are compromises within the majority, but rarely between the majority and the minority. I would say that here in Vicenza, the minority is somewhat older and out of touch. This is so because they are not part of the dialectics of the party because the battles are all fought out within the majority."

The view cited earlier that patronage differences within the majority were easily resolved was not echoed by other leaders. To cite a Doroteo. "Within the majority they seek to obtain as much as possible, until an agreement is reached." A left-wing leader commented at length on the divisions with the Dorotei.

> Within the majority, there are certainly compromises between the two groups. The compromises are based on the partition of power—that is, the determination of political offices. Sometimes there are ferocious battles within the majority over these positions of power. In general, there is a sense of competition. It is not casual. It is a very tense kind of competition. We must fight against this, especially against the form of clienteles which harm the party very much. Because they place the personal interest of some men over and above the interests of the party, they form a personalist and exclusivist consensus, not a common one, as we would like.
>
> The kind of competition that we have here in Vicenza, in which the minority is excluded from the policy-making positions and in which the relationships within the majority are very sharp and difficult is a bad thing. This should not occur within the party, especially one based on Christian principles. However, this is the climate within the party. Sadly, therefore, and especially on the local and administrative levels, the battles are not based upon political ideas or ideals but on personal issues.

Put simply, in Vicenza the minority factions are utterly frozen out of policy positions and patronage sources. Competition for them occurs between the majority's clientelist factions. In recent years, these divisions have been exacerbated with Antonio Bisaglia's rise to national faction leadership. Based in nearby Rovigo, Bisaglia used his control of national and regional patronage sources to attract followers in Vicenza and thereby to reduce Rumor's power.

Vicenza differs in some important ways from Potenza and Milan. As noted earlier, the majority in the southern province reflected a shift away from traditional governing patterns in Potenza. Led by a group of university-educated young friends, their mode of rule and the content of their goals were atypical. Not only did they strive to modernize the area, but they maintained a very high level of collegial rule based on their friendship ties. One young lawyer stated:

> We have a new situation here. A new generation of leaders has taken power and fought against the old personalist ways. Now members of the Secretariat meet frequently, some of us every day, all of us, four or five times a week. We seek to change the party and to involve the members in the party's decisions. We believe in the importance of the lower levels of the party.

Still, the desire and need to control governing positions clearly have conditioned their mode of rule. First, while they have dominated the party majority, they still have not controlled party positions within the local government bodies. "All the power positions are not in our hands, but in those of the old mentality in the party. We have to open a dialogue with these older groups and not to have discussions over power positions but of the new means of political leadership."

Second, and most important, the new leaders have sought to bring about collective benefits through clientelist means. Their attachment to Colombo and their obedience to his national and local demands have been predicated on an understanding of Italian political competition. Necessary for the control of policy, in general, and to bring about wide-ranging structural changes, in particular, is the control of the governing positions, not only to be part of a ruling majority. Only by using clientelist tactics is it possible to capture those positions. One leader succinctly outlined the problem resulting from the cohesion of clientelist factions into party majorities.

> This is the heart of the problem of the management of power in Italy. When a group constitutes a majority, there is a solidarity of action. It is highly unusual for a man in the majority to be accused by other leaders.

The only effective way to bring about new and generally beneficial policies is to control the majority. When that is accomplished, anything is possible.

> If there is a strong majority, as in our province, there is no need for compromises. If the majority is weak, compromises are necessary.

To be in the majority implies not only a voice in policies but control of positions to build political power. Patronage sources are used to increase the number of supporters and to block opponents. The modernizing group has sought to hook their political future to Colombo. They would provide him with voters and workers, even support among the new generation; he would allow them to rebuild Potenza. It has not worked. Sanza is no longer Colombo's follower, but firmly tied to the Base and the new party majority led by Zaccagnini. Perhaps this indicates that efforts to combine clientelist means and collectivist ends are most difficult, if possible at all.

Relations between the factions in Milan differed somewhat from the patterns observed in the other two provinces. In Milan, the majority was an alliance of two left-wing factions of equal size. The power of the party leaders was less tied to their factions. For the most part, their faction loyalty was based on ideological and policy affinities. Clientelist ties did not occur within the majority. Milan did not have a majority that ruled to conquer patronage resources.

As in all the policy-making units, though all respondents expressed preference for collegiality, this rarely happened. Most decisions were not made by the provincial committee or directorate, but by the members of the executive group, acting together as a committee of the majority or acting in their individual capacities as department heads. The independent political positions of these leaders assured them greater decision-making latitude over their departments' issues than in Potenza or

Vicenza. The relations within the majority were cordial and businesslike. They were neither a group of friends as in Potenza nor a group of competitors as in Vicenza.

In Milan, party splits came to the fore over policy, not patronage, issues. Almost all leaders agreed that it was the responsibility of the majority to govern even if the minority opposed the policy. At the same time, it was common to seek to reach compromise positions to which all could agree over patronage issues and to which all those within the majority could agree over policy issues. Within the Base and Forze Nuove majority, there was a strong willingness to grant patronage positions to those in the minority, but to monopolize the policy issues. Thus, when policy agreements existed within the majority there were few compromises. In the words of one leader,*"Il compromesso è una parola brutta"* ("Compromise is an ugly word"). Another majority faction leader described the decision-making process in the following terms.

> Concerning basic policy, we always seek to avoid making compromises, if there are some disagreements. For example, in university reform, relations with the Communists, problems of this type, we do not seek out compromises with the minority. We vote in the provincial committee and directorate and those who are in favor are in favor and those who are against are against. While for that which refers to the conduct of the party, above all the naming of men to the local governmental bodies, we always seek to reach agreements with the minority for a division of the positions. At least we do so in Milan. In other provincial committees they do things differently. That is, the majority takes all the positions in the local governmental bodies. We feel, however, that it is more correct, more democratic to give positions to the minority in the local governing bodies.

Very much unlike Vicenza, the only ones to express general dissatisfaction with the pattern of relations among the party leaders were members of the majority factions. They generally did not approve of the factional rivalries and condemned the isolation of the minority factions from the decision-making process and the essentially ratificatory functions of the provincial committee and directorate.

In contrast to Vicenza and Potenza, in Milan the members of

the competing factions of the majority and minority were on generally good personal terms. This may be explained by the rather generous patronage-sharing policies of the Base and Forze Nuove and the relatively few province-based policy differences between the factions. The basic divisions between many of the Milanese Dorotei and the Base and Forze Nuove were over national issues. As a Doroteo indicated,

> There are differences but not in relation to Milan but over the national party program, especially over relations with the Communists at the national level.

Several patterns of general applicability may be drawn from this survey of faction competition within the party.

> 1. Whether composed of clientelist factions or not, the majority groupings monopolize the control of policy-making positions within the party and the content of party policies.[1]
>
> 2. The maintenance of political alliances and the control of positions (within the party or government) are the primary concerns of the clientelist factions. Those interests take precedence over the professed collegial decision-making norms and the content of policy.
>
> 3. Even where they are not included in the policy majority, the clientelist factions maintain access to positions in the government.
>
> 4. The policy majority blocs within the party cut along the clientelist-left-wing cleavage. Given the relative size of these blocs, it is, therefore, easiest to maintain a clientelist majority alliance and most difficult to maintain a majority composed of a clientelist–left-wing alliance.

Since 1969, the clientelist factions have not excluded the left from the national party majority. The revolution at San Ginesio, which brought a new generation of party leaders to the fore, was spearheaded by an alliance between Forlani and DeMita. It gave the left, especially the Base, control over key party positions. Only the return to Fanfani in the summer of 1973 and the subsequent resistance to his leadership by the Forze Nuove threatened to restore the old majority-minority lines. With Zaccagnini's election as secretary in 1975, left-wing faction leaders were solidly in control of the party's policy-making positions in the Secretariat and through them the content of party policy.

During this period of shifting party majorities, several points crucial to my argument remain clear:

> 1. While outside the party majority, all clientelist factions have maintained access to positions in the parliament, cabinet, and bureaucratic agencies.
>
> 2. Clientelist factions have persisted as the bulk of the party. Thus, Zaccagnini's accumulation of a bit more than half the votes at the 1976 Party Congress required the support of the clienteles of Colombo, Rumor, and Taviani.
>
> 3. The new majority reflects the fragility of joining clientelist and nonclientelist factions in a policy majority.

DC Party Factions and Cabinet Coalition Behavior

Cabinet coalition behavior in Italy is described by a high rate of instability (frequent collapses and long and hard negotiations over their replacements) and the general inability of accepted theories to account for these patterns. Between the founding of the republic in June 1946 and the summer of 1976, thirty-three cabinets were formed. Formal theories of coalition behavior which focus on the political parties as the competitive units account for few of the party combinations that form the cabinets and are particularly baffled by the low durability of the cabinets. Hypotheses derived from Riker's "size principle" are confounded by the larger than minimal size of Italian coalitions. Browne argues that random predictions of coalition partners prove more useful and Dodd shows that only one of the Italian cabinets was a minimum winning coalition, while only Finland of all parliamentary democracies has had more oversized and undersized coalitions.[2] When the ideological or policy distance between potential partners is added to the calculation, the suggested hypotheses fare a little better. Although predictions about the subset of parties composing Italian cabinets have been both larger than actual, they have included the correct subsets thirteen of twenty-one times.[3] Even so, they do not account for the very high dissolution rate. Italian cabinets have rested on the support of large, predetermined, and solid parliamentary majorities, and yet most cabinets have dissolved easily and have not ruptured these interparty parliamentary alliances.

The most perplexing problem in Italy is that of low durability. Cabinets fall not only when the interparty agreements in parliament dissolve (as well as at elections), but most cabinets have ended without the demise of the interparty agreements. That is, the same parties form the next cabinet, while maintaining their alliance. Explanations of Italian cabinet coalition behavior which focus solely on party interactions fall short of completion. They are useful only in the relatively few cases when a cabinet and an interparty agreement dissolve together.

The primary analytic distinction required to account for the patterns of Italian cabinet coalition behavior is the difference between mass and elite political competition.[4] Parties are the appropriate units for analyzing electoral behavior. When the results of the parliamentary elections are clear, the need to form a governing coalition has produced a competitive arena with different units. Central to this second stage are party factions.

The extent of faction membership by Demochristian Deputies during the 1968-75 period is elaborated in table 6.1. It sets out their presence within the parliament and alludes to their control of cabinet positions. If all DC members of Parliament are members of

Table 6.1. Factions in the Chamber of Deputies

Factions	Legislature V (1968-72)	Legislature VI (1972-76)
Forze Nuove	26	28
Base	19	28
Morotei	34	32
Nuova Sinistra	3	1[a]
Tavianei	19	19
Fanfaniani	37	36
Rumor-Piccoli	64	84
Colombo-Andreotti	30	28
Forze Libere	18	10[a]
Not identified	14	
Total	264	266

Source: Adapted from Franco Cazzola, "Partiti, Correnti," in Un Sistema Politico alla Prova, Mario Caciagli and Alberto Spreafico, eds. (Bologna: Il Mulino, 1975), p. 133.
Note: Cazzola reports the relative faction sizes just before and after the 1972 national elections. Because it is difficult to pin down exact membership figures, these figures are best viewed as reliable estimates. They are, therefore, extended to cover both legislatures.
    a. By 1973, both these factions had dissolved—The Nuova Sinistra into the Fanfaniani and the Forze Libere into the Rumor-Piccoli.

Table 6.2. Stages of Cabinet Formation

Stage	Competitive Units	Competitive arena	Outcome
I	political parties	parliament	coalition formula: 1. agreement over division of cabinet position 2. agreement over cabinet policy
	party factions	each party	bargaining strategy and goals of each party
II	party factions	parties of the coalition formula	filling of the cabinet positions

factions, and all DC members of cabinets are members of Parliament, all DC cabinet officers are also faction members.

Table 6.2 outlines the process by which cabinets form.[5] For most of the postwar period the first stage has been characterized by the recurrence of the same outcomes. The results of national elections and the distribution of parliamentary seats to the parties have granted the pivotal role to the DC and have produced two possible coalition formulas and three types of cabinets: the Christian Democrats aligned with one or more of the center parties, the PRI, the Liberals, and the PSDI; the center-left in which the PSI replaces the PLI; and a single-party DC cabinet. All cabinets are composed of or are supported by the parties of the coalition formula.[6]

During both stages, party factions are crucial competitive units. They compete within the parties to set party policy and strategy and thereby control the formation of the coalition formula. Cabinet positions are distributed to the parties and to the factions according to the relative size and policy expertise of each. The factions are the vehicle for entering into the cabinet, and it is within the second stage that cabinets have proved so fragile. DC party factions are of particular importance because they determine which of the other political parties (and their factions) will be invited to form a cabinet and because their actions have brought down almost all the cabinets.

The persistence of faction coalitions, which exist within and across the parties of the coalition formula, is the necessary and sufficient condition for the survival of Italian cabinets. It is the dissolution of the interfaction agreements that ends the cabinets. Given the position of the DC factions, their behavior is the prime determinant of the pattern of competition for control of cabinet coalitions in Italy.

As shown in chapter 5, most of the DC factions are political clienteles and the two factions that are not have adopted much of the former's competitive goals and strategies. As political clienteles, in this contest they act according to three behavioral rules:[7]

1. They seek to control cabinet positions, strive to occupy more and better positions than previously, and defend those already controlled.
2. They seek to further the career of the leader and support him in his effort to achieve better positions.
3. They seek to obtain goods of value to those who are not faction members only when the persistence of the faction or the strength of the Christian Democratic party is at stake.

The conjunction of these behavioral rules with the absense of rules that protect the tenure of a cabinet and the fact that cabinet positions are primarily distributed at the formation of cabinets has two consequences: (1) party factions will dissolve a given cabinet when they have a chance to better the number and quality of positions controlled in the next formation; and (2) party factions will delay the formation of a cabinet until they obtain the best bargain possible. Winnings and losses in this political game are judged by the quality and number of offices controlled, given the rank-ordering of junior and senior cabinet posts and the relative size of each faction within its party.

The volatility of cabinet coalitions is further increased by their location in time and space. The interlocking nature of the factions' several competitive arenas—within the party as well as parliament—links faction coalition dissolutions in one arena to the others. The resignation of the Rumor-led coalition cabinet in July 1969 was directly related to the split in the reunited Socialist party and the reformation of the PSI and the Social Democrats as well as to internal DC divisions. The Demochristians' problems surfaced that fall and brought about the split in the Dorotei and the formation of a new governing coalition of DC factions. Given the shift within the Christian Democrats, the Rumor coalition cabinet, which was formed in March 1970, lasted less than four months and was replaced by a Colombo-led cabinet.

Other cabinet dissolutions and formations have been caused by similar internal DC divisions and arrangements. The collapse of a center-left coalition led by Rumor and its replacement by a Christian Democrat-Republican cabinet led by Moro in November 1974 has been attributed not only to a falling out between the Socialists and the Demochristians. Rather, as a prelude to the regional elections held six months later, DC leaders desired to shore up support for the party by providing second-level cabinet positions and their perquisites of office to the many party deputies and senators in electoral trouble at home. For the first and so far only time, a rule was applied to foster the entry into the cabinet of those who had never before served as undersecretaries.[8] Similarly, observers attributed the selection of Andreotti to form the cabinet after the 1976 national elections to the repayment of a favor owed him by the party chieftains. Three months earlier he had been passed over in party president selections in favor of Fanfani.[9]

As a set, the behavioral rules by which the party factions compete account for the fragility of Italian cabinets and the difficulties exhibited in their formations. Taken individually they may be used to deal with related phenomena. That the party factions act to further the political career of the leader underscores the personal bases of the Fanfani-Moro feud. This decade-long conflict between two former prime ministers, political secretaries of the DC, and candidates for the presidency not only divided their factions within the DC and constrained the formation of a new governing coalition within the party, but it had powerful repercussions in cabinet competitions and in the presidential election of December 1971.[10]

The third behavioral rule introduces electoral and policy factors into cabinet competitions and thereby ties the latter to the arena of mass politics. The choice of coalition formula partners is linked to electoral appeal and policy affinities. The DC left factions and the dominant factions of the PSI long proclaimed a common desire to join in a two-party coalition which would eliminate the "insufficiently progressive" PSDI and PRI from power. The clientelist factions of the DC along with the latter two parties succeeded in blocking the move and in maintaining the four-party coalition formula. When electoral and policy issues split a faction coalition, they will lead to an interparty alliance dissolution as well as to a cabinet collapse.

The link to electoral and policy factors introduces elements which reduce the fragility of cabinets. Not only do factions work together to assure Christian Democrat success at the polls but their hunger for governing posts is limited by fears of being perceived as unduly selfish. Cabinets are typically provided a period of grace, free from sniping. In addition, policy expertise is a requisite for the occupation of the most crucial cabinet positions—prime minister, foreign minister, and minister of the Treasury.

Other factors further support cabinet stability. Each cabinet formation is perceived to be a contest intimately tied to others in the past and future—a "rolling game"—and competitive tactics are toned down accordingly.[11] Participants remember past favors and arrange future ones. The use of proportional representation as the rule by which cabinet positions are distributed first to the parties and then to the factions emerges not as the determinant of the number or volatility of party and faction coalitions, but as a means by which conflict is modified, such as it is. Proportional representation provides a standard of fairness of distribution by holding out to each group within the coalition a portion of the positions roughly equivalent to its size in the party and the parliament. Given the position orientation of the factions and the need for the parliamentary support of all the factions to sustain the cabinet, a distribution rule by which only the members of a winning coalition occupied the governing posts would make it impossible for cabinets to form. Monocolore DC cabinets, examples of winning coalitions within the parliamentary alliance controlling all governing positions, are temporary expedients. They hold office only as long as the interparty faction coalition cannot form.[12]

> 1. At each stage of the cabinet formation process, the parties of the coalition formula and their factions obtain positions according to their relative size, bargaining skills, and policy

expertise. Each coalescing group is assured of at least one position.

2. As long as the interparty and interfaction alliances cohere, the cabinet will stay in office. If one dissolves, then the cabinet will resign.

3. The party-based coalition formula changed twice from 1948 to 1972.

4. Given the goals and competitive strategies of the party factions, their alliances are fragile. They are liable to dissolve at almost any time. A faction's reluctance to destroy a cabinet may be accounted for by the fear of losing positions in the cabinet reshuffle, the rolling game aspects of the competition, the fear of damaging the party in elections.

5. The demise of interfaction agreements rarely affects the persistence of the interparty coalition formula. It does so only on those infrequent occasions when the divisive issue is one of government policy or party election concern—that is, when the strategies of mass political competition contradict the maneuvers of elite contests. Thus, the difficulties within the center-left party coalition that began in 1974 were directly tied to Socialist gains and DC losses in the divorce referendum and the 1975 regional elections. Striving to capture what they saw as a new generation of radicalized voters, the Socialists sought to dissociate themselves from the DC.[13]

I have argued that clientelist factions seek to expand the number and quality of the positions they control and that only under a limited and specifiable set of circumstances do they act to help those who are not faction members. This view also provides a specification of the consequences for the process and content of public policy when they control cabinet positions. The control of cabinet positions provides not only the means to conquer other cabinet positions. It provides the ability to appoint members of bureaucratic and quasi-governmental agencies. All ministries have enormous patronage opportunities, but none more than the Fund for the South, State Participation, Posts and Communication, and Public Works. In addition, the local patronage that comes from Rome cements the power of all faction leaders. As Lombardo and others have argued, this has increased the autonomy of the factions from the party and other organizations.[14]

Factions in National Policy-Making

There is a direct link between the continuous faction competition for governing positions and the mode and content of government policy. Reacting to a long history of neglect, the Italian university students rioted in 1968, a most eventful year for such occurrences, in Rome. After much delay, the Minister of Education, Fiorentino Sullo, developed a plan for a wide-ranging reform of the universities. Before he could present his program to the cabinet, he resigned, an act which set back the policy-making process several more months. His resignation was provoked by a disagreement between Sullo and Flaminio Piccoli, then party secretary, over the date chosen for the party congress in Avellino, Sullo's home. In a bid to gain the national support of DeMita and his followers in the Base, Piccoli had arranged for the Avellino party congress to occur while Sullo was presenting the educational reform plan in Rome. Rather than lose his local power base, Sullo resigned.

Set out most generally and derived from the argument of this work, the presence of clientelist factions as the occupants of the governing positions have two consequences for the policy-making process: (1) primary concern will be with the controlling of governing positions and with using these positions to capture other positions; and (2) the factions will be unwilling to help others; they will be particularly unwilling to use their control of governing positions to pass laws that will harm actual and potential faction supporters.

In the preceding section, the characteristics of clientelist factions were used to account for the high rate of cabinet instability and the crucial importance of factional loyalty as the key to recruitment into decision-making positions in the cabinet and governmental agencies. Recent work by Italian and other scholars specifies additional consequences for making policy and laws.

1. Cabinets are unable to develop and pass through parliament coherent sets of policy packages.
2. There is a fractionalization of the policy-making process—

that is, separate majorities are formed to pass different laws.
3. Most bills become isolated laws, not parts of developed policy programs.
4. Most frequently, laws have only specific and limited sets of individuals as beneficiaries.
5. Very few laws affect large social groups in positive or negative ways.
6. A frequent object of laws are groups within the bureaucracy and others responsive to the appeals of highly visible patronage projects.

Alan R. Posner points to the DC party factions as well as interparty competition as causes of the personalist and improvisational character of foreign economic policy in Italy. DC control of recruitment into the bureaucracy and parastate corporations and the factional contests that goes with it have affected a set of policies that frequently contradict one another when they are made at all.[15]

Others have provided details on the decision-making process in the parliament. According to Alberto Predieri, the Italian parliament is "a working body: It does much work; makes many laws and hold many sessions."[16] In the twenty years spanning the first four legislatures, 8,000 laws were enacted, an average annual rate of 400—four times more than most other countries of Western Europe for which there are data. Only Sweden in 1966 with 285 laws and the sessions of the French Fourth Republic (which passed an annual average of 250 bills) are even close to the Italian totals. The Italian parliament is also distinguished by the relatively large number of laws that are initiated by members of parliament. Di Palma has shown that 25 percent of all laws were first presented by members of parliament, compared to 14.3 percent in Britain (1966-67), none in Ireland (1965), 3.9 percent in Sweden (1966), 9.5 percent in France (1966), and none in India (1965). Only West Germany, where 22.3 percent (1949-65) were presented by members of parliament, approached the Italian levels. The German case, argues Di Palma, is significantly different from the Italian, because most German laws were initiated by members of parliament at the suggestion or with the approval of the cabinet.[17] In Italy, however, the success of the private bills depends on the power of individual parliamentarians, not the

cabinet. "The parliamentary proposals must find votes by themselves; the search is easiest if the proposal is signed by a deputy or
senator of an important party or by members of parliament of
many parties."[18] Di Palma demonstrates that 50 percent of the
private bills passed were initiated by Demochristians and others
from the "center parties." Almost 25 percent of those initiated by
someone from that bloc were passed, as were nearly 30 percent of
those put forth by Demochristians and Communists and/or
members of parliament from the center and right blocs.[19]

In addition, while the success rate of government-sponsored
bills is high, Di Palma's analysis indicates that of the bills passed,
whether initiated by the cabinet or parliament, most have specific
and limited beneficiaries and that those presented by the cabinet
do not derive from cohesive policy packages.

> Government legislation submitted to parliament has little to
> do with the legislative programs that coalition partners agree
> upon at the outset of every new coalition. . . . A necessarily
> rough estimate from newspaper accounts of the period,
> comparing original coalition agreements with final legislative
> action, indicates that approximately 10% of the original
> legislative programs of the six cabinets during the Fifth
> Parliament (1968-72) ever arrived, in one form or another, in
> parliament. And it should be kept in mind that in most
> instances a cabinet adopts large parts of the unfinished
> program of a previous one."[20]

Also, as Predieri shows, while all bills have a gestation period of
nearly four months, the more important the bill (the more people
and issues it affects) the longer it takes to become a law.[21]

Drawing on a general study of the content of the laws enacted
by the Italian parliament, Di Palma has set out some defining
characteristics.

> 1. The laws are parts of highly particular legislation of
> immediate benefit to their subjects but with no effects on
> others.
> 2. The subjects of most laws are small, homogeneous
> groups.
> 3. Given Italy's highly politicized bureaucracy, it follows

that elements of the bureaucracy are the subject of many laws.

4. Very few laws are passed which are part of policy packages and which affect broad categories of citizens, such as constitutional reform or economic policies.[22]

Distinguishing favorable from unfavorable laws and immediate and external subjects of the laws, Di Palma demonstrates that 80 percent of all laws initiated by the cabinet had immediate favorable affects on their subjects and of those only 4 percent had negative affects on others; 88 percent of laws initiated by members of parliament had immediate favorable affects on their subjects and not even 2 percent of these had negative affects on others.[23] Di Palma's analysis of the level of the aggregation separates national, sectional, and microsectional subjects of laws. That is, 45.5 percent of the laws presented by the government and 56.5 percent of those presented by members of parliament influenced microsectional interests. Of the microsectional laws, almost 90 percent helped those affected by the laws, and of those somewhat more than 5 percent had negative or mixed consequences for others. Nearly 80 percent of the national and sectional laws helped their subjects, and of them, more than 16 percent hurt those who were not immediate beneficiaries.[24]

Di Palma's analysis further indicates the special position of bureaucrats and those in the public employ: Nearly 70 percent of the laws concerning them were microsectional, and the vast majority had no affect on anyone other than their subjects.[25] At the same time, very few laws dealt with constitutional reform or economic policy—that is, issues with widespread consequences. Constitutional reform legislation amounted to 2 percent of all laws enacted; economic planning accounted for an even smaller percentage. Similarly, only 3 percent of the laws dealing with the penal code covered basic revisions.[26]

To cite Di Palma, "The same observations can be made concerning the scarcity of projects dealing with the schools and the tax system, except that the last contain for the most part exemptions and not new taxes and that for the first category, as is easily understood, most are concerned not with educational reform but with the treatment of teachers, i.e., the largest and perhaps most clientelist of public employees (it is not for nothing that the number of parliamentary bills on schools is double that of the governments)."[27] Two general characteristics describe the content of the laws: very few deal with collective goods issues and an extraordinarily large number are directed specifically to improve the lot of those with clientelist ties to members of parliament and the cabinet.

The particular details of the policy-making process and the content of the laws bear out the general argument of this study.[28] Clientelist factions strive to enact laws of particular benefit to their members and to their political survival. The microsectional laws—*leggine* in Italian—typically touch none but those addressed by the laws, and in the tradition of pork-barrel legislation are the bills most likely to be enacted. Highly aggregative bills—those which affect large categories of individuals—are most prone to harm the clienteles' supporters and hence are most likely to be opposed. The bills passed benefit teachers and other members of the public and quasi-public bureaucracy; they provide specific tax benefits to some, and provide public demonstration through mass patronage of the importance of the local deputy. They are not meant to restructure the Italian polity and economy.

The result is a particular type of political competition: (1) Members of parliament strive to enact laws directly and specifically beneficial to their followers and, therefore, to themselves. (2) Institutionalized clientelist factions structure the vision of the members of parliament in regard to their own interests, who their followers are; and what they want. Because collective goods policy may hurt faction members, and, while over finite goods, the contest for the control of jobs is not yet zero-sum, majorities form easily over specific and limited issues and almost never over concerns with wide-ranging applications. Thus, the strength of a faction in electoral contests, for party votes and preference markers, rests on its ability to provide sufficient patronage opportunities for its voters. Contests within the political elite are over governing positions to be distributed among faction members. For the leaders, they involve cabinet and sub-cabinet offices, especially the ministries of State Participation, Public Works, Labor, Posts, and the Fund for the South, which in turn control hundreds of thousands of positions at all levels of Italian government. Control of these offices is the goal and reward of faction activists and voters.

*Clientelist Factions and the Place of Ideology in
Interparty Conflict*

By focusing upon the consequences of the interaction of
political clienteles within the political elite, I have proposed an
implicit interpretation of interparty conflict that runs counter to
the accepted wisdom. Nowhere in my presentation have I dealt
with ideological conflict between the political parties as a source
of either cabinet instability or haphazard policy-making. In part
this occurs because I have ignored cabinets that dissolve from the
rupture of interparty alliances. I contend, however, that it is
possible to explain the observed patterns without raising the issue
of ideological conflict, much less the view of Italian politics as the
conflict of two mutually antipathetic political cultures.

A political group must have two characteristics for a political
clientele to bargain and align with it: (1) it must be willing to
maintain the rules of the game of position control; and (2) it must
be crucial to the formation of a ruling majority—that is, the
clientelist faction must perceive the need of the other's political
support.

Thus, in a competitive arena composed solely of political
clienteles with potentially continuous competition for the control
of seats (that is, there are no formal time limits on political
contests), the following bargaining outcome and alliance may be
expected. All competitive actors will be given access to governing
positions. The logic of the minimum winning coalition does not
apply here; it serves as a threat to exclude any one faction from
the control of positions over a number of competitive interactions
and hence to destroy it. Since no faction can be certain that it will
not be the loser, the most probable outcome is for all to be
granted some access to governing positions. At the same time,
because the formal rules are such that the agreements may be
dissolved at any time and because the clientelist factions always
seek to improve their status, these alliances are highly fragile.

In a competitive arena composed of clientelist factions and
collective goods or categoric factions, the bargaining outcomes and
alliances will depend on the relative size of the groups and the
bases of division between the categoric factions. Where political
clienteles dominate, they will pursue several tactics. Because
collective goods factions are always a threat to revamp the rules of

the competitive game—for example, to reorganize the bureaucracy, to close off formerly accessible positions, to pass "harmful" collective goods policies—the clientelist factions will (1) prefer to bargain and align with each other and (2) join together with categoric factions when the latter express the willingness to maintain the game and/or when the categoric factions are' sufficiently strong to be necessary to the formation of ruling majorities.

The second scenario describes the pattern of internal DC conflict that has prevailed at the national level in party and cabinet contests. "It is no accident," to borrow a determinist phrase, that DeMita, a patron in his own right, led the Base entry into the governing alliance. The scenario also describes the patterns observed in Vicenza and Milan.

Particularly intriguing about the applicability of this argument is that it describes a DC left that was excluded from party majorities much as the Communists have been omitted from government majorities. There is a striking parallel between the way Alan Stern describes the DC monopoly government control in a commune in the Veneto and my description of the Dorotei's monopoly within the party in neighboring Vicenza.[29] Similarly, the exclusion of the Communist party from national majorities (and the Socialists in the earlier period) is parallelled by the exclusion of the Base and Forze Nuove from national party majorities until San Ginesio. In all these instances, the clientelist factions were able to maintain the dominance over positions to the absolute exclusion of the others. They had no need to involve those who would not play the game. A question to which I will turn in the next chapter follows from this parallel: did Communist control of key parliamentary positions in the summer of 1976 herald a fundamental shift in the governing alliance?

In sum, it is not necessary to introduce issues of ideological difference to explain the exclusion of the PCI from national and local governments. To reiterate the description of the clientelist factions by a leader of the DC left in Vicenza, "Because they place the personal interests of some men over and above the interests of the party, they form a personalist and exclusivist consensus, not a common one, as we would like." The issue is not conflict over the content of policies but the requirements of maintaining access to governing positions.

Not only is it more parsimonious to exclude ideological factors from the analysis, but there is very little evidence that DC leaders ever allow ideological consideration to affect their decisions.[30] While Putnam's analysis demonstrates Italian politicians to be more ideological than their British counterparts, the Italians placed at the center and center-right receive "moderate" scores on the ideological style index and appear to be not particularly more ideological than comparably placed British politicians.[31] Most important, there is no evidence that DC leaders have ever sought to apply as policy the principles of Christian Democracy. This, of course, is the critical cry of the radical Catholic *Comunione e Liberazione* movement.

This point bears elaboration. If, as it is sometimes argued and frequently presumed, the heads of the DC act as the leaders of a highly ideological political subculture and if, as I have demonstrated, the party has dominated Italian policy-making positions, how does one account for the absence of policies that are both coherent and Christian-inspired? If the party has had both an agreed on set of goals and the means to fulfill them, why has its rule been characterized by policy incoherence? The response contained within my argument is that they are not at all ideological. Indeed, what sounds like ideological pronouncements is the propaganda of electoral appeals. Most DC leaders are political patrons using the control of government positions to further personalist ends.

This argument also provides a response to an anomaly in Putnam's findings: while DC leaders are not especially ideological (using Putnam's measures), they are the least willing of all Italian politicians to compromise with political opponents.[32] Given their tactics, as long as the DC dominates (as the leaders certainly thought they would at the time of Putnam's interviews), compromise with political opponents is politically unnecessary and a gratuitous waste of resources.

Putnam analyzes a final problem in the analysis of bargaining in making governmental policies. It is not that Italian politicians are unwilling to compromise—his data show them as amenable to that form of political negotiation as the British leaders, and my analysis has provided additional examples of its frequent occurrence—but they bargain over "the spoils of office," not the content of policies, and most important do not engage in "problem-solving." They compromise over positions but not policy:

> What is lacking among Italian political leaders is not, it seems, a willingness to cooperate for mutual benefit, but rather a

> belief that such cooperation is possible on major social issues. The sense that these issues involve irreconcilably opposed interests, the fear that society may virtually fly apart if they are raised and faced openly, might lead a prudent politician to put them aside as quietly as possible. . . .[33]

Putnam unnecessarily introduces the issue of ideological cleavages. The problem is not that Italian politicians bury divisive issues—and evidence from the divorce referendum and abortion issues run counter even to this notion—but that general policies are not even formulated. As Di Palma's analysis of the parliament and my examination of the DC show, coherent policies are rarely formed within those parties and alliances which share issue positions.

DC leaders do not always bury issues, especially when they can win and approve of the consequences. Nor are they unwilling to compromise. They bargain incessantly to maintain and increase their control over governing positions. They most certainly have been able to reach agreements over particular laws—those which are in the limited interests of each of the competing political groups, as analyses of parliamentary bills clearly indicate. They have been unable to reach agreement over laws which may adversely affect any one or all factions, hence the absence of substantial collective goods policies and coherence in government programs.

There is a final link to this chain of arguments: if clientelist factions are particularly concerned with controlling governing positions and are successful in reaching those goals, they will continuously increase their position control and even create new jobs to help themselves. In doing so, they will drive out of the competitive arena those categoric factions without the proper tactical skills—a point first made by Mosca.[34] Given this, and the contention that clientelist factions block the formation of general policies, categoric factions must first conquer governing positions to be able to influence policy. Without the direct control of the relevant positions, they will be thwarted by the clienteles' vetoes. It seems clear that this was the logic of the modernizing group led by Sanza in Potenza. Those outside the DC have no political power. Indeed, only through the support of Colombo could positions be controlled and policies effected to benefit the province. Hence, join his faction and use his patronage. A similar logic applies to the DeMita-Forlani alliance.

There is an undeniable power to this tactical logic. Its ability to succeed within the DC is open to much doubt. Sanza is no longer a Colombiano having despaired of the ability to affect policy change through clientelist factions. With others in the Base, he is an ardent supporter of Zaccagnini.

7. The Future of Clientelist Rule in Italy

I began the discussion of the Christian Democratic party by detailing its dominance over the Italian polity. It may appear paradoxical to conclude its analysis with the question of the party's (and regime's) ability to survive. It is not. The mode of governing ascribed to the DC and its factions is best summed as the enactment of laws which are in the short run particularistic interests of their supporters, without regard for long-run interests. The question raised by observers in several recent articles, and implicit in my analysis so far, is whether the short-run game has finally reached its long-run consequences. Specifically, has the party's policy of distributing resources to a limited sector of the populace angered enough of the others for them to drive the DC from power?

Several recent political events give these questions political as well as theoretical significance. The results of the June 1976 national election as well as the May 1975 regional elections and the divorce referendum, in addition to recent patterns in survey responses, point to the presence of important changes in the Christian Democratic party's electoral position.[1] The surveys taken indicate a realignment underway among the Italian electorate:

> 1. For the first time polls show that the DC did not receive a plurality among young voters, but was surpassed by both the Communist and Socialist parties.[2]
>
> 2. Attachment to the Catholic church has declined as has the willingness of those who maintain their religious beliefs to transfer them into political deeds.
>
> 3. There is evidence of a weakening of the DC's ability to attract women voters. Females appear no more likely than males to vote Demochristian, a marked change from past patterns.

The DC's recovery to nearly 39 percent of the vote in the 1976 election provides at best ambiguous indications for the future. It is impossible to know the extent to which its electoral successes depended on the losses of the Liberals and Neo-Fascists and hence the future of the bloc that together with the DC has secured enough votes to deprive the left of a possible parliamentary majority. It is also impossible to know the extent to which the DC benefited from a "one last chance" feeling among those still unwilling to support a Communist government. Most important, new voters composed an extraordinarily high portion of the electorate and strongly favored the Communist and Socialist parties, a potentially fatal weakness.[3]

Changes are also present within the DC supporters as well. The maneuvering that preceded the 1976 Party Congress displayed a major growth in the number of activists claiming to reject the clientelist ways of the past and seeking to redirect the party towards greater policy goals. They are the supporters of Zaccagnini. It also showed a decline in the power of such old-line party patrons as Rumor and Gioia, the split in the Fanfaniani, as well as the end of the Colombo-Andreotti alliance.[4] Certainly the most remarkable demonstration of change were the whistles, insults, and catcalls that greeted the party's grand leaders: Colombo, Andreotti, Rumor, Piccoli among many others, including Donat Cattin, and the applause for Zaccagnini at the National Congress.[5] Table 7.1 outlines startling shifts in the distribution of preference votes among the party leaders. Indicated are substantial declines for some, especially Rumor and Piccoli, but also Forlani, Gaspari, and Natali. Even Andreotti, who scored extremely well, suffered the loss of many preference supporters. At the same time, Cossiga, a major Base supporter of the Zaccagnini group, scored big gains as did Zaccagnini himself. Last, Rossi di Montelera who swamped Donat Cattin in Torino, and De Carolis and Barusso, both from Milan, emerged as strong gatherers of preference votes.

The Crisis of the DC as a "Regime Crisis"

In separate but complementary essays, Sidney Tarrow[6] and Gianfranco Pasquino[7] have argued that these events indicate not only the weakening of the DC but of the regime itself. Pasquino argues that the key problem facing the Christian Democrats is the contradictions engendered by a changing society and an increasingly rigid party. He maintains that particularly since 1968 Italy has been characterized by the spread of "modern" values and with them the effects of the joint realization of the "crises of participation and distribution." At the same time the Christian

Table 7.1. Preference Vote Totals for Selected DC Leaders

	1972	1976
Rumor	266,000	74,000
Bisaglia	138,000	103,000
Andreotti	367,000	200,000
Piccoli	84,000	37,000
Forlani	156,000	110,000
Gaspari		(−50,000)
Natali		(−50,000)
Zaccagnini		101,000
Cossiga	94,000	178,000
Donat Cattin	72,000	50,000
Rossi di Montelera		143,000
De Carolis		150,000
Borrusso		100,000
Gioia	123,000	111,000

Sources: Adapted from Franco Cazzola, "Partiti, Correnti," in *Un Sistema Politico alla Prova,* Mario Caciagli and Alberto Sprefico, eds. (Bologna: Il Mulino, 1975), p. 130; and *Panorama,* July 6, 1976, and January 18, 1977.
Note: Numbers rounded.

Democratic party has become even more monopolistic of its power and closed to the outside. Using data which add to those cited in preceding chapters, Pasquino details the growing bureaucratization of the party and shows that its recruitment patterns are out of touch with the changes in the society. It persists with the same individuals at the top of the party and, therefore, the government, and its incessant internal competition, makes it unable to govern effectively. At the same time, because of the changes occurring within the electorate its old electoral appeals no longer suffice. The calls of "God, Fatherland, and Family" are unable to assure it of sufficient voters to hold onto the levers of power.

Because the DC is the governing, "dominant" party, Pasquino argues, its crisis is a regime crisis. The party cannot reform itself or its method of governing Italy. How is it possible, asks Pasquino, to expect the Christian Democrat regime to destroy its bases of power through a reform of the bureaucracy and the para-state organizations, which feed the clientelistic arrangements? To do so would be tantamount to political suicide.[8]

Tarrow also utilizes the hegemonic qualities of the DC as the key to the current crisis of the regime: "Immobility of personnel leads to immobility in policy because the existing political class is so absorbed in protecting its positions that it either loses control of policy—to the bureaucracy, to private actors—or remains incapable of modernizing its policies to cope with the rapidly changing problems of the society." Thus, the problem of Italy is "survival in the face of immobility in leadership and policy direction at the summit of the political system."[9]

Like Pasquino, Tarrow derives the current crisis from the internal contradictions of the political system itself. His argument is especially powerful because it ties the regime's problems not only to the DC but also to the arrangements between the Christian Democrats and the Communist party. Responding to a sharply divided political system, Tarrow argues, Italian political leaders have developed a mode of cooperative political exchange that belies the visible ideological pyrotechnics. Both the DC and the PCI have successfully captured the state resources and spread them among their electoral followers. While the DC because it controls so many more positions is better able to dominate those resources, the PCI where it is in power does so as well. "Since not policy, but distribution is the key to power, the great party and factional leaders and their machines can remain in power by maintaining their hold on their bases of patronage: the great state monopolies, the public-works producing ministries, and the local *enti* which provide public employment to grassroots supporters."[10]

Tarrow derives two crucial consequences from this pattern. The first, as was also noted in the previous chapter, is the government's inability to deal with general issues of reform and the provision of collective goods. The second ties these patterns to mass disaffection and, thereby, strengthens the contention that the regime is in imminent danger. Tarrow bears citing at length:

> This disjuncture between the mercantilist nature of Italian political exchange and the ideological flavor of the public debate reveals a major contradiction in the system's functioning. Because resources are distributed to private groups, economic sectors and local governments through well-functioning networks of political exchange, the party system is able to maintain the consent of broad groupings of the population. But because the policies which result from such politicized decision-making are irrational and contradictory, there is little tendency among the citizens to ascribe

legitimacy to these structures, even those who profit from them. Thus the very mechanisms of political exchange that have been developed to carry out the public business of the country are themselves inimical to the legitimacy of the system as a whole.[11]

Thus it would seem, given the analyses of Tarrow and Pasquino as well as that of the previous chapters, that there is support for the hypotheses detailing the instability of clientelist regimes. The arrangements reviewed mesh with Mosca's theoretical predictions: the increasing monopolization of governing positions by a limited group, policy-making in their selfish interests, increasing distance from the masses, and therefore cultural divergencies between mass and political elite will lead to a revolution led by those theretofore excluded from political leadership. One might say that the PCI appears to be coming into power on the theoretical coattails of Mosca.

Taken together, these are very powerful theoretical and empirical reasons to conclude the analysis with a prediction of the imminent demise of the DC and "its" political system. While the party has not yet lost its dominant position, the logic of my argument and the analyses of others predict that in a very short time the party will fall from power. Surveys taken before the 1976 elections, though proved wrong by the electoral results, showed more than 70 percent of the voters opposed to the DC.[12] It would follow that the Demochristian leaders will be unable to end their game of musical chairs until the floor collapses beneath them.

This attempt to argue that recent events—initiated by the divorce referendum and highlighted by the 1975 and 1976 elections—mark a crisis for the Christian Democratic regime must resolve two additional issues. The first is the timing of the crisis. How does the argument account for the marked increase in the perceived severity of party and regime difficulties in the mid-1970s? The second is the meaning of the crisis. Our sources, whether analyses of current Italian politics or the theoretical works that set out the consequences of clientelist rule refer to "survival," "collapse," and "contradictions of the system"—all terms without clear empirical referents. They do not specify whether the problem is to account for a general alteration of the regime or some less drastic alternative in the mode of rule. The first issue deals with the explanatory power of the theory, its ability to specify the timing of its predictions. The second issue requires an operationalization of one of the dependent variables—regime change.

When will a clientelist regime reach its point of crisis? Beyond pointing to the long run, most analyses do not deal with the problem. Mosca's only answer focuses on the coming-to-power of the patrons' children. Two points should be made about this response: it is not useful to tie the analysis to the actual children of the political elite; not all patrons have children active in politics. Hence, a more general time reference is required. However, evidence from Italy supports even this particular contention. The political ascendancy of the sons of Gava and Gioia have been followed by their political clienteles' loss of local power.[13] Still, I will use a more general specification of the onset of the crisis.

One way to do so—which also follows from Mosca's point—is to link the timing to generational change. The current Italian crisis is then associated with the advent of an extraordinarily large number of new voters into the electorate at large and into the ranks of the DC in particular. The electorate of 1976 (and 1975) was very different from that of 1972. Seven million voters who were new to national elections took part in 1976, one quarter of all those voting. As I noted earlier, as a group these voters were much less disposed than the others to be religious, to tie their votes to their religious convictions, to see the Communists as evil incarnate, and to want to join the clientelist arrangements within the DC.[14] The supporters of Zaccagnini, controlling the Christian Democratic party in the wake of the electoral debacles of the divorce referendum and the 1975 regional elections, appear to reflect these same changes within the ranks of the DC. The children born in the early 1950s—products of the postwar baby boom—occupy a very large share of the population and appear to have values very different than their parents. In this view, the timing of the crisis is accounted for by the onset of a new political generation of exceptionally large size, to whom the party's old electoral claims and electoral methods do not appeal. It is not just the monopolization of governing positions by the patrons' "political" children nor the indifference of the leaders. These are continuously present. Rather, the crisis is a product of generational change in political values.

A second way of explaining the advent of the crisis—in general and in the Italian case—is to tie it to the sudden inability of the clienteles to provide the necessary goods and services required by their followers. Clientelist politics is inflationary politics. It requires the economic outbidding of one's opponents to stay victorious. In particular, the longer they have been in power, the greater the number tied to their mode of governing, the more that is expected of them, and the greater the consequences of the failure to produce. In times of economic recession, such as that which began in 1973, the clienteles were faced with increased demands by their supporters and the decreased ability to meet those demands. Not only could they not respond adequately to their clients, but these factions were now even more vulnerable to the anger of those excluded from the patronage arrangements. The latter generally turned against the DC to vote Communist and Socialist. The first sign of these changes were the results of the 1975 regional election.

Both factors, generational change and economic downturn, resulted in massive shifts within the electorate. They also further exacerbated the problems of the DC and the clientelist factions. The PCI's and PSI's electoral gains in 1975 removed the Christian Democrats from office in many regional, provincial, and communal governments, reduced their control of governing positions, and further weakened their ability to reward their clients with jobs and contracts.

Thus, one response specifies "long-term" (and hence explains the current crisis) by substantial change in the composition of the electorate and party activists. In Italy that occurred between 1972 and 1976. The second points to the affects of the economic recession that began in 1973 on the clientelist factions. The confluence of the two explanatory factors might additionally be used to account for the extreme severity of the crisis. At the same time, the confluence of the factors makes it impossible to select one over the other hypothesis. In addition, each factor may be derived from two rather different theories of political change, which makes it even more difficult to choose one of the hypotheses over the other. The link between economic downturns and crises for clientelist regimes is predicted by Pareto's theoretical speculations.[15] The association between generational change and electoral transformation meshes with some recent analyses of European voting patterns.[16] Hence, the timing of the crisis can be explained by two hypotheses, both of which may be linked to the general argument of the essay. Crises of clientelist regimes will occur when one or both of the following are present: (1) major economic downturns which follow periods of economic expansion; and (2) the entry into the political arena of an extraordinarily large number of voters, generally uninterested in the appeals of the clientelist party.

It is perhaps easier to account for the timing of the crisis than to specify its nature. Put vaguely at first, the claim is that the Italian government is unable to handle the policy problems and that the method of rule will soon change (or is now changing). Any analysis of this issue must detail the content and speed of change.

There are two very different interpretations of the current crisis. The first implies radical, abrupt change in the general character of the political system. The second implies the end of Christian Democratic dominance. The first type is illustrated by violent revolutions, coups, and the imposition of a new regime by outside political forces. The rise of DeGaulle and the shift from the Fourth to the Fifth Republic, the establishment of the postwar regimes in West Germany and Italy, as well as the coup in Greece are obvious examples of this form of regime change in the countries of Western Europe. The second type is exemplified by the shift in the relative position of the German Social Democrats and Christian Democrats after 1959. The formation of a grand coalition of the two parties ended the SPD's isolation and moved the German party system from one dominated by the CDU/CSU to the competition of two equally large parties. The first interpretation raises the issue of sudden regime change. The second focuses on change in the party system. It only raises the potential of long-term change in the structure of the regime through the policies of a new governing coalition.

Few observers view Italy as on the brink of a violent revolution, military coup, or regime change imposed by outsiders. Stated most generally, given the military power of the ruling government in an advanced industrial society, violent revolutions are highly unlikely. The outcome of the student demonstrations in March 1977 and even the terror that killed Aldo Moro underline the futility of violent revolution in Italy. In addition, the impossibility of violent revolutions in these societies is sustained by the strategy of the Communist parties. Despite the numerous rumors of military and

police plots against the Italian regime, it is equally unlikely that
the Italian crisis will end with the solution exemplified by the
coming-to-power of the Greek colonels. The power of the Communist and Socialist forces and the widespread lack of willingness
of Italians to engage in military coups exclude this possibility. In
addition, the mix of political personalities in Italy offers no Italian
candidates for the mantle of De Gaulle or Indira Gandhi. Hence,
for reasons particular to Italy and to other advanced industrial
societies, but contrary to the theoretical argument that I have
been following, I will set aside the possibility of sudden, radical
change in the Italian regime. Arguments derived from Mosca as
well as Marx run aground on the shoals of changes in the political
conditions.

Thus the questions are whether the DC is losing its dominant
position; how this will occur, and what its long-term consequences
will be. Will it share power with the Communists? Will the DC
enter the opposition for the first time in the history of the Italian
Republic? Will the new government be able to increase the
efficiency of the Italian bureaucracy and remove the clientelist
arrangements within it? Will the government seek to restructure
the Italian economy and society, provide more social services, and
reorder the tax system? In all, will it address the problems of
general policy, which the DC has long ignored? These questions
may be reduced to two. Will the period of DC rule be replaced
with an era of control by the left-wing parties, particularly the
PCI? Or can we look forward to a period of grand coalition in
which the DC and PCI rule together? If the second, will their joint
rule be based on a formal agreement to share power or the
informal arrangement that followed the June 1976 elections? It is
useful to restate these questions in terms of my general argument.
When an instance of prolonged clientelist rule reaches the point of
collapse, will the governing party, here the DC, lose power and, if
so, how?

Because a grand coalition requires only the decision of Christian
Democratic and Communist leaders, it is more easily analyzed
within my argument than the formation of a left-wing government, which also requires electoral shifts. Will the DC and PCI
agree formally to govern together? I think not. It is highly unlikely
that the DC will relinquish control over governing positions to
Communists. The logic of clientelist politics counsels against the

"unnecessary" sharing of governing positions. The PCI will certainly demand more control than did the Socialists during the center-left governments, and the DC still is not driven by the laws of electoral numbers to share power with the Communists. In addition, until the party develops an electoral appeal other than its anti-Communist position, it will be unwilling to legitimate the PCI through an open and formal sharing of power. For their part, the Communists appear to be torn by the desire for complete legitimation, as received by the German SPD after 1959, and the fear of being blamed for government failures, during a period of joint rule. More likely, then, is the continuation of parliamentary collaboration. It is the solution to the current crisis that minimizes the potential losses to both parties. In turn, it follows that the next election will be one in which the DC and the PCI face each other in a contest for dominance. Given all that I have contended so far, it is most likely that the DC will be unable to organize itself adequately to maintain its controlling position. Hence, the predicted outcome is the inauguration of a Communist-led government to follow the next national elections. In Italy, and in other advanced industrial societies, regime change means not violent revolution but the defeat of the dominant party and a new mode of rule.

Will the DC Save Itself?

Two potential sources of arguments complicate the analysis's theoretical simplicity and deny that the DC will lose power after the next election. The first has to do with the DC's leaders' abilities to set aside their conflicts in order to engage successfully in electoral contests. The second is tied to internal changes within the party, as exemplified by the new leadership under Zaccagnini.

Throughout this book I have attached a limiting condition to the aggrandizing goals of the clientelist factions. They act in the general interest of the party when their own survival and the party's strength is at stake. Over the years, they have set aside their battles to work together in electoral campaigns. It is especially but not exclusively, during those contests that the interests of each particular faction is tied to the survival of all of them within the party. Election appeals even where cutting against the concerns of some of the factions, particularly the left, are devised to best maintain the party in power and are adhered to by all. Indeed, the occasional willingness of the dominant factions to compromise with the left, as exemplified by the one instance of compromise in Vicenza and Sanza's ability to keep a place on the ballot even after leaving Colombo's clientele, attest to the factions' willingness to work together to save themselves through the party's victory at the polls. Only the divorce referendum seems to have broken with this pattern. There is indication that the Base and Forze Nuove did not actively support Fanfani's campaign leadership. Here, however, there was no threat to faction or of party survival. A leader of the Forze Nuove outlined to me the point where internal opposition ends and cooperation must begin.

> Because a political vacuum persisting for a long time would have hurt the party, we agreed to accept the current [Rumor-led] center-left government. Even if we did not have many reasons to facilitate the formation of the government, we would have preferred a Party Congress first. We did so for the good of the party, while declaring that we were disposed to participate if the DeMartino faction of the PSI also participated in the cabinet.

The DC leaders will face the crucial issues of strengthening the party's electoral base as faction leaders. Their primary concerns are with their factions, through which the party makes decisions. The critical question is whether the leaders will set aside their search for particularistic rewards to act together. Are there the incentives and means present to reorganize the party? Given the logic of the argument that I have been pursuing, the determinant issues are:

> 1. Do the leaders interpret the current crisis as sufficiently dangerous to the party's health to entail collective action?
> 2. If they do, are there adequate personnel and organizational resources to revamp the party and improve its electoral ability, and perhaps most important, to govern effectively?

Events since the disastrous regional elections of May 1975 provide no clear answers to these questions. The election of Zaccagnini brought to power a man not of the old ways. His close ties to Moro were not clientelist. The battles for delegate positions to the 1976 Party Congress by supporters of "Zac" and their successes in controlling party and government positions are all signs of internal change.[17] In addition, DC activists who lost or who fear for the loss of governing positions have a strong incentive to reinvigorate the party. Without such efforts their political careers will be over. However, the bitter battles between Piccoli and Zaccagnini over access to positions in the RAI-TV, the ascension of Fanfani to the party presidency and the reliance on God, fatherland, and family as electoral appeals indicate the old ways are not gone. In additonal the results of preference voting in the 1976 election are ambiguous. Rumor and Piccoli suffered massive losses and Andreotti's supporters, though still very large in number, declined. Zaccagnini and Cossiga, symbols of the new order, gathered many new preference votes as did several new and conservative DC leaders in the north. Finally, are the catcalls that greeted faction leaders at the Party Congress to be viewed as the end of their power or indications by their followers that they had better produce?

Other factors indicate that the DC leaders need not interpret current events as necessarily disastrous for themselves. If so, they will not change their ways. The results of the 1976 elections point to both the strength of the PCI and the grave weakness of the Socialists. It is the latter party which suffered the most, in actual results and political image. Together, the PCI and PSI cannot form a governing coalition, and given the divisions within the Socialist leadership and electorate they will not coalesce with the Communists lest they risk their political futures for very little gain. Unless national elections seriously weaken the Christian Democrats, no cabinet can form without it as the dominant party. If so, then there is no threat to the political lives of the particular Christian Democratic party and faction leaders because no one else can govern. They will not change their current behavior patterns, therefore, and will neither revamp the party nor enact sweeping new policy packages. True, the long-term consequences, as specified previously, of their behavior will catch up to them, but there is little reason to expect these particular leaders to be especially concerned with the long-term fate of the party. After all, they have been playing a short-term game for a long time, a game whose limited particularistic goals are major sources of the current crisis. Fanfani, Rumor, Piccoli, Colombo, and Andreotti have very few personal incentives to act in the long-term interests of the party. They have already conquered the heights of political power in Italy and the best parts of their careers are behind them.

The same logic applies to the assumption that the party leaders do interpret the current problems as being of crisis proportions. Given their primary concerns for their own aggrandizement and the fact that they have operated in this manner for well over a decade, it is highly probable that each will fear that the others will take advantage of his acts in the collective interest. In this contest, there is danger attached to being the first to give up a particularistic strategy. If so, they will not put aside their overriding concern with their own factions.

DC leaders, themselves, have made these same points. Antonio Gava, often usually frank about the factions, likened efforts to eliminate them to disarmament negotiations. "The truth is that the problem of the factions is like disarmament. No one wants to disarm first."[18] Leaders of the new majority despair over the problem of factions: "No one should be fooled. The factional cancer must be destroyed, if the *Democrazia Cristiana* is to function. . . . If at the next meeting of the National Council the factions lose control of the membership lists, we will have won. If not, the old way to suicide will have won."[19] Angelo Sanza has served as my example of the new DC leaders. His response was the most pessimistic of all: "I am convinced that a number of years in the opposition would be enough to liberate us from Colombo, Rumor, Fanfani, among other anachronistic ornaments."[20]

Thus, there is additional support for my general argument. As long as the clientelist factions predominate within the party, there is little reason to expect the party to do anything but lose power after the next elections.

A central question then is whether any groups can now defeat the clientelist factions. Within the DC, there is another set of leaders present with sufficient incentive but perhaps insufficient power to effect the necessary changes in the party. While its long-term demise may not directly threaten the clientelist leaders, it most certainly endangers their lieutenants and the left-wing faction leaders. Given their more limited accomplishments and their relative youth, their political careers require concern for long-term developments. In addition, it is the left-wing leaders who have been most likely to set aside personal and factional goals in the general interests of the party. Unlike the senior party leaders, these Demochristians have strong incentives to break with patterns of the past and to reorganize the party, as Arnaud's split from the Fanfaniani to support Zaccagnini indicates.

The problem with this solution is that it was attempted at San Ginesio only to fail when Fanfani returned to power. Why argue that it may succeed now? Its particular and paradoxical strength is that is ties a reinvigorated DC to ongoing changes within Italian society which have been cited as the potential source of the party's downfall. Pasquino argues for the presence of the post-1968 changes in Italian society and moral values. These clearly surfaced in the divorce referendum and in the survey results gathered by Sani. If Zaccagnini and his policy adherents are to maintain control of the party they require the sustained support of large numbers of new party activists. Such support occurred prior to the 1976 Party Congress, where many youthful workers were crucial to his victory. It was also evident among the 200,000 at the party's "festival" in September 1977. The large numbers of new voters that have entered the electorate particularly since the 1972 elections need not necessarily become a source of left-wing strength. Most come from homes in which DC voting is the rule, and there are some recent polls giving the DC a plurality of their votes.[21] I do not argue that these changes will occur, but that they are necessary for the DC to maintain its dominant position.

This presence of sufficient numbers of the new DC activists is not just a pious hope of Zaccagnini's supporters. Some studies of the party, including my own fieldwork, point to their presence within the party, albeit in small numbers, during recent years. A study of party activists carried out by the Carlo Cattaneo Institute in the mid-1960s locates the presence of such Demochristians in the south as indicative of sources of change within the party. As one such leader was quoted:

> One night I said to my colleagues in the Communal Council: "In order to straighten things out, each of us in decision-making positions must have the following frame of mind." I said that you must think that you are here to help others. You must convince yourselves that whoever becomes mayor, assessor, or communal counsellor stands to serve. He

must put it into his head that he is to serve and not to be
served—because many people think that when they have a
position they become *padroni*.[22]

My analysis of Potenza depicted the presence of an age-related
division, in which the younger group had very specific policy goals
and had succeeded in gaining control of party. This age-related
policy split was not at all limited to the provincial level but played
itself out in a fascinating incident that I witnessed. I accompanied
Sanza, then provincial secretary and a secretary of a zone, to a
meeting in a tiny commune near the border with Calabria, a
four-hour car ride from Potenza. An extraordinary meeting with
an exceptionally large turnout and much local interest had been
called because of a generational split in the local section.

The meeting was held in a room of the local church. The room
itself was rather bare, and the only decoration on the grimy yellow
walls was a crucifix. Over the table, which at other times was used
for table tennis, hung a single light bulb which provided the only
light in the room. Only those seated close to the lone gas
room-heater were able to escape the biting cold.

In this commune of approximately 1,000 residents, there were
100 members of the DC, 25 of whom were present for the
meeting. The section's secretary who opposed the calling of the
meeting was conspicuous by his absence, having refused to await
our rather belated arrival. During the past several years there had
been few, if any, meetings and little or no response on the part of
the leaders to the desires of the members, especially the youth.
The secretary of the zone noted that the party organization was so
moribund that he had to come to the town to organize the
electoral campaigns. The section leaders replied: "This has always
been the case, so why the present concern?"

The basic issue revolved around the desire of a group of young
men in their early twenties to enter the party and to be granted
full voting rights at the coming party assembly. Opposition was
voiced by some of the older leaders. The most striking aspects of
the meeting were the strong differences based on age and the
apparently deeply held democratic attitudes of the vast majority
of those present. Most members, except the oldest, seemed to
desire politics to be based on principled leadership and not on the
old methods of personalism.

To return to the description of the DC in the mid 1970s, not only was the Party Congress filled with new faces but so was the party's list of candidates in the June election. In 1976, 49 of 266 Christian Democratic deputies (18.4 percent) and 55 of 135 senators (40.7 percent) did not stand for reelection. Slightly more than one-third of the Demochristians elected to the Chamber of Deputies and more than one-half of those elected to the Senate were newcomers.[23] The total of 40 percent of the Demochristians elected for the first time to the parliament is the highest portion of the party's delegation since 1948. In that first legislature, 46 percent of the Christian Democrats were new (that is, had not served in the Constituent Assembly); in 1953, 30 percent were freshmen; as were 35 percent in 1958; 22 percent in 1963; 31 percent in 1968; and 22 percent in 1972.[24]

In addition, these shifts were in large part of the results of the changes within the DC just outlined. Table 7.2 shows that nearly two-thirds of those who did not return were not permitted to run for reelection, a figure in line with, but substantially greater than, past trends. Finally, Richard Dalton has located additional age-related changes with the party leadership and has argued that a new generation is coming to predominate.[25] These data on changes within the DC delegation to parliament provide further evidence of marked shifts in political goals. The results of the 1976 Congress and the contests for the control of parliamentary nominations show clear changes from past patterns in many dimensions.

There is good reason to believe that the new breed of DC activists that has controlled the party since the 1976 Congress is more interested in the collective fate of the party and nation than are those in the clientelist factions.[26] If so, and if they maintain their control, the DC will increase its efficiency as a governing and campaigning party. It can be expected to develop coherent policy packages as well as efficient campaign techniques. Both should enable it to maintain its position of dominance in Italy.

Will the DC fall from power? My analysis provides two conflicting responses. If the clientelist factions maintain their strength, they will continue their past practices. They will compete constantly for governing positions. Their contests will have the same consequences for the formation and content of policies in the party and the government. If so, the probability will

Table 7.2 How Christian Democrats Have Left Parliament

	1953		1958		1963		1968		1972		1976	
	%	N	%	N	%	N	%	N	%	N	%	N
Defeated at election	84	(91)	65	(48)	75	(41)	62	(32)	51	(28)	35	(56)
Replaced on party list	16	(17)	35	(26)	25	(14)	38	(30)	49	(27)	65	(104)
		(108)		(74)		(55)		(52)		(55)		(160)

Sources: Adapted from Marizio Cotta, "Classe Politica e Istituzionalizzazione del Parlamento: 1946-1972," *Rivista Italiana Di Scienza Politica* (April 1976), p. 93; and Gianfranco Pasquino, "Ricambio Parlamentare E Rendimento Politico," *Politica del diritto* (September–October 1976), p. 556.

increase that the party will lose the next election. If there is continued change within the DC—if Zaccagnini and his supporters are able to defeat the old factions—then policy cohesion and efficiency will improve. There will be a decrease in anger at the DC and an increase in its ability to attract new voters. With this would come an increased likelihood of its maintaining power.

I have taken my analysis of the DC's future as far as it will go. The outcome of the next elections will depend only in part on the actions of the DC leaders and hence only in a limited way on the variables used in my argument. I do not deal sufficiently with the determinants of electoral behavior to be able to further specify the predictions.

The limits of my argument not only pertain to voting decisions. By examining the "selfish" aspects of the DC's rule, I do not mean to imply that the rule of other parties would have been or would be "better." Because of the specificity of my argument, I have had to ignore perhaps the most important of the DC's accomplishments, the institutionalization of democratic rule in Italy. Clientelist rule permits large areas to be free of government control. If it also suffers because so many general issues are left to government by indirection, it does not sin by forcing others to do what the political leaders decree to be best for them.

My analysis raises some final speculations about how the Italian Communist party will rule if and when it comes to power. The DC's political clienteles now inhabit vast areas of the government not affected by elections. The Communists will find them in strength in the state and parastate organizations. Only a thoroughgoing purge could root them out. However, if the Communists were to attempt summary dismissals, they would raise questions about the legality of their rule. Even if they were to oust or limit the DC's political clienteles, that would not rule out the growth of Communist or Socialist clienteles, whether in place of or alongside those of the DC. If the clientelist factions are not eliminated and if clientelism continues its present course, other problems are raised. The PCI's ability to govern effectively will be blocked. The clientelist factions will certainly stop attempts to transform the society and the economy. If the Communist party, which now has greater access to patronage, develops its own political clienteles, that will add to its difficulties.

Obviously the advent of Communist rule in Italy will raise a series of questions. It is difficult to know whether the party will significantly improve policies. To the extent that PCI rule does not, its government will prove no better than the DC's. To the extent that its policies are frustrated by the bureaucracy, the Communist party leaders will be tempted to "turn the screws" on their opponents. Even more, Communist rule must seek to resolve questions of the collective good, its primary claim to legitimacy and political support. It must strive to bring social justice with its rule. To the extent that they do not reach that goal, they will remove counterrevolutionaries from the population. Even at its worst, clientelist rule does not seek and destroy its opponents.[27]

8. Conclusion: The Argument in Cross-National Perspective

I have sought to demonstrate that the numerous clientelist factions within the Italian political elite affect various elements of political competition, policy-making, and regime survival. My argument omits other explanatory factors as it pushes on with the implications of its own logic. How do I justify the resulting limited description of Italian politics? Only by presenting simple arguments can one hope to produce theoretical statements with wide explanatory power. Rising above some of the peculiarities of Italian politics and phrasing others in general terms allows the analysis to be applied to other countries. Hence, by focusing on a limited set of explanatory factors I not only have been able to account for various elements of Italian politics. Rather, and more generally, I maintain that wherever clientelist factions abound within a regime the same consequences that I specified in Italy will be found as well. An elaboration of my general argument shows that it applies to other countries particularly Japan and India.[1]

Several factors hinder the accumulation of information of political clienteles. Underpinning them all is the theoretical approach that relegates clientelist politics to a stage of economic development, and assumes political clienteles will be destroyed by industrialization. This structures the available information. Most studies are of village politics; very few deal with clientelist factions in other surroundings, whether cities, regional, or national governments. Because these arrangements are frequently seen as immoral, to raise them is to cast aspersions on the character of the people, their polity, and level of economic development. As a result, many such descriptions are the work of local muckrakers. In turn, not only do they always condemn the clientelist ties, but each writer also seems to feel that the arrangements are unique to his own country, and another indication of its backwardness. Neither perspective is helpful. The former condemns this most common form of political association to a purported transitional stage, to out-of-the-way areas, and to local politics. The latter limits the cross-national analysis of the issue, always explaining it is as an embarrasing local peculiarity.

Political Clienteles in Japan

The political clienteles that I have described in the Christian Democratic party of Italy have their counterparts in Japan. To start with the first link of the chain, voters and Liberal Democrats in the Diet are tied to the *koenkai,* the Japanese term for the clientele. Defined as the Diet member's "support organization," the koenkai, many of which have as many as 50,000 members, provide campaign work and votes in return for personal favors, jobs, patronage assistance, loyalty, and money. When the member of the Diet is in the cabinet, the voter is thereby tied to the highest levels of government. More likely, the Diet member himself is tied as a client to national faction leaders in the cabinet. In many instances as well, local assemblymen are part of the koenkai, linking voter and Diet member. What ties together those in the party's several national factions? To cite Nathaniel B. Thayer, "The faction, then, from its inception, has been a contract between faction leaders and faction followers. What the faction follower gives is his vote in the presidential election; what he gets in return is campaign support in elections, political funds, and assistance in securing a high post in the party or government."[2] Compared even to the Italian DC, the weak national organization of the Liberal Democrats has increased the autonomy of the Diet members from the national party and heightened their dependence on the factions. Not only their nominations rest on faction support, but just as important, the money to run their extraordinarily expensive election campaigns, also comes from the national patron.[3] Voters demand and expect tangible rewards— money as well as jobs and assistance with the bureaucracy. The required resources come from the faction leaders. The result is intense loyalty by each to the next person in the chain: voters to political acticists and koenkai; activists to koenkai and factions. Very few, except the national leaders, feel tied to the party as such.

Structured like pyramids, the factions also reproduce the traditional patron-client relations of rural Japan and the political clienteles that competed in prewar Japanese politics. Factions then were also well organized, and captured cabinet positions, which, along with "pocket money," were distributed among followers. However, the prewar factions were less central to the political process. Thayer cites Robert K. Reischauer's description of the formation of Japanese parties in the 1880s. The Liberal party and the Constitutional Progressive party, forerunners of the current LDP, were founded to block samurai monopoly over key government positions. The leaders "used their parties as tools to pry open posts in the administration for themselves and their loyal henchmen."[4] Social relations in rural Japan were characterized by the power of the landlord over his village. The same paternalistic control described in Italy was also found in Japanese villages, as was the bond between families as well as individuals. Postwar years have changed these ties. The economic power of the landlords was destroyed by the land reforms imposed by the United States after the war. Control of political resources now determines who are the local patrons. Also, as in Italy, the patron-client in rural areas has become more specialized, and there are examples of "horizontal clienteles."[5]

Thayer cites Japanese scholars and newspaper reporters to underline the parallels between the structures of the factions and traditional Japanese behavior:

> They have adopted the social values, customs, and relationships of an older Japan. The newsmen, when they write about the factions, frequently draw on examples in *sumō*, Japanese wrestling, or the *han*, the feudal clans, to make their points. This vocabulary is particularly apt in describing the factions. The old concepts of loyalty, hierarchy, and duty hold sway in them. And the Dietman (or any other Japanese) feels very comfortable when he steps into this world.[6]

Political Clienteles in India

With some differences, this description fits political clienteles in India as well. There, as in Japan and Italy, analysts have located the clientelist faction as the basic unit of party and government competition. Weiner's statement finds echoes in numerous studies of Indian politics:

> We shall suggest that politicians have affiliations to factional groups, which are in fact multi-caste, and that these affiliations are durable rather than transitory. We shall suggest that factions are the units of political action both within the parties and within villages, and that the relationship between party faction and village faction is the single most important

variable affecting the outcome of many (but not all) elections. We shall also suggest that it is the intricate relationship among factions which affects the stability of the Andhra government, determines who becomes state chief minister, and affects the relative electoral standing of Congress as against the opposition parties in the state.[7]

Through political clienteles, voters are tied to district and village politics, to state factions, and at times to national politics. The first and last links of the chains are different in India. Village factions may be based on caste or other loyalties as well as clientele arrangements. The most frequent locus of faction activity is in district and state governments. No matter what the basis of the first link, the ties of cohesion in district and state factions are personal and patronage, linking local patrons to higher activists within the Congress party. They are rarely caste, economic class, or other categoric bases.

Paul Brass describes the party factions in Uttar Pradesh as "very loose coalitions of local, district faction leaders, tied together at the state level party by personal bonds of friendship, partly by caste loyalties, and most of all by political interest."[8] He then outlines the group's internal structure:

> The inner circle of the faction remains with the leader through thick and thin, for the members of the clique are attracted to the leader by the character of his personality. The larger, fluctuating membership remains with the leader only so long as he can provide material benefits in a not too distant future. These men represent the "floating vote" of internal Congress politics.[9]

The "guru-disciple" relationship that Brass finds within the inner circle does not apply to all clientelist factions in India. Close personal ties and the exchange of political resources do. Pettigrew emphasizes the similarity between the factions that she observed among the Sikh Jats in village and state politics in the Punjab and those described by Brass.[10] In both, personal friendships and enmities as well as political exchanges cement the bonds. To retain their statewide character, the factions require political resources:

> Actually, the links of villagers, local area leaders and the CM [the state's chief minister], or whoever was the senior

political leader, were based on certain types of exchanges. . . . They could continue only so long as the unit of
which all three were a part retained the image and the reality
of power. . . . It was in this sense that a faction centered on
its leader: a faction had as much power as its political patron.
The leaders of the faction could not retain effective control
of their own downward links were they without political
patronage.[11]

Although Indian factions are less active in national politics than
those in Italy or Japan, there are strong parallels between the
political clienteles and the traditional patron-client ties that have
characterized rural areas. Also, each person gives his primary
loyalty to those with whom he is personally tied: voter to local
patron; local patron to district and state faction leader. More like
Japan than Italy, political attachments extend to the faction,
indeed the particular portion linked, less to the party as such. The
party factions are manned by political activists; the voters' ballots
are resources to be exchanged for political assistance, patronage,
and power rendered by the faction leader.

Others have noted these same parallels.[12] Some have compared
the ties that bind members of Japanese factions to godparent
relations in the Philippines.[13] Some have noted the similarities
between the Japanese and Indian party factions.[14] Other parallels
may also be drawn. The *caciquismo* frequently found in Spanish-
speaking societies on both sides of the Atlantic has also been
located in India.[15] Similarly, Pettigrew describes the development
of these relationships in areas like Hobsbawm's "anarchic
order."[16] In India and Japan, as well as Italy, observers have found
highly competitive and distrustful norms. In all these countries,
traditional patron-client ties not only abounded but they linked
families as well as individuals.

The Sources of Political Clienteles in Japan and India

Throughout this volume, I have engaged in a running battle with
those who associate the presence and amount of political clienteles
with the level of economic development. I located clientelist
factions not only within the political elite, but also in villages
throughout Italy as well as the appropriate social values in Italians
all over the peninsula. I found clientelist factions in all areas of

economic development. If my presentation had a weakness it was the inability to show the very same clientelist politics in Milan that were found in Vicenza and Potenza. Analyses of local politics in India and Japan correct that weakness.

No matter the level of economic development, from traditional rural areas to Calcutta, clientelist factions abound within India. There are differences among them. The political clienteles in Calcutta are tied by government patronage resources and those in the rural areas combine access to land and government positions. As in Italy, categoric political groups are also present, but still clientelist factions are everywhere. Because evidence from India might be questioned on the grounds that India is even less industrialized than Italy, the location of political clienteles in relatively industrialized areas of the subcontinent may not convince doubters. No matter, there is sufficient support from Japan to clinch my argument.

Using the koenkai to indicate local political clienteles in Japan, I find no association between their strength and the level of industrialization. Benjamin and Ori describe koenkai abounding in the politics of Kanagawa prefecture, which is among the most urban, populous, wealthy, and industrialized in Japan.[17] Thayer details their presence in an area of mixed farms and industry that has a growing population.[18] Curtis shows them to pervade areas based on tourism as well as rural prefectures with declining populations. In a cross-local analysis of koenkai, Curtis finds them everywhere. He shows only the slightest relationship to where the respondent lives, his age, or his occupation. Residents of medium-sized cities, older people, merchants, administrators, and LDP voters are a bit more likely than others to report membership in or contact with a koenkai.[19] The koenkai pervade local political life in Japan. They structure elections to local assemblies and to the Diet, all over Japan without regard to an area's level of industrialization. Not surprisingly, the incidence of factions within the party elite also do not vary with the level of local economic development.

In addition, in India and Japan as well as Italy, analysts agree that clientelist factions have increased, not decreased, in political importance. Factions in the Indian Congress, even through the early 1950s, were more likely to be based on issue agreement than now. The same conclusion applies to Japanese factions, when comparing prewar and contemporary politics. Not only are issue factions less important, but there are fewer of them as well. Both cross-sectional and longitudinal perspectives reveal very little association between growth in industrialization and decline—not to mention absence—of political clienteles. Finally, in both as in Italy, clientelist factions pervade the political elite of the dominant party.

What accounts for the very high levels of clientelism in politics and whatever variations in those levels which are found in the three countries? Given cultural norms and a long history of patron-client ties are partial answers. They account for the location of political clienteles, but without detailed information not yet available, they cannot account for variations in their strength. They cannot explain why members of the Japanese House of Representatives are much more likely than those in the House of Councillors to be in clientelist factions. Similarly, cultural norms as such cannot explain the relative weakness of Indian party factions in New Delhi compared to the state governments.

As in Italy, political factors are also keys to the variations in the strength of political clienteles. The government in New Delhi provides fewer patronage opportunities, because of a more independent bureaucracy, than lower levels of the Indian government. Elections to the House of Councillors in Japan are much less frequent than to the lower House, where members are much more dependent on faction leaders for reelection. Additional evidence supporting the importance of political factors comes from local clientelist factions. Using party membership in India and the koenkai in Japan to indicate their presence, I find their variation dependent on the amount of faction conflict. Koenkai provide and gather votes for Diet members. The greater the number of candidates competing and the more frequent the contest, the greater the size and importance of koenkai.[20] In India, as in Italy, numbers of votes gathered identifies the patron's political strength. Not only is this true for elections to government but to party offices as well. Unlike Italy, the object of faction conflict in India is much more likely to be in the municipal, village, district, or state governments. Thus the determinant is the requirements of local party and state contests. In Italy, it is national contests. In both, not only does actual size of the personal followings vary along these lines, but so do incidences of phony figures.[21] The greater the local conflict in India and the greater the national aspirations of the local patron in Italy, the greater the incidences of padded membership lists as well as local clientelist factions.

The importance of political factors must be emphasized in the explanation of clientelist factions. Where there are no limits on contests and where there are resources to distribute, there are political clienteles. The discrepancies from my argument result more from the particular rules in each country than from the weakness of the analysis. In Ireland, as well as India, patronage resources are located at the local level and political clienteles prosper there.[22] In Italy, they struggle hardest in Rome. In all these countries, where there are no effective time limitations on the contests, political clienteles are found. The rule in Japan is that party and government offices may be occupied for no more than two years without an election. This law does not limit contests but ensures the constant maneuvering and the strength of the factions. Where the time rule is different, as in Japan's House of Councillors, whose members serve for six years, the factions are less important.[23]

In Italy, India, and Japan, clientelist party factions within the dominant party are the primary units of competition within the political opportunities. Earlier, I cited the claim that faction membership is a requisite for participation in DC party politics. Given the majority status of the LDP in Japan, it is not surprising that the factions are said to structure all Japanese politics: "It's not too much to say that entering a faction is an essential condition for becoming a politician (Dietman)."[24] The same applies to Indian local and state government, if not as much to New Delhi. In India, too, access to the national parliament requires the support of party factions. There, however, the relative absence of patronage opportunities and Nehru's prolonged dominance turned the Lok Sabha into a dumping ground for some faction leaders who were in the minority in their states. In all three cases, primary loyalty is given to the clientelist faction, not the party that houses it.

*The Consequences of Clientelist Factions in
Japan and India*

If clientelist factions pervade in India and Japan, what are their effects on political competition, policy-making, and regime survival? To what extent do the patterns that I found in Italy apply to those countries as well?

Contests over cabinet positions in Japan may be distinguished from those in Italy in two ways. The Liberal Democratic party has always controlled a majority of the seats in parliament. It has not needed to form coalitions with other parties. In addition, the rules limit cabinet tenure to two years. Neither affects the applicability of the argument. Cabinets in Japan change slightly more frequently than once a year, just about the Italian average. Thayer reports that between 1945 and 1966, there were twenty-two cabinets. There has been, as well, a slight though continuous increase in the rate of cabinet change since prewar times.[25]

Not only does the rate of cabinet change in Japan match that of Italy but observers agree that the source of instability is also the behavior of the dominant party's factions. As political clienteles they compete to control more and better cabinet positions. They are always willing to bring down a government to improve their potision in the next one. If necessary, a faction will join with other parties to collapse a cabinet. But the interparty cooperation stops there. All other parties are excluded from controlling cabinet positions and from influencing policies. Within the party, competition between the factions is limited by the practice of allowing all who want to obtain cabinet positions. The conflict is over the rank and number of portfolios received.[26] Senior cabinet positions are obtained by the faction leaders and their closest lieutenants. Second-ranking positions in the ministries are apportioned on the basis of faction balance, with an eye to giving them to younger politicians who have served one or two terms in the Diet. "The posts' chief attraction is that they furnish the politicians a chance to use the ministry's facilities to do favors for their constituents (thus bettering themselves in the elections), and for other politicians (thus bettering themselves in the party)."[27] One result is that the turnover rate within the cabinet is much higher than in Italy. Thayer reports that in 1966, one-fourth of all Diet members had served in a cabinet.[28] The parallel to Italy is restored by noting that top leaders stay in the cabinets and new politicians are offered junior positions in ministries to improve the latter's election chances.

However, the links between party and government contests are much closer in Japan than in Italy. The president of LDP is the prime minister. There are no separate contests for the offices. The president's faction controls the top offices of the party, most importantly the office of secretary-general, which controls cabinet appointments and distributes the party's vast financial resources for election campaigns. Here, too, however, all other factions are appointed to party committees and the secretary-general does 'not try to eliminate the other factions. As in Italy, the party factions compete to obtain nominations to the Diet for their members.

In India, this pattern of cabinet coalitions occurs in state and local government but less frequently in New Delhi for several reasons, including the dominant position of Nehru through much of the period and the factions' access to patronage founts at the lower levels. Also, even though there has been intense competition for nominations to the Lok Sabha and the state parliaments, leaders of the major state factions prefer to stay at home. The intense competition, in turn, has led to a generally high turnover rate for members of the national parliament. The result is that the conflict among clientelist factions within the state governments is not matched in the national capital. Be that as it may, a coalition of state factions, through alliances of chief ministers competed for control of the national government after Nehru's death.[29]

In the states, competition among the political clienteles, primarily though not exclusively within the Congress party, produced patterns similar to those described in Italy and Japan.[30] Where there were several competing factions, alliances included them all and were fragile. Where one was large enough to prevail, its dominance generally lasted only a few years, falling prey to maneuvers between its subfactions and the other factions. Dominant factions were not those which controlled a simple majority. Indeed, to prevail they needed a near-monopoly on party and government positions. Where this was not the case, all factions within the dominant party were included in the coalition. Other factions or parties were excluded. Conflict among the coalescing political clienteles pertained to the rank and number of government positions obtained. As in Italy and Japan, ruling coalitions were frequently brought down by alliances of Congress factions and the other parties.

Unlike the other two countries, on occasion party factions in the Indian states would leave their party to better their own positions. Decisions to leave the Congress, to rejoin it, or, for those clienteles that originated outside the ruling party, to associate with Congress, resulted from several factors. Most important among them were personal pique of the faction's patron and tactical considerations. After the 1967 elections, when the Congress party lost its governing majority in several states, the rate of shifts between the parties increased as each faction sought maximum political advantage.[31]

As in Italy and Japan, the clientelist factions sought positions within the party. With the death of Nehru, their strength in the party's center in New Delhi rose as well.[32] Since Indian independence, they have controlled the party's nominations to elected and appointed office. One difference: the vast number of local clientelist factions, not linked to national politics, increased the severity of these competitions. Sethi reports an average of four or five candidates per seat in the Lok Sabha.[33] One result, as noted, was that most members of parliament served but one term.

Although the factions may share some points of agreement over policy and cast their public statements in terms of issues and principles, what binds and concerns their members is the control of patronage and government positions. I have described this in Italy. The sources on India and Japan echo this point.[34] If so, what do they do when in power, when they control those positions? As in Italy, they try to control more and better positions. They expand beyond the parliament and cabinet, to subcabinet offices and the bureaucracy. They do so in the national capital and in regional, state, and local governments wherever the rules of appointment and competition make it possible. In national politics in Japan, this has meant a proliferation of commissions in the Diet and faction ties within the bureaucracy, if not a comparable expansion of positions.[35] Two examples from state politics show the Indian patterns. Paul Brass reports on faction control over ministries in Kanpur:

A more general consequence of factional conflict for the functioning of the state government has been not the shedding of the patronage power of the ministries, but the division of patronage by the splitting of ministries and ministerial responsibilities. . . . In order to satisfy all of his

prominent district supporters and also to foster unity in the
state party organization by bringing into the government
some of his political opponents, C.B. Gupta formed a
government of 46 members. . . .[36]

Weiner describes the municipal government in Calcutta as the
near-monopoly of clientelist factions. Municipal councillors control the municipal administration, so that each member of the
bureaucracy is more frequently loyal to his councillor than the
executive officer.[37] In addition, few of the 25,000 to 30,000
employees in the municipal administration obtained their jobs
without patronage ties.[38]

In power, the clientelist factions use their positions to provide
particularist benefits to their supporters. The literature provides
numerous evidence of this in India and Japan (and elsewhere
where these patterns apply). For example, in Calcutta: "Inspectors
making house assessments, engineers responsible for locating street
lights, and other technical personnel are readily influenced by the
councillors."[39] The cases abound. The distribution of government
contracts and jobs, the location of roads, and the rearrangement of
train schedules are but some cases of factions influencing administrators to aid supporters. And these are found throughout Japan
and India, as well as Italy. Indian and Japanese sources establish
expediting or interceding with the bureaucracy as one of the
primary activities of faction leaders and activists. In Japan, the
activity proceeds through the koenkai in local government and the
deputy and his faction in national government. In India, the
factions more frequently operate through the Congress party.
Weiner describes one area in which the party is but one of the
objects of faction conflict: "The Congress party is simply one
object of power, along with the District Local Board, the taluka
development boards, and the banking and credit institutions. The
desire to maintain control over land, to have access to credit, to
influence the local market, and to obtain licences and permits for
oneself and more often for one's relatives and friends constitutes a
powerful motive."[40]

I cannot claim that the influence of factions on national policies
that I found in Italy applies to India and Japan, primarily because
the same kinds of detailed analyses of government laws for the
latter two countries have not been made. What is available
indicates that the national bureaucracies in India and Japan are

much more powerful than in Italy and that the bills of individual members of parliament are much less likely to become laws. There are also some sources that describe coherent Japanese policies produced by a generally effective bureaucracy.[41]

Still, there are parallels. To deal with Japan, about which there are analyses of policy-making in Tokyo, there is support for claiming some similarities with Italy and for noting that some of the differences derive from the particular legal and political circumstances. First of all, submitting private bills is technically cumbersome in Japan. It is also politically unnecessary. There are no coalition parties which must agree on the content of the bills. In addition, the private bills that are submitted and passed are almost all like the Italian *leggine,* of benefit to a particular group.[42] However, the primary locus for the factions to affect policy is through contacts with the bureaucracy. This is particularly important in Japan, where the administration is permitted to pass many laws as bureaucratic ordinances. In effect, to control the decisions of the bureaucrats in Japan is the equivalent of passing laws in Italy.[43] Japanese politicians strive mightily to those ends, and they succeed.

Japanese administrators play enormously powerful roles in the making of policy. Most bills are devised and drafted by the civil service and then presented by the ministers to the Diet. At the same time, the highest levels of the civil service are intensely political. Given the predominance of the LDP, it is not surprising that promotion within the administration requires the approval of the party. Perhaps even more important, there are direct clientelist ties between the leading bureaucrats and faction leaders. Thayer describes the reason for this bond. Senior officers generally retire at about fifty years of age. Some move to the large business firms with which they had close dealings; others move to the public corporations which they used to oversee, and still others move into politics. To succeed politically, they must develop election districts and have the backing of the party. To receive the party's nomination, they must join factions.[44] Citing a former bureaucrat, Thayer adds:

> Many of the top bureaucrats become politicians. They are good at running the country but terrible at winning elections. They need the help of professional politicians, campaign funds, and the party endorsement. If a bureaucrat is consider-

ing going into politics he must have close connections with the party from the time he is promoted to be a section chief. . . . He will usually be about forty years of age at that time. Although there are exceptions, most bureaucrats won't be in a position to run for office until they have become division chiefs. . . . They usually make this post at forty years of age. This gives the bureaucrat ten years to establish himself with the politicians.[45]

In 1968, those who succeeded amounted to almost 30 percent of the members of the lower house and more than 40 percent of the ministers.[46] As faction leaders, they frequently return as ministers and maintain influence over the policies of their areas of experience.

Numerous studies of India emphasize the increasing politicization of the bureaucracy, though without the detail available in studies of Japan or Italy. One source of this growth has been government decentralization, which added to the number of positions available through electoral contests, which ensured predominant control over them to the Congress party and its factions. To control local administrations is to control the resources of their agencies. One result is that factions have used the possession of a particular ministry in their contests with other factions.[47] In some areas, controlling the police has permitted factional conflict to include assaults and murders.[48] Politicizing the police provides ultimate political power. Most common of all is simple intercession with bureaucrats to favor the factions' supporters, the expediting noted previously.

As in Italy, government-supported efforts at economic development provide patronage opportunities in India. An important arena of faction conflict has been the control of local land reform projects. The distribution of seed, credit, tools and jobs in new industries has also been closely tied to place in the Congress party and its factions.

The District Cooperative Development Federation (DCDF) . . . is the apex institution in the district for most of the local cooperative societies engaged in production, marketing, and distribution. The DCDF distributes fertilizers, builds and operates brick-kilns, distributes iron and cement, and sometimes has a hand in the distribution of consumers' goods as well. The DCDF is, thus, an important agency for the distribution of goods, services, and patronage; for this reason, it is a prize for contending factions.[49]

Political influence over bureaucratic positions and decisions are paralleled by bribery and instances of apolitical corruption in each country. Money plays a particularly central role in Japan. The financial resources to run campaigns come from the business community to the LDP, and more importantly, to each faction. Money is also used to maintain the legislative support of some Diet members to ease the passage of some bills.[50] These actions are not explicitly illegal. However, as in Italy, financial scandals have been said to have reached into the cabinet itself. The same international corporation, Lockheed, has been implicated in successful bribes of members of both governments.[51]

Where political clienteles predominate, the absence of coherent policy programs can be expected. Factions are not only primarily interested in short-term aggrandizement but their policies typically result from political compromises. In turn, reaching these agreements means that issues are frequently ignored. Analysts differ over the quality of policy-making in Japan. Some have found haphazard and incoherent policies behind the rapidly expanding economy. Policies taken have frequently been to divert resources into political subsidies to maintain LDP support among various sectors of the economy.[52]

The much smaller economic base in India as well as its much slower rate of expansion has made it more difficult to use resources to buy political support. But attempts to do so have been magnified the attendant negative effects. Weiner associates the patronage politics in Calcutta with one of the worst municipal governments in India. Not only was it unable to provide badly needed municipal reform, but because the balance of power within the faction lay in the state government more attention was given to rural than urban issues.[53] In rural Kanpur, "To accommodate such a huge Council of Ministers and also to prevent any single minister from gaining too much power, authority and responsibility had to be fragmented." The result was "confused lines of administrative control" and "truncation of once powerful departments."[54] Brass ties the problems of Kanpur—its absence of orderly, honest, and efficient government, immobilism, and logrolling—to the party factions.[55]

Kanpur and Calcutta are but extreme examples of a pervasive phenomenon, one not located solely within the government. Rather, it may be found wherever the clientelist factions are able to gain predominance over institutions. Brass locates these effects within some trade unions [56] and Kochanek describes their increasing presence within Congress. After Nehru's death the factions fought "in the struggles for succession, which, the immediate succession crisis overcome, created renewed problems of party-government coordination."[57] Most important, the party could not agree on policies to deal with the prevailing economic stagnation.[58] An equally revealing example of the inability to agree on general reforms was the fate of the Kamaraj plan, which banned individuals from holding both party and government positions. In keeping with the strength of the state factions and the weakness of the national Congress party leadership, the directive was generally ignored in practice. By maintaining the control of local patronage, state factions severely limited the power of national party leaders. The contest between the branches of the party has been played out in the ongoing struggle between Indira Gandhi and her opponents.

How has faction conflict affected economic development in India? Although analysts differ on specific points, the consensus is that is has inhibited long-term growth and efficient planning. Jobs and resources have been produced and distributed with an eye to their political rather than economic benefits. Even Weiner, who generally praises the Congress party's efforts, cites the negative consequences of the factions:

> The danger to government performance lies less in the composition of the party than in the prospect of intense factional rivalries within the party distrupting the functioning of the government. A few of the state Congress governments have sought to maintain party unity in part by allocating ministerial posts to representatives of all important factions within the party. The result is that state cabinets are politically well balanced but incapable of working together. One can point to several states where factional rivalries within the party have prevented coordination among community development, irrigation, and agricultural ministries and to situations where chief ministers have been fearful of

taking actions which might destroy a precarious political balance.[59]

Weiner finds an increase in these patterns in national politics, beginning toward the end of Nehru's rule. Faction conflict, there, too, he reports, blocked effective ministerial coordination on military and agricultural policies. Francine Frankel presents a more damning critique. The short-run and particularist concerns of the clientelist factions inhibit the government's ability to govern in the general interest. As a result, "scarce public resources were siphoned off by projects to benefit local elites. While they in turn were unwilling to make any significant contributions to government development programs or social policies designed to benefit the poor."[60] The greatest casualty was the absence of new investments.[61]

Writing before Mrs. Gandi's emergency rule, some analysts pointed to the negative consequences for the regime itself from the persistence of these patterns. In terms reminiscent of Mosca, Sethi bemoans the decline in the quality of those who engage in politics. "People of some genuine commitment find this power game too dirty and too expensive and hence opt out of politics."[62] Frankel concludes her essay by warning of the dire consequences of the politics of patronage, which "can end only in the complete breakdown of the parliamentary system of government."[63] To push this point to the limit of speculation, I might note parallels between the collapse of democratic regimes in Greece and the Philippines with that of India.[64]

There is no evidence that Japan faces problems of regime collapse or change. The ongoing economic miracle has fueled this pattern of political, if not economic, inflation. If the kind of politics that I have described requires the political patrons always to increase the resources under their control, the success of the Japanese economy has produced the required benefits. Indeed, the LDP and its factions seem to have weathered the political storms occasioned by the economic problems of the mid-1970s even better than the DC in Italy. They have not lost political control, nor have they had to share political power with other parties. The parallels between the Japanese Liberal-Democrats and the Italian Christian Democrats are striking. In both, the middle years of the 1970s saw the first effective runs taken at their dominance. At the same time, a new generation of party leaders apparently less given to joining and acting through the factions emerged in both parties. The 1976 elections saw the largest turnover in both parties' representatives in parliament,[65] as well as claims that the factions have disbanded.[66] The parallel continues: leaders of both parties reacted to the crises, among them the Lockheed scandal, by electing new and "clean" party heads. Miki was Zaccagnini's counterpart.[67] And, in the face of apparent changes in the electorate, the Liberal-Democrats and the Christian Democrats have been able to hold on to their respective share of power.

Clientelist Factions and Political Clienteles

The information on India and Japan added to my material on Italy describe political clienteles in societies in different parts of the world, at different levels of economic development, and with different cultures. Together, the sources also present information on clientelist factions throughout those societies, from villages to national capitals, from general elections to maneuverings within cabinets.

Clientelist factions seek to control available political resources, not policies as much as positions. Leaders and followers, patrons and clients, join to pursue more and better tangible benefits for themselves. In particular, they follow the leader in his quest for greater amounts and more prestigious governing positions. These factions have generally persisted as structured political groups over relatively long periods. On the whole, individuals do not shift between factions in response to the bids of competing patrons. Important as the tangible benefits are, personal loyalties bind the members. In all cases, political activists generally retain primary loyalty to the faction itself. In India, this is exemplified by some of the factions moving en bloc in and out of the Congress party. In Japan, members of the koenkai typically do not also belong to the Liberal Democratic party. In Italy, there is no evidence of choices made between party and faction, but there, too, the political activist's central loyalty goes to his faction.

The drive to control more and better positions means that political clienteles form fragile alliances. They are always willing to end an arrangement if they can improve their position in the new one. In all of these cases, as factions of the dominant party, political clienteles have brought about frequent cabinet crises. In

Italy, Japan, and India, cabinet resignations have been occasioned most frequently not by policy disagreements between coalescing political parties, but rather by the maneuvers of clientelist factions.

With whom does a political clientele ally? It forms a political bond with a group that ensures its access to the governing positions. Thus, where the political arithmetic allows, they align with other political clienteles. Given a choice, they do not join with categoric factions, which are always a threat to redo the political game into one attuned to the needs of broad issues. The categoric faction's claim to political legitmacy and support is that it will govern in the general interest. Put specifically, it will appoint to office those who will govern efficiently, not only those with the correct partisan attachments. From the perspective of the clientelist faction, to deal with categoric factions is to risk losing their permanent access to office. With regard to cabinet coalitions, the clientelist party factions maneuver their party to align with other parties controlled by political clienteles.

When coalescing, political clienteles assure each other access to the alliance. The rule of minimum-winning coalitions does not apply here. It threatens a faction's survival. Because no faction can be certain that it will not be in the minority and thereby, without control of political resources, they allow all political clienteles who desire to be part of the governing majority. The result is to assure to all continued access to governing resources. This rule of "all in who want in" is paralleled by allowing past arrangements and future hopes to condition behavior. Favors are repaid and future payments planned in each coalition. In turn, these factors affect the outcome of particular contests. Who is to be prime minister, minister of the treasury, or minister of the posts is as much a product of current bargaining skill and power as past favors rendered and future ones expected. At the same time, these rules provide elements of order to what might otherwise be seen as a war of all against all.

When in power, clientelist factions use their positions to control additional political resources. As minister of state participation, for example, the faction leader appoints friends and clients to positions within the various state holdings. He allows them to appoint their friends and clients to positions as well. As a result, his clientele, from laborers employed in particular factories to the heads of government conglomerates, is expanded. Similarly, development funds are viewed as ideal when they produce a series of jobs, not ongoing employment free from political control. The point is always to maximize the political clientele's political benefit.

Thus, when in power, factions also use those positions to pass laws and bureaucratic ordinances to benefit their followers. The cases here abound in the political clienteles' organized interference in the bureaucracy. Most laws passed are designed to help particular groups of political supporters. More generally, governments controlled by clientelist factions emphasize the distributive aspects of government economic policy. Because they prefer to use the government's economic resources to help their followers, the clientelist factions are loath to plow capital back into investments.

Finally, political clienteles are particularly vulnerable to sudden downturns in the economy. They prosper when they can distribute portions of a large and expanding economy. Recessions, particularly when they follow a period of marked economic growth, make it very difficult for the political clienteles to meet the demands of their followers: They make the collectivist appeals more attractive to those outside the political clienteles, and they increase the competition between the clientelist factions for the remaining resources. Here is where alliances among these factions come undone. Some will opt to save themselves by joining with categoric factions. Others will seek to save themselves by increasing their control of whatever resources remain.

It is important to bear in mind a general point. Although political clienteles always put their particular interests first, these are not the only interests of the members. Patrons also want to be statesmen and national leaders. Where statesmanlike decisions do not hurt their factions, they make them. They provide collective goods, but only where there is no political cost to their faction or only when the threat to their political survival is so high that they see no other choice. In the absence of these two factors, they do not. It is not, however, a question of malevolence, but of political priorities.

At the same time, what I have described is not a unique form of behavior. Certainly, not only politicians strike bargains, maneuver and, deflect the general good to their personal ends. The issue has been to analyze these arrangements as structured political groups. Even as factions, they are not unique. They do not exist solely in out-of-the-way areas, backward, or even transitional states of development.

Several factors confound the claim that there is an inverse relationship between the presence of political clienteles and industrialization. Some are methodological with theoretical consequences. The claims entail a marked secular decline, where the bulk of the information provides cross-sectional descriptions, locating political clienteles in places of different levels of economic development. Also, few have searched for political clienteles in other than rural areas. Their theoretical lenses have precluded seeing them, where they were not expected.

When information is available, there is evidence of the persistence of political clienteles in the face of much economic and social change. There are alterations in the bases of patronage. Government resources have become more important than the control of land or access to the society's center. Clients, too, are not primarily found among peasants. That political clienteles are still in rural areas should not be used to argue that they are not also found in industrial areas. I found increases in preference voting and clientelist factions in the DC in areas of industrial Italy as well as in the south. Koenkai pervade Japanese politics no matter the level of industrialization, as do village and state factions in India. In all cases, the personal norms associated with patron-client ties pervade. Italians living in the northern and southern parts of the peninsula share more values with each other than with those who live in the center. Finally, there has been a decline in the politics of issues and a corresponding growth in the importance of political clienteles. In all three countries, the immediate postwar period was characterized by more conflict over policies than in the years that followed. To return to the theoretical level, the prevailing wisdom omits the theoretical possibility—and here the apparent reality—of values and beliefs that are not simply translations of social positions and economic factors. What seems to have occurred is a decline in traditional patron-client ties but no consequential decrease in the norms and general behavior patterns associated with them.

At the same time, what stands out in the analysis of Italy, Japan, and India (as well as other countries) is *both* the presence of traditional patron-client ties and the norms of clientelism and the political factors that assure the availability of political resources.

The argument that cultural factors alone account for political clienteles does not hold. More precisely, it does not explain the variations in the presence of clientelist factions within these countries. There is no reason to argue that those in the two Houses of the Japanese Diet do not share general political values. Yet clientelist factions are present in greater abundance in the House of Representatives than in the House of Councillors. The same holds for the differences between the location of political clienteles at the local, state, and national levels of the Indian government. In both cases, the differences apply to variations in the availability political resources. Elections to the lower house in Japan are more frequent than to the upper house. Given the demands of electoral competition in Japan clientelist factions are more important among representatives than councillors.

Still, one must be careful not to assign all the explanatory power to political factors. First, the evidence depicting what is actually available at the different levels of government is still sketchy. My conclusions derive from a limited number of cases. Second, political factors are themselves not only causal phenomena but the products of decisions by political leaders. Using proportional representation as the rule to decide how positions are distributed increases the availability of political resources and, hence, the persistence of the clientelist factions. But that decision rule was chosen in Italy to assure just those results. In this particular chicken-and-egg puzzle, the political clienteles came first.

There is then not just the possibility, but the practice of clientelist factions in governing positions arranging the rules to sustain their persistence. Where they predominate, the political rules will be established to keep them going. The rules emerge as products of clientelist design, as well as independent explanatory factors in their own right. Thus, where political clienteles are present at the institutionalization of a regime, they strive to establish formal rules that enable them to conquer governing positions. Where will that occur? Where clienteles are an accepted, widespread form of actual groups and a model for all associations.

Where political clienteles are permitted to do so, they structure the formal rules of governing to assure their survival.

The traditional use of clientelism is crucial to the presence of political clienteles in another, perhaps even more important, way. In all societies where clientelist factions predominate, the exchange of personal favors and loyalty is an accepted and even expected mode of human interaction. Put broadly, Japanese voters expect their political leaders to provide them with gifts when they have children or open new businesses. Italians and Indians expect to be helped by their friends. Most expect their contacts to use their positions of authority to help them, even at the expense of others. And they demand that they do so. If it is not part of the explicit public morality of the society—it is condemned when others do it—it is an expected relationship. Personal favors are required. These expectations are found whether or not patron-client ties in their pristine form still pervade explicitly economic relationships. Patrons may no longer be landlords or mediators. Clients may no longer be peasants. The mode of behavior persists.

In these societies, political activists are attuned to these expectations and demands. They understand that their supporters expect them to produce particularistic benefits and if they do not they will lose their supporters. They understand that their competitors are under the same demands. To engage in political competition is to wage a constant battle over political resources, while presuming that others have those same goals. Those who do not are vulnerable to the designs of the clientelist factions. To lower one's guard, to produce collective benefits at the expense of particularist ones, is dangerous. As one DC patron put it, it is like disarmament negotiations. Each side is afraid to be the first to play by new rules. To disarm first, here too, is a gratuitous act that risks political suicide.

For political clienteles to pervade a government both factors need be present. If political resources are available but the appropriate cultural expectations are not, particular clientelist factions will be sustained by those resources. They will not abound within the government, but will exist alongside other arrangements, categoric factions, and individuals outside structured groups. In those circumstances, political clienteles are vulnerable to public exposure and to the statesman in each politician. Their voters do not demand particularist benefits. Their opponents are more willing to share. The dynamic of their competition that resembles disarmament negotiations is missing. Political clienteles will remain localized as they feed on particular political resources. They will not pervade the political system. In Italy, Japan, and India, local clientelist factions have sustained ties to national factions. United States political machines, though powerful in particular areas of government at whatever level, do not form national factions. In a society without the proper normative supports, political clienteles form where there are available political resources, but they remain an embarrassment to themselves and to others. As such, they remain vulnerable to the ultimate political embarrassment: defeat.

Where few political resources are available—for example, where the rules ensure long tenure to elected and appointed officials— even where patron-client ties and their attendant expectations prevail, there will be relatively few clientelist factions. Where patrons cannot produce, they lose their followers. However, this is an unlikely occurrence. In the first instance, political rules may be changed. In office, political patrons will rewrite those formal bars on their access to patronage. As I argued earlier, where clientelism pervades a society, it is most likely that the political leaders will enact the initial laws to aid the political quest of the political clienteles. In the second instance, even strong and independent bureaucracies as in India and Japan are prone to fall to the battering of the clientelist factions. The logic of the behavior of political clienteles and the cases that I have examined attest to this.

Notes

Preface

1. Giovanni Sartori, "European Political Parties: the Case of Polarized Pluralism," in *Political Parties and Political Development,* eds. Joseph La-Palombara and Myron Weiner (Princeton: Princeton University Press, 1966), pp. 136-76; and Sartori, *Parties and Party Systems: A Framework for Analysis* (New York: Cambridge University Press, 1976), vol. 1, chap. 6; and Giuseppe Di Palma, *Surviving without Governing: The Italian Parties in Parliament* (Berkeley: University of California Press, 1977), chap. 6.

2. From apparently divergent sources James Q. Wilson and Carl H. Landé have arrived at the same conceptualization of categoric group. See Wilson, *Political Organization* (New York: Basic Books, 1974), p. 98; and Landé, "Networks and Groups in Southeast Asia: Some Observations on the Group Theory of Politics," *American Political Science Review* (March 1973), pp. 103-28.

3. See Charles Hendel, *David Humes's Political Essays* (New York: Liberal Arts Press, 1953), p. 81. Setting out types of "real factions," Hume writes, "Parties from *principle,* especially abstract principle, are known only to modern times and are, perhaps, the most extraordinary and unaccountable phenomenon that has yet appeared in human affairs."

4. Giovanni Sartori, "Concept Misformation in Comparative Politics," *American Political Science Review* (December 1970), pp. 1033-53, emphasizes the importance of unambiguous definitions in concept formation, and, hence, concept as "data container."

5. Here, I follow Robert D. Putnam, *The Beliefs of Politicians* (New Haven: Yale University Press, 1973), p. 2. See also Putnam, *The Comparative Study of Political Elites* (Englewood Cliffs, N.J.: Prentice-Hall, 1976), p. 11.

6. Gabriel A. Almond and Sidney Verba, *The Civic Culture* (Princeton: Princeton University Press, 1963).

7. Samuel H. Barnes and Giacomo Sani, "Mediterranean Political Culture and Italian Politics: An Interpretation," *British Journal of Political Science* (July 1974), 289-313. For a detailed analysis of the 1968 survey, see Samuel H. Barnes, *Representation in Italy* (Chicago: University of Chicago Press, 1977).

8. Many dissertations, articles, and books have been published by the Workshop's members. The major volume is Harry Eckstein and Ted Robert Gurr, *Patterns of Authority: A Structural Basis for Political Inquiry* (New York: Wiley Inter-Science, 1975).

Chapter 1

1. For elaborations of Marx's conceptualization of class see Ralf Dahrendorf, *Class and Class Conflict in Industrial Society* (Stanford: Stanford

University Press, 1967), p. 25; Shlomo Avineri, *The Social and Political Thought of Karl Marx* (New York: Cambridge University Press, 1970); and Alan Zuckerman, "Political Cleavage: A Conceptual and Theoretical Analysis," *British Journal of Political Science* (April 1975), especially pp. 231-35. Marx's development of social class as a theoretical concept is clearest in *The Eighteenth Brumaire;* see Karl Marx and Friedrich Engels, *Selected Works* (Moscow: Foreign Languages Publishing House, 1962), p. 334

2. Seymour M. Lipset, *Revolution and Counterrevolution* (Garden City, N.Y.: Doubleday, Anchor, 1970), pp. 321 ff.

3. Ibid., pp. 270 ff.

4. Richard Rose and Derek Urwin, "Social Cohesion, Political Parties, and Strains in Regimes," *Comparative Political Studies* (April 1969), p. 39.

5. Lipset, *Revolution and Counterrevolution,* pp. 242-43.

6. Ibid., p. 243.

7. Rose and Urwin, "Social Cohesion, Political Parties, and Strains," pp. 40-42.

8. See, for example, Arend Lijphart, "Typologies of Democratic Systems," in *Politics in Europe* (Englewood Cliffs, N.J.: Prentice-Hall, 1969), pp. 46-80; and Eric A. Nordlinger, *Conflict Regulation in Divided Societies* (Cambridge: Harvard University Center for International Affairs, 1972).

9. The literature on "cross-cutting cleavages" is voluminous. In addition to those cited in the text, see also David Truman, *The Governmental Process* (New York: Knopf, 1951); and William Kornhauser, *The Politics of Mass Society* (Glencoe, Ill.: The Free Press, 1959).

10. Douglas Rae and Michael Taylor, *The Analysis of Political Cleavage* (New Haven: Yale University Press, 1970), pp. 87-88.

ll. Seymour M. Lipset, *Political Man* (Garden City, N.Y.: Doubleday, Anchor, 1963), pp. 77-78.

12. Lipset, *Revolution and Counterrevolution,* pp. 276 ff.

13. Robert A. Dahl, ed., *Political Oppositions in Western Democracies* (New Haven: Yale University Press, 1967), p. 395.

14. Rae and Taylor, *Analysis of Political Cleavage,* p. 14.

15. For a general critique of the plausibility of this argument, see Nordlinger, *Conflict Regulation,* pp. 93-104.

16. Robert A. Dahl, *Who Governs?* (New Haven: Yale University Press, 1961), p. 90.

17. Ibid., p. 95.

18. Gaetano Mosca, *The Ruling Class,* ed. A. Livingston (New York: McGraw-Hill, 1939), p. 332. For a conceptual analysis of the political elite in Mosca and Pareto as well as more recent sources, see Alan Zuckerman, "The Concept 'Political Elite': Lessons from Mosca and Pareto," *The Journal of Politics* (May 1977), pp. 324-44.

19. See especially, *Teorica dei Governi e Governo Parlamentare,* new ed. (Varese: Giuffre, 1968). In chapter 2, I describe Mosca's (and Pareto's) analysis of divisions within the Italian political elite at the turn of the century.

20. Dahl, *Who Governs?,* pp. 85-95.

21. Hans Gerth and C. Wright Mills, *From Max Weber* (New York: Oxford University Press, 1958), p. 99.

22. Ibid., p. 86.

23. Ibid., p. 108.

24. See chapter 2 for an elaboration of Mosca's analysis of this point.

25. Gerth and Mills, *From Max Weber,* pp. 108-09.

26. James Q. Wilson, *The Amateur Democrat* (Chicago: University of Chicago Press, 1966), p. 3.

27. Ibid., p. 4. A source of this typology may be found in Peter B. Clarke and James Q. Wilson, "Incentive Systems: A Theory of Organization," *Administrative Science Quarterly* (September 1961), pp. 592-615. The attempt to classify political activists by personality characteristics is found and examined in numerous studies of American party politics. See Margaret Conway and Frank Feigert, "Motivation, Incentive Systems, and the Political Party Organization," *American Political Science Review* (December 1968), pp. 1159-73; Conway and Feigert, "Incentives and Task Performances among Precinct Party Workers," *Western Political Quarterly* (December 1974), pp. 693-710; C. Richard Hofstetter, "The Amateur Politician: A Problem in Construct Validation," *Midwest Journal of Political Science* (February 1971), pp. 31-56; and Hofstetter, "Organizational Activists: The Bases of Participation in Amateur and Professional Groups," *American Politics Quarterly* (April 1973), pp. 244-76. Because so much of this literature derives as generalizations from patterns found in American local politics, the location of nonliberal, purposive individuals and groups has surprised some. For that finding, see Aaron Wildavsky, "The Goldwater Phenomenon: Purists, Politicians, and the Two-Party System," *Review of Politics* (July 1965), pp. 386-413.

28. I. William Zartman, "The Study of Elite Circulation: Who's on First and What's He Doing There?" *Comparitive Politics* (April 1974), p. 477.

29. See especially Lewis Edinger and Donald Searing, "Social Background in Elite Analysis: A Methodological Inquiry," *American Political Science Review* (June 1967), pp. 428-45.

30. Ibid.

31. Robert D. Putnam, *The Beliefs of Politicians* (New Haven: Yale University Press, 1973).

32. The first position is exemplified by much of the literature that applies game theory to the analysis of cabinet coalition behavior. The second position is set out by Giovanni Sartori, when he contends that politics within the elite is closest to "pure politics": "Compared with visible politics, then, intra-party politics is *pure politics*—in two respects: It is more simple, and it is more genuine. It is more simple in the sense that many exogenous factors and disturbing variables may be set aside: Pure politics is made of, and explained by fewer variables." *Parties and Party Systems: A Framework for Analysis* (New York: Cambridge University Press, 1976), vol. 1, p. 96.

33. Giovanni Sartori, "From the Sociology of Politics to Political Sociology," in *Politics and the Social Sciences,* ed. Seymour M. Lipset (New York: Oxford University Press, 1969), p. 84.

34. Giuseppe Di Palma, *The Study of Conflict in Western Society: A Critique of the End of the Ideology* (Morristown, N.J.: General Learning Press, 1973), p. 3.

35. Lijphart, "Typologies of Democratic Systems."

36. Nordlinger, *Conflict Regulation.*

Chapter 2

1. Giovanni Sartori, *Parties and Party Systems: A Framework for Analysis* (New York: Cambridge University Press, 1976), vol. 1., provides the best analysis of the faction concept. He sets out its intellectual antecedents and distinguishes between faction and party; see especially pp. 3-13 and 71-82. Sartori argues strongly that the term *faction* carries a pejorative connotation and, hence, efforts to provide it with a special political science meaning are wrong. Because my concern is with the kind of subparty grouping that Sartori labels a faction, my use of the label does not conflict with Sartori's analysis: "I shall follow, therefore, the wording of Hume with the understanding that factions of interest subsume two distinguishable referents: Naked *power factions* (power for power's sake), on the one hand, and *spoils factions* (side payment more than power oriented) on the other. . . . Unscrupulous power and/or spoils groups point to what is generally understood by 'faction'" (italics in original) p. 77. My use of the adjective "clientelist" is meant to indicate that the factions under study have a particular structure. I will elaborate on these points later in the chapter.

For other overviews of the voluminous literature on factions see Norman K. Nicholson, "The Factional Model and the Study of Politics," *Comparative Political Studies* (October 1972), pp. 291-315; Giovanna Zincone, "Accesso Autonomo alle Resorse: le Determinanti del Frazionismo," *Rivista Italiana di Scienza Politica* (April 1972), pp. 239-59; and Alan Zuckerman, "Hierarchal Social Divisions and Political Groups: Factions in the Italian Christian Democrat Party," Ph.D. dissertation, Princeton University, 1971, chap. 2.

2. Charles Hendel, ed., *David Hume's Political Essays* (New York: Liberal Arts Press, 1953), p. 101.

3. Norman Frolich, Joe A. Oppenheimer, and Oran Young, *Political Leadership and Collective Goods* (Princeton: Princeton University Press, 1971), p. 3.

4. Hendel, *David Hume,* p. 77.

5. Ibid., pp. 77-78.

6. Raymond E. Wolfinger, *The Politics of Progress* (Englewood Cliffs, N.J.: Prentice-Hall, 1974), p. 105. Wolfinger develops a typology of political groups based on the incentives to political participation as routine/substantive and tangible/intangible. Political machines are characterized by routine/ tangible incentives. See p. 102. For another typology of political groups based on the incentives of participation in the group, see James Q. Wilson, *Political Organizations* (New York: Basic Books, 1974), chap. 3.

7. Wolfinger, *Politics of Progress,* p. 97.

8. That is, the presence of these groups derives not only from the theoretical assumptions of the economic analyses of politics. These may be

seen in Mancur Olson, Jr., *The Logic of Collective Action* (New York: Schocken, 1968).

9. F. G. Bailey, *Stratagems and Spoils* (New York: Schocken, 1969(, p. 53.

10. Wolfinger, *Politics of Progress*, p. 79.

11. Recent studies have begun to detail the vast number of positions in the United States at the national, state, and local government levels controlled by patronage. See Martin and Susan Tolchin, *To the Victor* (New York: Random House, Vintage, 1971); and Michael Pinto-Duschinsky, "Theories of Corruption in American Politics," paper presented to the Annual Meetings of the American Political Science Association, 1976, in Chicago. I shall elaborate on this point later in the chapter.

12. Wolfinger, *Politics of Progress,* p. 99.

13. Ibid., p. 99.

14. René Lemarchand and Keith Legg, "Political Clientelism and Development," *Comparative Politics* (January 1972), p. 149.

15. Carl H. Landé, "Networks and Groups in Southeast Asia: Some Observations on the Group Theory of Politics," *American Political Science Review* (March 1973), p. 105.

16. Eric Wolfe, "Kinship, Friendship, and Patron-Client Relations in Complex Societies," in *The Social Anthropology of Comples Societies,* ed. Miahael Banton (London: Tavistock, 1966), pp. 16-17.

17. Though James Scott, "Patron-Client Politics and Political Change in Southeast Asia," *American Political Science Review* (March 1972), pp. 91-113, argues that only the first type is properly labeled patron-client ties, and Emrys Lloyd Peters, "Patronage in Cyrenaica," in *Patrons and Clients* ed. Ernest Gellner and John Waterbury (London: Duckworth, 1977), pp. 275-90, provides an even more limited definition; others cite both as examples of clientelism. See Michael Kenny, *A Spanish Tapestry* (Bloomington: Indiana University Press, 1962); Sydel Silverman, "Patronage and Community-Nation Relationships in Central Italy," *Ethnology* (1965), pp. 172-89; and Jeremy Boissevain, "Patronage in Sicily," *Man* (October 1966), pp. 18-33. This is not to argue that Scott's or Peters's definition is wrong, but that the theoretical utility of each has not yet been established so as to warrant the more limited denotation.

18. Julian Pitt-Rivers, *The People of the Sierra,* 2d ed. Chicago: University of Chicago Press, 1971), p.,140.

19. Eric Hobsbawm, *Primitive Rebels* (New York: Norton, 1965), pp. 32-33.

20. For analyses of *caciquismo,* see ibid.; and Robert Kern, ed., *The Caciques* (Albuquerque: University of New Mexico Press, 1973).

21. For examples of clientelism in Africa, see René Lemarchand, "Political Clientelism and Ethnicity in Africa," *American Political Science Review* (March 1972), pp. 68-90; in Spain, see Kenny, *A Spanish Tapestry,* and Juan Linz, "The Party Systems of Spain: Past and Future," in *Party Systems and Voter Alignments,* ed. Seymour M. Lipset and Stein Rokkan (New York: The Free Press, 1967), pp. 197-282; in India, see F. G. Bailey, *Politics and Social Change: Orissa in 1959* (Berkeley and Los Angeles: University of California

Press, 1963), Adrian Mayer, "Quasi-Groups in the Study of Complex Societies," in *The Social Anthropology of Complex Societies,* and Oscar Lewis, *Village Life in Northern India* (New York: Random House, Vintage, 1958). Analyses of changing patron-client relations in Latin America are found in George Foster, "The Dyadic Contrast in Tzintzuntzan: Patron-Client Relations," *American Anthropologist* (December 1963), pp. 1280-94; John Duncan Powell, "Peasant Society and Clientelist Politics," *American Political Science Review* (June 1970), pp. 411-26; and Dwight Heath, "New Patrons for Old: Changing Patron-Client Relationships in the Bolivian Yungas," *Ethnology* (January 1972), pp. 75-98.

22. James Scott, "Corruption, Machine Politics, and Political Change," *American Political Science Review* (December 1969), pp. 1142-58. See also Alex Weingrod, "Patrons, Patronage, and Political Parties," *Comparative Studies in Society and History* (July 1968), pp. 377-400.

23. Maurice Duverger, *Political Parties,* rev. ed. (New York: Wiley, 1967), p. 20.

24. Myron Weiner, *Party Politics in India* (Princeton: Princeton University Press, 1957); Robert Scalapino and Junnosuke Masumi, *Parties and Politics in Contemporary Japan* (Berkeley: University of California Press, 1962); Michael Leiserson, "Factions and Coalitions in One-Party Japan: An Interpretation Based on the Theory of Games," *"American Political Science Review* (September 1968), pp. 770-87; and Scott Johnston, "A Comparative Study of Intra-Party Factionalism in Israel and Japan," *Western Political Quarterly* (June 1967), pp. 288-307.

25. Giovanni Sartori, "Proporzionalismo, Frazionismo e Crisi dei Partiti," *Rivista Italiana di Scienza Politica* (December 1971), pp. 629-55.

26. Stefano Passigli, "Proporzionalismo, Frazionismo e Crisi dei Partiti: Quid Prior?" *Rivista Italiana di Scienza Politica* (April 1972), pp. 126-39.

27. Carl Linden, *Khrushchev and the Soviet Leadership, 1957-1964* (Baltimore: The Johns Hopkins University Press, 1966). Classic studies of personalist groups within the Soviet Communist party are Franz Borkenau, "Getting at the Facts Behind the Soviet Facade," *Commentary* (April 1954), pp. 393-400; and Boris Nicolaevsky, *Power and the Soviet Elite* (New York: Praeger, 1965). See also Philip Stewart et al., "Political Mobility and the Soviet Political Process," *American Political Science Review* (December 1972), pp. 1269-91, for an attempt to detail the presence of political clienteles within the party.

28. Perhaps the best critical summary of this vast literature may be found in Wolfinger, *Politics of Progress,* chap. 4. In two recent studies, Martin Shefter has made significant theoretical and empirical advances in the study of political machines. See Martin Shefter, "The Emergence of the Political Machine: An Alternative View," in *Theoretical Perspectives in Urban Politics,* ed. Willia Hawley and Michael Lipsky (Englewood Cliffs, N.J.: Prentice-Hall, 1976), and "Parties, Patronage, and Political Change," paper presented at the Annual Meetings of the American Political Science Association, 1976, in Chicago.

29. Duverger, *Political Parties,* p. 152.

30. Ibid.

31. Bailey, *Stratagems and Spoils,* p. 43.

32. V. O. Key, *Southern Politics* (New York: Knopf, 1949).

33. Landé, "Networks and Groups."

34. P. A. Allum, *Politics and Society in Post-War Naples* (Cambridge, England: Cambridge University Press, 1973), p. 10.

35. Sidney Tarrow *Peasant Communism in Southern Italy* (New Haven: Yale University Press, 1967)

36. Luigi Graziano, "Patron-Client Relationships in Southern Italy," *European Journal of Political Research* (April 1973), pp. 3-34.

37. Scott, "Corruption, Machine Politics, and Political Change," p. 106.

38. Key, *Southern Politics.*

39. Wilson, *Political Organization,* p. 98.

40. Karl Marx and Friedrich Engels, *The German Ideology* (New York: International Publishers, 1966), p. 46.

41. Karl Marx and Friedrich Engels, *The Eighteenth Brumaire of Louis Bonaparte,* vol. 1, in *Selected Works* (Moscow: Foreign Languages Publishing House, 1962), p. 334.

42. Ralf Dahrendorf, *Class and Class Conflict in Industrial Society* (Stanford: Stanford University Press: 1967).

43. Antonio Gramsci, *Selections from the Prison Notebooks* (New York: International Publishers, 1971), p. 93.

44. Ibid., p. 94.

45. Ibid., p. 227.

46. Dahrendorf, *Class and Class Conflict.*

47. Gramsci, *Prison Notebooks,* p. 227.

48. Cited in Shlomo Avineri, *The Social and Political Thought of Karl Marx* (New York: Cambridge University Press, 1970), pp. 61-62.

49. Gramsci, *Prison Notebooks,* p. 129.

50. Landé, "Networks and Groups," p. 117.

51. Boissevain, "Patronage in Sicily," pp. 30-31.

52. Weiner, *Party Politics in India.*

53. Chie Nakane, *Japanese Society* (Berkeley: University of California Press, 1970) provides a general analysis of Japanese social structure and makes this argument; and Scalapino and Masumi, *Parties and Politics.*

54. Paul Martin Sacks, *The Donegal Mafia: An Irish Machine* (New Haven: Yale University Press, 1976), pp. 57-58.

55. Boissevain, "Patronage in Sicily," p. 30.

56. Linden, *Khrushchev and the Soviet Leadership.*

57. Sartori, "Proporzionalismo," p. 15, and *Parties and Party Systems,* pp. 93-106.

58. Pinto-Duschinsky, "Theories of Corruption," p. 50.

59. Ibid., pp. 57-58.

60. Mosca, *The Ruling Class,* p. 154. See also *Teorica dei Governi e Governo Parlamentare,* new ed. (Varese, Italy: Giuffre, 1968), pp. 246-47.

61. *The Ruling Class,* pp. 254-60.

62. Hans Gerth and C. Wright Mills, *From Max Weber* (New York: Oxford University Press, 1958), p. 125.

63. Sachs, *The Donegal Mafia,* p. 22, maintains that patron-client ties were

not present in traditional rural Ireland. Hence he emphasizes general political culture. Mart Bax, "The Political Machine and Its Importance in the Irish Republic," *Political Anthropology* (March 1975), pp. 6-20, does locate traditional clientelism in Ireland. Because of this and because Sachs hints at the presence of clientelist ties between priest and parishioners, storekeepers and farmers (as well as patron-client ties among Protestant landlords and peasants), I have retained clientelism as an explanatory factor.

64. Mosca, *The Ruling Class*, p. 259. See also Alan Zuckerman, "The Concept 'Political Elite': Lessons from Mosca and Pareto," *Journal of Politics* (May 1977), pp. 324-44.

65. Mosca, *The Ruling Class*, pp. 260-61.

66. Gerth and Mills, *From Max Weber*, p. 113.

67. Mosca, *The Ruling Class*, p. 283.

68. Ibid., p. 284.

69. Ibid., p. 285.

70. Ibid., p. 287.

71. Satori, *Parties and Party Systems*, pp. 89-90.

Chapter 3

1. The arguments do not reflect the work of any one theorist, but have been ordered for the purposes of this analysis.

2. As quoted in Luigi Graziano, "Patron-Client Relationships in Southern Italy," *European Journal of Political Research* (April 1973), p. 4.

3. The following discussion draws on numerous sources, especially Carlo Levi, *Christ Stopped at Eboli* (New York: Farrar, Straus, 1963); Danilo Dolci, *Report from Palermo* (New York: Viking, 1970); Giuseppe Di Lampedusa, *The Leopard* (New York: New American Library, Signet, 1961),; Sidney Tarrow, *Peasant Communism in Southern Italy* (New Haven: Yale University Press, 1967); P. A. Allum, *Politics and Society in Post-War Naples* (Cambridge, England: Cambridge University Press, 1973); Joseph Lopreato, *Peasants No More* (San Francisco, Chandler, 1967); F. G. Bailey, ed., *Gifts and Poison* (Oxford: Basil, Blackwell, 1971); Jeremy Boissevain and John Friedl, eds., *Beyond the Community: Social Process in Europe* (The Hague: Department of Educational Science, the Netherlands, 1975); Edward Banfield, *The Moral Basis of a Backward Society* (New York: The Free Press, 1958); A. L. Maraspini, *The Study of an Italian Village* (The Hague: Mouton, 1968); Frederick G. Friedmann, *The Hoe and the Book* (Ithaca, N.Y.: Cornell University Press, 1960); and Jane Schneider, "Patrons and Clients in the Italian Political System" (Ph.D. dissertation, University of Michigan, 1965), as well as Leonard W. Moss and Stephen C. Cappannari, "Estate and Class in a South Italian Hill Vaillage," *American Anthropologist* (1962), pp. 287-300; Leonard W. Moss and Walter H. Thompson, "The South Italian Family: Literature and Observation," *Human Organization* (1959), pp. 35-41; Paul Stirling, "Impartiality and Personal Morality (Italy)" in *Contributions to Mediterranean Sociology* ed. J. G. Peristiany (The Hague: Mouton, 1968) pp. 49-64; Jeremy Boissevain, "Patronage in Sicily," *Man* (1966), pp. 18-33; Alex Weingrod, "Patrons, Patronage, and Political Parties," *Comparative*

Studies in Society and History (July 1968), pp. 377-400; Anton Blok, "South Italian Agro-Towns," *Comparative Studies in Society and History* (April 1969), pp. 121-35; Donald Pitkin, "Land Tenure and Family Organization in an Italian Village," *Human Organization* (1960), pp. 169-73; J. Davis, "Morals and Backwardness," *Comparative Studies in Society and History* (July 1970), pp. 340-53; Alessandro Pizzorno, "Amoral Familism and Historical Marginality," *International Review of Community Development* (1966), pp. 55-66; Leonard W. Moss, "The Passing of Traditional Peasant Society in the South," in *Modern Italy,* eds. Edward R. Tannenbaum and Emiliana P. Noether (New York: New York University Press, 1974), pp. 147-70.

4. See especially Boissevain, "Patronage in Sicily"; Weingrod, "Patrons, Patronage"; John S. and Leatrice MacDonald, "Institutional Economics and Rural Development: Two Italian Types," *Human Organization* (Spring 1959), pp. 113-8; and Levi, *Christ Stopped at Eboli.*

5. See especially Dolci, *Report from Palermo.*

6. John S. and Leatrice MacDonald, "Institutional Economics," p. 114.

7. J. S. MacDonald, "Agricultural Organization, Migration, and Labor Militancy," *Economic Development and Cultural Change* (July 1964), pp. 368-74.

8. Moss and Cappannari, "Estate and Class," p. 287.

9. John S. and Leatrice MacDonald, "Institutional Economics," p. 114.

10. Dolci, *Report from Palermo,* pp. 168-69, 171.

11. Banfield, *Moral Basis of a Backward Society,* p. 83.

12. Maraspini, *Study of an Italian Village,* p. 197. See also Roy A. and Maria Gabriella Miller, "The Golden Chain: A Study of the Patterning of *Comparatico* in the South Italian Village," *American Ethnologist* (February 1978), pp. 116-36.

13. Maraspini, *Study of an Italian Village,* p. 200.

14. Ibid., p. 202.

15. John S. and Leatrice MacDonald, "Institutional Economics," p. 115.

16. Lopreato, *Peasants No More,* p. 66.

17. Ibid., p. 103.

18. See, for example, J. Davis, "Passatella": An Economic Game," *British Journal of Sociology* (September 1964), pp. 191-205; and Roger Vailland, *The Law* (New York: Knopf, 1958).

19. Levi, *Christ Stopped at Eboli,* p. 77.

20. Ibid., p. 130.

21. Ibid., p. 28.

22. Boissevain, "Patronage in Sicily."

23. Herman G. Finer, *Mussolini's Italy* (New York: Universal Library, 1965), p. 82.

24. Quoted in A. William Salomone, *Italy in the Giolittian Era* (Philadelphia: University of Pennsylvania Press, 1960), p. 17. Salomone's volume stands as the best general analysis of the Giolittian period. See also Salvatore Saladino, "Politics in the Liberal Era, 1861-1914," in *Modern Italy,* eds. Tannenbaum and Noether, pp. 27-51; and Giovanni Giolitti, *Memoirs of My*

Life (London: Chapman and Dodd, 1923); and Brunello Vigezzi, *Da Giolitti a Salandra* (Firenze: Valecchi, 1969).

25. Vilfredo Pareto, *The Ruling Class in Italy* (New York: Vanni, 1950), p. 31.

26. Gaetano Mosca, *Teorica dei Governi e Governo Parlamentare,* new ed. (Varese: Giuffre, 1968), p. 157.

27. Ibid., p. 157.

28. Ibid., p. 158.

29. Pareto, *The Ruling Class in Italy,* p. 32.

30. Mosca, *Teorica dei Governi,* pp. 248-9.

31. Ibid., p. 249.

32. Ibid.

33. Ibid.

34. Ibid.

35. Ibid., p. 252.

36. Gaetano Mosca, *Partiti e Sindacati Nella Crisi del Regime Parlamentare* (Bari: Laterza, 1949), p. 190.

37. Ibid., p. 191.

38. Ibid., pp. 201-2.

39. Mosca, *Teorica dei Governi,* pp. 254-55.

40. Pareto, *The Ruling Class in Italy,* p. 56.

41. Mosca, *Teorica dei Governi,* p. 255. For an analysis of the *Camorra* as the Sicilian Mafia, see Eric Hobsbawm, *Primitive Rebels* (New York: Norton, 1965).

42. Pareto, *The Ruling Class in Italy,* p. 60.

43. Ibid.

44. Quoted in Salomone, *Italy in the Giolittian Era,* p. 110.

45. Pareto, *The Ruling Class in Italy,* p. 55.

46. Quoted in *L'Espresso* (December 2, 1973), p. 11.

47. Stirling, "Impartiality and Personal Morality," p. 60.

48. Ibid., p. 51.

49. Ibid.

50. Ibid.

51. Boissevain, "Patronage in Sicily," p. 23.

52. Weingrod, "Patrons, Patronage," p. 398.

53. Joseph LaPalombara, *Interest Groups in Italian Politics* (Princeton: Princeton University Press, 1964), p. 344.

54. Ibid.

55. Tarrow, *Peasant Communism,* p. 331.

56. Cited in Francesco Alberoni et al., *L'Attavista di Partito* (Bologna: Il Mulino, 1967), p. 246.

57. Ibid., p. 247.

58. Luigi Barzini, *The Italians* (New York: Bantam, 1965).

59. Ibid., pp. 237-38.

60. Ibid., p. 238.

61. Ibid., p. 239.

62. Ibid., p. 240.

63. Ibid., p. 240.

64. Schneider, "Patrons and Clients," p. 252.

65. LaPalombara, *Interest Groups,* p. 40.

66. Sydel Silverman, "Patronage and Community-Nation Relationships in Central Italy," *Ethnology* (April 1965), p. 173.

67. Ibid., p. 183.

68. Weingrod, "Patrons, Patronage," pp. 382-84.

69. F. G. Bailey, "What Are Signori?" pp. 231-51, in *Gifts and Poison* (Oxford: Basil Blackwell, 1971).

70. Joseph Lopreato, "Social Stratification in an Italian Town," *American Sociological Review* (1961), pp. 585-96; and *Peasants No More.*

71. Bailey, "What Are Signori?" p. 236.

72. Ibid., p. 241.

73. Robert Wade, "Political Behavior and World View in a Central Italian Hill Village," pp. 252-80, in *Gifts and Poison,* ed. Bailey; and Banfield, *Moral Basis of a Backward Society.*

74. Wade, "Political Behavior," p. 254.

75. Ibid.

76. Ibid., p. 267.

77. The survey responses analyzed were taken from Almond and Verba's "Five Nation Study" and were made available through the Inter-University Consortium for Political Research. The major published work produced from the study is *The Civic Culture* (Princeton: Princeton University Press, 1963).

78. Samuel H. Barnes and Giacomo Sani, "Mediterranean Political Culture and Italian Politics: An Interpretation," *British Journal of Political Science* (July 1974), especially p. 301.

79. Allum, *Politics and Society,* p. 148. For a view of the use of the preference vote in the north, see Alberoni et al., *L'Attavista,* pp. 246–47.

80. For an analysis demonstrating the presence of major north-south differences on political, especially policy, variables, see Robert Fried, "Communism, Urban Budgets, and the Two Italies: A Case Study in Comparative Urban Government," *Journal of Politics* (November 1971), pp. 1008-51.

81. Though it should be emphasized that preference votes are best used as a rough indicator of clientelist ties, the data presented support the reliability of the measure.

82. Franco Cazzola, "Partiti, Correnti, e Voto di Preferenza," in *Un Sistema Politico alla Prova,* eds. Mario Caciagli and Alberto Spreafico (Bologna: Il Mulino, 1975), pp. 127-52.

83. Ibid., p. 148.

84. Ibid., p. 147.

85. Ibid., pp. 148-49.

86. Ibid., p. 130.

87. See note 2.

Chapter 4

1. Maurice Duverger, *Political Parties,* rev. ed. (New York: Wiley, 1967), pp. 308-09.

2. Alan Arian and Samuel Barnes, "The Dominant Party System: A

Neglected Model of Democratic Stability," *Journal of Politics* (August 1974), pp. 582-615. There are a few excellent studies of the Catholic political movement before World War II. See Richard Webster, *The Cross and the Fasces* (Stanford: Stanford University Press, 1960); Gabriele De Rosa, *Storia del Movimento Cattolico in Italia* (Bari: Laterza, 1966); and Elsa Carillo, "Christian Democracy," in *Modern Italy,* eds. Edward R. Tannenbaum and Emiliana P. Noether (New York: New York University Press, 1974), pp. 78-101; A. William Salomone, *Italy in the Giolittian Era* Philadelphia: University of Pennslvania Press, 1960), remains a most useful overview of the period preceding World War I. For a general survey of the history of the Christian Democratic party, see Franca Cervellati Cantelli et al., *L'Organizzazione Partitica del PCI e della DC* (Bologna: Il Mulino, 1968), pp. 197-230.

3. Among many sources, see Raphael Zariski, *Italy: The Politics of Uneven Development* (Homewood, Ill.: Dryden, 1972), p. 156.

4. The following discussion is drawn from the histories of the Catholic political movement in Italy.

5. Webster, *The Cross and the Fasces,* p. 62.

6. Vittorio Capecchi et al., *Il Comportamento Elettorale in Italia* (Bologna: Il Mulino, 1968), pp. 78-79.

7. Webster, *The Cross and the Fasces,* p. 200.

8. Gianfranco Poggi, *Italian Catholic Action* (Stanford: Stanford University Press, 1967). A product of this period in which Catholic and Fascist social thought are linked, is a brief volume by Amintore Fanfani, the dominant DC personality. See Fanfani, *Catholicism, Protestantism, and Capitalism* (New York: Sheed and Ward, 1935).

9. Among important leaders of the Christian Democratic party active in resistance movement were Taviani in Genoa and Marcora in Milan.

10. The classic study remains Giovanni Sartori, "European Political Parties: The Case of Polarized Pluralism," in *Political Parties and Political Development,* eds. Joseph LaPalombara and Myron Weiner, (Princeton: Princeton University Press, 1966), pp. 137-76. Sartori has reworked some of these ideas in "Rivisitando il 'Pluralismo Polarizzato," in *Il Caso Italiano,* eds. F. L. Cavazza and Stephen R. Graubard, (Milan: Garzanti, 1974), pp. 196-223; and Sartori, *Parties and Party Systems: A Framework for Analysis,* chap. 6.

11. Capecchi et al., *Il Comportamento,* p. 217.

12. Giacomo Sani, "Determinants of Party Preference in Italy: Toward the Integration of Complementary Models," *American Journal of Political Science* (1974), p. 322.

13. Samuel H. Barnes and Giacomo Sani, "The New Politics and the Old Parties in Italy," paper presented to the 1973 meetings of the Midwest Political Science Association, Chicago, p. 15.

14. Samuel H. Barnes and Giacomo Sani, "Partisan Change and the Italian Voter: Some Clues from the 1972 Election," paper presented to the World Congress of the International Political Science Association, Montreal, August 1973, pp. 14-15.

15. Ibid.

16. Joseph LaPalombara, *Interest Groups in Italian Politics* (Princeton: Princeton University Press, 1964), p. 306.

17. Ibid., p. 309.

18. Ibid., p. 326.

19. Ibid.

20. Cited in *The Economist* (February 14-20, 1975), p. 55.

21. Giuseppe Tamburrano, *L'Iceberg Democristiano* (Milan: Sugarco, 1974), pp. 121-24. I can provide no estimate of reliability for the data presented here and in the following news sources.

22. Ibid., p. 124, which draws its evidence from *L'Espresso* (May 2, 1971), financial supplement, p. 5. See also *Panorama* (September 21, 1976).

23. *L'Espresso* (May 23, 1976; July 24, 1977; September 11, 1977; and October 16, 1977).

24. Tamburrano, *L'Iceberg Democristiano,* p. 124.

25. *L'Espresso* (April 25, 1976).

26. Ibid.

27. Tamburrano, *L'Iceberg Democristiano.*

28. Capecchi et al., *Il Comportamento;* Mattei Dogan, "Political Cleavage and Social Stratification in Italy and France," in *Party Systems and Voter Alignments,* eds. Seymour M. Lipset and Stein Rokkan (New York: Free Press, 1967), pp. 129-96; and Gianfranco Poggi, *Le Preferenze Politiche Italiane* (Bologna: Il Mulino, 1968).

29. Capecchi et al., *Il Comportamento,* p. 304.

30. Ibid., pp. 275-303.

31. Ibid., p. 272.

32. Dogan, "Political Cleavage and Social Stratification," p. 156.

33. Poggi, *Le Preferenze Politiche.*

34. Samuel H. Barnes, "Italy: Religion and Class and the Italian Voter," in *Electoral Behavior,* ed. Richard Rose (New York: Free Press, 1974), pp. 217-18.

35. There is growing evidence that in recent years the Communist party has attempted with some success to spread its electoral net into the middle classes. For an analysis of this, see Stephen Hellman, "The PCI's Alliance Strategy and the Case of the Middle Classes," in *Communism in Italy and France,* eds. Sidney Tarrow and Donald Blackmer (Princeton: Princeton University Press, 1976), chap. 10.

36. Duverger, *Political Parties,* pp. 133-202; and Raphael Zariski, "Intra-party Conflict in a Dominant Party: The Experience of Italian Christian Democracy," *Journal of Politics* (February 1965), pp. 3-34.

37. The description of the formal organization of the party is drawn from C. E. Traverso, V. Italia, and M. Bassanini, *I Partiti Politici: Leggi e Statuti,* (Milan: Cisalpino, 1966); as well as Cantelli et al., *L'Organizzazione Partitica del PCI e della DC;* and numerous internal DC sources, especially *Statuto del Partito: Democrazia Cristiana* (Rome, 1968).

38. *Statuto del Partito,* p. 59.

39. Ibid., p. 60.

40. Ibid., pp. 62-63.

41. At the Party Congress in March 1976, the secretary was elected by all the delegates for the first time.

42. *Statuto del Partito,* p. 65.

43. Ibid., p. 67.

44. Gianfranco Pasquino, "Contro il Finanzimento dei Questi Partiti," *Il Mulino* (March-April 1974), pp. 233-55, cites research by Giacomo Sani.

45. *Statuto del Partito,* p. 18.

46. Cantelli et al., *L'Organizzazione Partitica,* pp. 390-91.

47. Ibid.

48. Ibid.

49. Ibid.

50. A DC official, Giovanni Galloni, echoed this view in the spring of 1977: "The problem is not to know if all members are physically alive. The problem is to arrange mechanisms for them to be alive, vital, and participating." Quoted in Paolo Franchi, "Le Ambiguità della DC," *Rinascita* (April 8, 1977), p. 4.

Chapter 5

1. Giovanni Sartori, *Parties and Party Systems: A Framework for Analysis,* vol. 1 (New York: Cambridge University Press, 1976), pp. 89-90.

2. See the numerous compilations of the party leaders' speeches and articles. For example, works by Amintore Fanfani, *Da Napoli a Firenze* (Milan: Garzanti, 1959); *Dopo Firenze:Azione per lo Sviluppo Democratico dell'Italia* (Milan: Garzanti, 1963); and *Centro Sinistra '62* (Milan: Garzanti, 1963); Aldo Moro, *Una Politica per I Tempi Nuovi* (Rome: Agenzia "Progetto," 1967); Paolo Emilio Taviani, *Principi Cristiani e Metodo Democratico* (Florence: Le Monnier, 1965), and *Per Il Progresso e la Liberta D'Italia* (Rome: Eliograf, 1972) as well as his work published in the journal *Civitas,* which he has edited; among many of Base faction leader Luigi Granelli's position papers are the following: *Politica di Potenza e Strategia di Pace,* 1968; *Per un Mondo della Liberta Scelta,* 1968; *Nuova Frontiera in Europa,* 1968; and *Il XII Congresso del PCI,* 1968 (all published in Milan: Centro di Carlo Puecher). See also *Libro Bianco Sullo Scioglimento di "Impegno Democratico": No a Queste Correnti* (Rome: Edizioni N.P., 1969).

3. The following analysis draws primarily on Sartori, *Parties and Party Systems,* chap. 4; Sartori, "Proporzionalismo, Frazionismo e Crisi dei Partiti," *Rivista Italiana di Scienza Politica* (December 1971), pp. 675-88; Stefano Passigli, "Proporzionalismo, Frazionismo e Crisi dei Partiti: Quid Prior?" *Rivista Italiana di Scienza Politica* (1972), pp. 126-39; Giovanna Zincone, "Accesso Autonomo alle Resorse: le Determinanti del Frazionismo," *Rivista Italiana di Scienza Politica* (1972), pp. 239-59; Gianfranco Pasquino, "Le Radici del Frazionismo e Il Voto di Preferenza," *Rivista Italiana di Scienza Politica* (1972), pp. 353-68; Franco Cazzola, "Partiti, Correnti, e Voto di Preferenza," in *Un Sistema Politico alla Prova* eds. Mario Caciagli and Alberto Spreafico (Bologna: Il Mulino, 1975), pp. 127-52; Antonio Lombardo, "Sistema di Correnti e Deperimento dei Partiti in Italia," *Rivista Italiana di Scienza Politica* (April 1976), pp. 139-62; Zariski, "Intraparty Conflict in a

Dominant Party: The Experience of Italian Christian Democracy," *Journal of Politics* (February 1965), pp. 3-34; and Robert Leonardi, "Opinioni Politiche delle Correnti Democristiana in Emilia-Romagna," *Rivista Italiana di Scienza Politica* (1974), pp. 387-408.

4. Lombardo, "Sistema di Correnti," pp. 144-45

5. Sartori, *Parties and Party Systems,* pp. 97-104.

6. Passigli, "Proporzionalismo, Frazionismo," pp. 126-39.

7. Pasquino, "Le Radici del Frazionismo," p. 355.

8. Lombardo, "Sistema di Correnti," p. 151; and Pasquino, "Le Radici del Frazionismo," pp. 355-60.

9. On the use of highway construction as a major source of patronage for these and other DC leaders, see Giuseppe Tamburrano, *L'Iceberg Democristiano* (Milan: Sugarco, 1974), pp. 111-16.

10. Ibid., and *Panorama* (May 4, 1976), where it is also argued that the highway was constructed solely for patronage reasons.

11. See *L'Espresso* (November 18, 1973) for a description of the Gaspari clientele in Chieti (as well as that of Natali in the same province) and *Panorama* (November 13, 1975) for the description of Bosco's activities in his area. The latter source also reports Bosco's so far successful efforts at getting his son Manfredi to follow in his political footsteps. Also, the elder Bosco was reported to have obtained a university professorship for Manfredi and to have had the son's marriage annulled, after several years, on the grounds that the son's wife suffered from vaginism.

12. Tamburrano, *L'Iceberg Democristiano,* pp. 114-15.

13. Ibid.; see also *Panorama* (October 16, 1975) for another analysis of Gioia's power in Sicily. That Gioia's political fortunes have declined with the party's recent problems is noted in *Panorama* (January 14, 1976).

14. Cited in P. A. Allum, *Politics and Society in Post-War Naples,* (Cambridge, England: Cambridge University Press, 1973), pp. 166-67.

15. Tamburrano, *L'Iceberg Democristiano,* p. 115. On DeMita's power base see also *L'Espresso* (December 2, 1973). The most extensive study of Gava's position in Naples is Allum, *Politics and Society.* See also Tamburrano, *L'Iceberg Democristiano,* p. 115, and *Panorama* (December 4, 1975). Analyses of Bisaglia's power base and growth may be found in *L'Espresso* (February 4, 1976), as well as Gian Paolo Pansa, *Bisaglia: Una Carriera Democristiana* (Milan: Sugarco, 1975). Cossiga, a Base leader who rose to national prominence as minister of the Interior in the Andreotti government, combines a left-wing DC policy position with a clientelist control over much of Sardinia. See *Panorama* (March 22, 1977).

16. The importance to the political clienteles of controlling positions in the radio and television corporation is easily seen in the bitter fight between Piccoli and Zaccagnini in the fall of 1975. At a time of much concern for the future of the party, Piccoli insisted on the right to control such positions in the face of Zaccagnini's efforts to play down those concerns. See *L'Espresso* (November 2, 1975) and *Panorama* (November 6, 1975).

17. Pansa's study, *Bisaglia,* provides information on DC politics in the entire region of the Veneto. For an analysis of politics in a village outside of Padua, within the area generally controlled by Gui, see Robert H. Evans, *Life*

and Politics in a Venetian Community (Notre Dame, Ind.: University of Notre Dame Press, 1976).

18. See *Panorama* (May 4, 1976).

19. Cited in Allum, *Politics and Society,* p. 330.

20. *L'Espresso* (October 28, 1973). Calleri's political demise after the 1976 election is described in *Corriere della Sera* (May 29, 1977), p. 2.

21. *L'Espresso* (January 11, 1976).

Chapter 6

1. Alan Stern, "Political Legitimacy in Local Politics: The Communist Party in Northeastern Italy," in *Communism in Italy and France,* eds. Sidney Tarrow and Donald Blackmer (Princeton: Princeton University Press, 1976), pp. 221-58, indicates that this is true not only within the DC but also holds for interparty relations.

2. Eric Browne, "Testing Theories of Cabinet Formation in the European Context," *Comparative Political Studies* (January 1971), p. 403. Lawrence C. Dodd, *Coalitions in Parliamentary Government* (Princeton: Princeton University Press, 1976), pp. 168-69.

3. Abraham DeSwaan, "An Empirical Model of Coalition Formation as an *N*-Person Game of Policy Distance Minimization," in *The Study of Coalition Behavior,* eds. Sven Groennings, E. W. Kelley, and Michael Leiserson (New York: Holt, Rinehart and Winston, 1971), p. 427. Robert Axelrod, *Conflict of Interest* (Chicago: Markham, 1970) chap. 8; Adriano Pappalardo, "L'Analisi delle Coalizioni," *Rivista Italiana di Scienza Politica* (1974), pp. 197-230; and Giuseppe Di Palma, *Surviving without Governing: The Italian Parties in Parliament* (Berkeley: University of California Press, 1977), pp. 243-46, show that the requirements of shared policies have made most cabinets in Italy larger than minimum winning coalitions. However, the substantive knowledge that must be added to specify which parties share policy positions detracts from the mathematical simplicity of formal coalition theories.

4. Alan Zuckerman, "Social Structure and Political Competition: The Italian Case," *World Politics* (April 1972), p. 429. See also Gianfranco Pasquino, "Per Un'Analisi Delle Coalizioni di Governo in Italia," in *Continuità e Mutamento Elettorale in Italia* eds. Arturo Parisi and Pasquino (Bologna: Il Mulino, 1977), p. 252.

5. Other analyses emphasizing the role of DC factions in the formation of cabinets include Alfred Grosser, "The Evolution of European Parliaments," *Daedalus* (Winter 1964), pp. 153-68; and Antonio Lombardo, "Sistema di Correnti e Deperimento dei Partiti in Italia," *Rivista Italiana di Scienza Politica* (1976), pp. 139-62. Although I emphasize the independence of the DC and its factions from the coalition partners, Lombardo contends that the Christian Democrats have increasingly lost power to the Socialists within the arena of cabinet competition.

6. Thus, Lombardo argues that the need for the support of the other parties, particularly the Socialists, has made the latter the keys to the process.

7. For the derivation of these propositions, see chapter 2.

8. The source for this observation is a DC Member of the Chamber of Deputies who declined to serve in the cabinet.

9. *Corriere della Sera* (July 13, 1976).

10. Leo Wollemborg, *Italia al Rallentore* (Bologna: Il Mulino, 1966), pp. 438-85. See news sources for that election. The party divisions are closely tied to personal disputes which implies equally that the professions of unity can be affected by the agreement of the leaders as well. This will result in highly fragile alliances.

11. Giovanna Zincone, "Accesso Autonomo alle Resorse: le Determinanti del Frazionismo," *Rivista Italiana di Scienza Politica* (1972), pp. 239-59, also emphasizes the rolling game aspects of the competition.

12. See also Pasquino, "Per Un'Analisi Delle Coalizioni," pp. 263-65.

13. See *L'Espresso* (May 23, 1976) and *Panorama* (October 2, 1975).

14. Lombardo, "Sistema di Correnti,'" pp. 140-41; and Gianfranco Pasquino, "Le Radici del Frazionismo e Il Voto di Preferenza," *Rivista Italiana di Scienza Politica* (1972), pp. 359-60.

15. Alan R. Posner, "Italy: Dependence and Political Fragmentation," *International Organization* (Autumn 1977), pp. 809-39.

16. Alberto Predieri, "Mediazione e Indirizzo Politico nel Parlamento Italiano," *Rivista Italiana di Scienza Politica* (1975), p. 409.

17. Giuseppe Di Palma, "Contenuti e Comportamenti Legislativi nel Parlamento Italiano," *Rivista Italiana di Scienza Politica* (1975), p. 19. See also Predieri, "Mediazione e Indirizzo," p. 411.

18. Di Palma, "Contenuti e Comportamenti."

19. Ibid., p. 10.

20. Giuseppe Di Palma, "Institutional Rules and Legislative Outcomes in the Italian Parliament," *Legislative Studies Quarterly* (1976), p. 154.

21. Predieri, "Mediazione e Indirizzo," p. 413.

22. Di Palma, "Contenuti e Comportamenti," pp. 25-26.

23. Ibid., pp. 28-31.

24. Ibid.

25. Ibid., pp. 32-33.

26. Ibid., pp. 36-38.

27. Ibid., p. 36.

28. However, Di Palma, *Surviving without Governing: Italian Parties in Parliament* (Berkeley: University of California Press, 1977), explains these patterns with a very different argument.

29. Stern, "Political Legitimacy in Local Politics."

30. Except as it involves the tactics and consequences of visible, electoral politics.

31. Robert D. Putnam, *The Beliefs of Politicians* (New Haven: Yale University Press, 1973), pp. 53 and 60, displays tables comparing the two countries on a left-right continuum and the index of ideological style and the index of partisan hostility.

32. Ibid., p. 61: "Statistical evidence that the Left maintains greater support for compromise comes from the questionnaire item: 'To compromise with our political opponents is dangerous because it usually leads to the

betrayal of our own side.' Seven of eight Communists and nine of thirteen
Socialists disagreed with this item. Sixteen of twenty-three Christian Democrats and all six other rightists agreed with it. Nearly all other indicators of
orientations toward compromise that were built into the interview confirm
this finding."

33. Ibid., pp. 153-54.

34. See chap. 2, note 61.

Chapter 7

1. See the surveys gathered and analyzed in Giacomo Sani, "Secular Trends
and Party Realignments in Italy: The 1975 Election," presented to the
Annual Meetings of the American Political Science Association, San
Francisco, September 2-5, 1975, and published as "Ricambio Elettorale e
Indicazioni Partitiche: Verso Una Hegemonia delle Sinsistre?" *Rivista Italiana
di Scienza Politica* (1975), pp. 515-44; and Arturo Parisi and Gianfranco
Pasquino, "20 Giugno: Struttura Politica e Comportamenti Elettorali," *Il
Mulino* (May-June 1976), pp. 342-86.

2. See Sani, "Secular Trends and Party Realignments," p. 10, which
reports a DOXA survey indicating a PCI plurality among those below age
thirty-five. See also Parisi and Pasquino, "20 Giugno," p. 352.

3. Ibid.; see also Giacomo Sani, "The Italian Election of 1976: Continuity
and Change," presented to the Conference Group on Italian Politics, Meetings
of the American Political Science Association, Chicago, September 2-5, 1976,
table 1.

4. See *Panorama* (January 14, 1976); *L'Espresso* (February 8, 1976); and
Panorama (December 4, 1975); among many sources.

5. See *L'Espresso* (March 28, 1976) and *Corriere della Sera* (March 22,
1976) for reports describing the treatment of the leaders.

6. Sidney Tarrow, "Italy: Political Integration in a Fragmented Political
System," presented to the Meetings of the American Political Science
Association, San Francisco, 1975.

7. Gianfranco Pasquino, "Crisi della DC e Evoluzione del Sistema Politico,"
Rivista Italiana di Scienza Politica (1975), pp. 443-72.

8. Ibid., p. 469.

9. Tarrow, "Italy: Political Integration," p. 3. Tarrow has reworked this
paper in "The Italian Party System between Crisis and Transition," *American
Journal of Political Science* (May 1977), pp. 193-224.

10. Tarrow, "Italy: Political Integration," p. 12.

11. Ibid., p. 9.

12. See the Pragma survey published in *L'Espresso* and cited in Parisi and
Pasquino, "20 Giugno," p. 345.

13. See, especially, *Panorama* (December 4, 1975) and (January 14, 1976).

14. See also Arturo Parisi and Gianfranco Pasquino "Relazioni Partiti-
Elettori e Tipi di Voto," in *Continuità e Mutamento Elettorale in Italia*
(Bologna: Il Mulino, 1977), pp. 215-49.

15. Vilfredo Pareto, *Mind and Society* vol. 3 (New York: Harcourt and Brace, 1935), pp. 1642-44.

16. Alan Zuckerman and Mark Irving Lichbach, "Stability and Change in European Electorates," *World Politics* (July 1977), pp. 523-51.

17. Zaccagnini's candidate, Berthè, now heads RAI-TV (see *L'Espresso,* July 24, 1977) and the membership lists in Naples have been reduced from 28,000 to 5,500 (see *Panorama,* July 4, 1978).

18. *Corriere della Sera* (October 12, 1977), p. 2.

19. Ibid., p. 1.

20. *Panorama* (June 4, 1976), p. 12.

21. *Panorama* (February 14, 1978).

22. Francesco Alberoni et al., *L'Attivista di Partito* (Bologna: Il Mulino, 1967), p. 310.

23. Gianfranco Pasquino, "Ricambio Parliamentare e Rendimento Politico," *Politica del diritto* (September-October 1976), p. 556.

24. Maurizio Cotta, "Classe Politica Istituzionalizzazione del Parlamento: 1946-1972," *Rivista Italiana di Scienza Politica* (1976), p. 87.

25. Richard Dalton, "Generational Change within the Italian Christian Democratic Party Elite," *European Journal of Political Research* (June 1977), pp. 155-78.

26. See also the letter-writing campaign to Zaccagnini that opposed a cover-up of a scandal involving Gioia; *Panorama* (January 18, 1977).

27. Giuseppi Di Palma, *Surviving without Governing: The Italian Parties in Parliament* (Berkeley: University of California Press, 1977), especially pp. 227-85, incisively analyzes the place and prospects of the PCI in government.

Chapter 8

1. In addition to the sources cited in chap. 2, notes 24 and 53, my description of clientelist factions in Japan and India draws on: Roger W. Benjamin and Kan Ori, *Some Aspects of Political Party Institutionalization in Japan* (Tokyo: Institute of International Relations, Sophia University, 1971); Gerald L. Curtis, *Election Campaigning Japanese Style* (New York: Columbia University Press, 1971); Haruhiro Fukui, *Party in Power: The Japanese Liberal-Democrats and Policy-Making* (Berkeley: University of California Press, 1970); Nobutaka Ike, *Japanese Politics: Patron-Client Democracy,* (New York: Knopf, 1972); J. A. Stockwin, *Japan: Divided Politics in a Growth Economy* (London: Wiedenfield and Nicolson, 1975); Nathaniel B. Thayer, *How the Conservatives Rule Japan* (Princeton: Princeton University Press, 1969); Hans Baerwald, "An Aspect of Japanese Parliamentary Politics," *Japan Interpreter* (Summer, 1970), pp. 196-205; Gerald Curtis, "The Koenkai and the Liberal Democratic Party," *Japan Interpreter* (Summer 1970), pp. 206-19; Roger W. Gale, "The 1976 Election, the LDP—Edge of a Precipice?" *Japan Interpreter* (Spring 1977), pp. 433-47; Ronald H. Hrebenar, "Money, the LDP, and the Symbolic Politics of Reform," *Japan Interpreter* (Winter 1976), pp. 340-50; Chalmers Johnson, "Japan: Who Governs? An Essay on Official Bureaucracy," *The Journal of Japanese Studies* (Autumn 1975), pp.

1-28; Fukuda Kan'ichi, "Grass-roots Base of Money Politics," *Japan Interpreter* (Spring 1975), pp. 495-98; and Kan'ichi, "Parliamentary Democracy and Political Corruption," *Japan Interpreter* (Autumn 1976), pp. 159-66; Matsushita Keiichi, "Politics of Citizen Participation," *Japan Interpreter* (Spring 1975), pp. 451-65; Michael Leiserson, "Coalition Government in Japan," in *The Study of Coalition Behavior,* eds. Sven Groennings, E. W. Kelley and Michael Leiserson, (New York: Holt, Rinehart and Winston, 1970), pp. 80-102; T. J. Pempel, "The Bureaucratization of Policymaking in Postwar Japan," *American Journal of Political Science* (November 1974), pp. 647-64; T. J. Pempel, "Japanese Foreign Economic Policy: The Domestic Bases for International Behavior," *International Organization* (Autumn 1977), pp. 723-74; Daniel I. Okimoto, "The LDP in Transition: Birth of the Miki Cabinet," *Japan Interpreter* (Spring 1975), pp. 385-402; Shiratori Rei, "Conservative Rule in Japan Self-Destructs," *Japan Quarterly* (January-March 1977), pp. 44-54; and Miyazaki Yoshikazu, "Conspiracy of Silence," *Japan Interpreter* (Autumn 1976), pp. 161-71. For India: Paul Brass, *Factional Politics in an Indian State* (Berkeley: University of California Press, 1965), Mary C. Carras, *The Dynamics of Indian Political Factions* (Cambridge, England: Cambridge University Press, 1975); Samuel J. Eldersveld, N. Jaggannadham, and A. P. Barnabas, *The Citizen and the Administrator in a Developing Democracy* (Glenview, Ill.: Scott, Foresman, 1968); Stanley A. Kochanek, *The Congress Party of India: The Dynamics of a One-Party Democracy* (Princeton: Princeton University Press, 1968); Rajni Kothari, *Politics in India* (New Delhi: Orient Longmans, 1970); Bruce Bueno de Mesquita, *Strategy, Risk, and Personality* (Cambridge, England: Cambridge University Press, 1975); Joyce Pettigrew, *Robber Noblemen: A Study of the Political System of the Sikh Jats* (London: Routledge and Kegan Paul, 1975); J. D. Sethi, *India's Static Power Structure* (Delhi: Vikas, 1969); Richard Sisson, *The Congress Party in Rajasthan* (Berkeley: University of California Press, 1972); Myron Weiner, *Party Building in a New Nation: The Indian National Congress* (Chicago: University of Chicago Press, 1967); Paul R. Brass, "Party Systems and Government Stability in the Indian States," *American Political Science Review* (December 1977), pp. 1384-1405; Francine R. Frankel, "Democracy and Political Development: Perspectives from the Indian Experience," *World Politics* (April 1969), pp. 448-68; and L. Michael Hager, "Bureaucratic Corruption in India: Legal Control of Maladministration," *Comparative Political Studies* (July 1973), pp. 197-221. The material provides information on the period before Mrs. Gandhi's rule by emergency decree.

2. Thayer, *How the Conservatives Rule Japan,* p. 21.

3. See, especially, ibid., pp. 26-30; Hrebenar, "Money, and LDP, and Symbolic Politics"; Curtis, *Election Campaigning,* pp. 231-35; and Fukui, *Party in Power,* pp. 74-77 and 130-33.

4. Thayer, *How the Conservatives Rule Japan,* p. 4. See also Fukui, *Party in Power,* p. 30; and Stockwin, *Japan: Divided Politics,* pp. 105-10.

5. Curtis, *Election Campaigning* pp. 179 and 209, describes the use of established organizations as parts of koenkai and of developments much like Tarrow found in Italy.

6. Thayer, *How the Conservatives Rule Japan*, p. 41. See also Stockwin, *Japan: Divided Politics*, p. 105. Chie Nakane, *Japanese Society* (Berkeley: University of California Press, 1970), especially pp. 50-58, shows how the clientelist factions reproduce the underlying structure of all Japanese groups.

7. Weiner, *Party Building*, p. 134.

8. Brass, *Factional Politics*, p. 55.

9. Ibid., p. 56.

10. Pettigrew, *Robber Noblemen*, p. 63.

11. Ibid., p. 73.

12. Keith R. Legg, *Politics in Modern Greece* (Stanford: Standford University Press, 1972), describes clientelist politics in local and national Greek politics and also notes the similarity between political clienteles in Greece and elsewhere.

13. Yoshikazu, "Conspiracy of Silence."

14. Brass, *Factional Politics*, p. 56.

15. Compare the descriptions in Wayne A. Cornelius, *Politics and the Migrant Poor in Mexico City* (Stanford: Stanford University Press, 1975), pp. 135-65, and especially 159-60, of caciquismo and its links to local politics to Pettigrew, *Robber Noblemen*, pp. 208-12 and the sources noted in chap. 2, notes 19 and 20.

16. Pettigrew, *Robber Noblemen*, p. 204.

17. Benjamin and Ori, *Some Aspects of Political Party Institutionalizations*, p. 19.

18. Thayer, *How the Conservatives Rule Japan*, p. 89.

19. Curtis, *Election Campaigning* especially pp. 134-35; see also Curtis, "The Koenkai and the Liberal Democratic Party."

20. Benjamin and Ori, *Some Aspects of Political Party Institutionalizations*, p. 33.

21. Weiner, *Party Building*, p. 57; Kochanek, *Congress Party of India*, pp. 213-23; and Brass, *Factional Politics*, p. 24.

22. Mart Bax, "The Political Machine and Its Importance in the Irish Republic," *Political Anthropology* (March 1975), pp. 6-20.

23. Thayer, *How the Conservatives Rule Japan*, pp. 48-53, 159; Stockwin, *Japan: Divided Politics*, pp. 82-87; and Fukui, *Party in Power*, p. 122.

24. Quoted in Thayer, *How the Conservatives Rule Japan*, p. 36.

25. Ibid., p. 182.

26. See especially Leiserson, "Coalition Government in Japan," pp. 86-89; and Thayer, *How the Conservatives Rule Japan*, pp. 189 and 197.

27. Ibid., p. 279. See also Fukui, *Party in Power*, pp. 127-30.

28. Thayer, *How the Conservatives Rule Japan*, p. 279.

29. Kochanek, *Congress Party of India*, pp. 84-85.

30. Paul Brass, "Party Systems and Government Stability," especially pp. 1401-05, shows the weak explanatory ability of general theories of coalition behavior in Indian state politics and argues for the need to include leadership and party factions as important explanatory factors.

31. Kothari, *Politics in India*, pp. 181-84. Sethi maintains that the major opposition parties are best seen as clientelist factions—see *India's Static Power Structure*, p. 93; and Bueno de Mesquita, *Strategy, Risk, and Personality*,

shows the utility of analyzing coalition politics between 1967 and 1972 as if the parties were solely interested in redistributing government resources to their own benefit.

32. Kochanek, *Congress Party of India*, pp. 286-98; and Sethi, *India's Static Power Structure.* pp. 6-7.

33. Ibid., p. 29.

34. Of all the sources that I used, only Carras, *Dynamics of Indian Political Factions,* stays with the counterargument.

35. Thayer, *How the Conservatives Rule Japan*, p. 216; and Stockwin, *Japan: Divided Politics,* pp. 127-30.

36. Brass, *Factional Politics*, p. 215.

37. Weiner, *Party Building*, p. 332.

38. Ibid., p. 333.

39. Ibid.

40. Ibid., p. 274.

41. Baerwald, "An Aspect of Japanese Politics"; Johnson, "Japan: Who Governs?"; and Pempel, "Japanese Foreign Economic Policy"; make this general claim.

42. Thayer, *How the Conservatives Rule Japan*, p. 214; Pempel, "The Bureaucratization of Policymaking," pp. 649-51; Fukui, *Party in Power*, p. 93; and Stockwin, *Japan: Divided Politics*, p. 78.

43. Pempel, "The Bureaucratization of Policymaking," pp. 653-64.

44. Thayer, *How the Conservatives Rule Japan*, p. 227.

45. Ibid., p. 228.

46. Ibid., and Fukui, *Party in Power*, p. 66.

47. Brass, *Factional Politics*, pp. 96 and 215.

48. Pettigrew, *Robber Nobleman*, pp. 69-70, 112.

49. Brass, *Factional Politics*, p. 75.

50. Thayer, *How the Conservatives Rule Japan*, p. 165; and Fukui, *Party in Power*, pp. 130-33, 145-59.

51. Gale, "The 1976 Election," especially pp. 438-41.

52. Rei, "Conservative Rule," describes the "nonpolicy" of the Sato governments in the mid-1960s. Decisions on agricultural issues particularly were used to gain votes. See also Ike, *Japanese Politics*, pp. 122-23; Stockwin, *Japan: Divided Politics*, p. 136; and Fukui, *Party in Power*, pp. 220-24, 265, for similar arguments.

53. Weiner, *Party Building*, p. 368.

54. Brass, *Factional Politics*, pp. 215-16.

55. Ibid., pp. 194-95.

56. Ibid., pp. 194 ff.

57. Kochanek, *Congress Party of India*, p. 186.

58. Ibid., p. 187.

59. Weiner, *Party Building*, p. 488.

60. Frankel, "Democracy and Political Development," p. 459.

61. Ibid., p. 466; and Sethi, *India's Static Power Structure*, p. xlii.

62. Ibid., p. 121.

63. Frankel, "Democracy and Political Development," p. 468.

64. Sources on the Philippines provide evidence of the same general patterns that I have described in Italy, Japan, and India. See especially Robert B. Stauffer, *The Philippine Congress: Causes of Structural Change* (Beverly Hills: Sage Research Papers in the Social Sciences, nos. 90- 024, 1975) and the sources cited therein; Carl H. Landé, *Leaders, Factions, and Parties: The Structure of Philippine Politics* (New Haven: Yale University Southeast Asia Studies, 1965); Landé, "Networks and Groups in Southeast Asia: Some Observations on the Group Theory of Politics," *American Political Science Review* (March 1973), pp. 103-28; and Richard A. Styskal, "Philippine Legislators' Reception of Individuals and Interest Groups in the Legislative Process," *Comparative Politics* (April 1969), pp. 405-23. For relevant information on Mexico, see Merillee Serrill Grindle, *Bureaucrats, Politicians, and Peasants in Mexico* (Berkeley: University of California Press, 1977); Cornelius, *Politics and the Migrant Poor in Mexico City;* and Kenneth F. Johnson, *Mexican Democracy: A Critical View* (Boston: Allyn and Bacon, 1971), especially pp. 67-80; as well as the sources cited in chap. 2, notes 19 and 20.

65. Okimoto, "The LDP in Transition," p. 398.

66. See Hrebenar, "Money, the LDP and Symbolic Politics"; and Gale, "The 1976 Election."

67. Hrebenar, ibid., and Okimoto, "The LDP in Transition," emphasize Miki's political cleanliness.

Selected Bibliography

Books and Articles in English

Allum, P. A. *Politics and Society in Post-War Naples.* Cambridge, England: Cambridge University Press, 1973.

Almond, Gabriel A., and Verba, Sidney. *The Civic Culture.* Princeton: Princeton University Press, 1963.

Arian, Alan, and Barnes, Samuel. "The Dominant Party System: A Neglected Model of Democratic Stability." *Journal of Politics,* August 1974, pp. 587-615.

Avineri, Shlomo. *The Social and Political Thought of Karl Marx.* New York: Cambridge University Press, 1970.

Axelrod, Robert. *Conflict of Interest.* Chicago: Markham, 1970.

Baerwald, Hans. "An Aspect of Japanese Parliamentary Politics," *Japan Interpreter,* Summer 1970, pp. 196-205.

Bailey, F. G. *Politics and Social Change: Orissa in 1959.* Berkeley and Los Angeles: University of California Press, 1963.

_____. *Stratagems and Spoils.* New York: Schocken, 1969.

_____. ed. *Gifts and Poison.* Oxford: Basil Blackwell, 1971.

Banfield, Edward. *The Moral Basis of a Backward Society.* New York: The Free Press, 1958.

Barnes, Samuel H. *Party Democracy.* New Haven: Yale University Press, 1965.

_____. "Italy: Religion and Class and the Italian Voter." In *Electoral Behavior: A Comparative Handbook,* edited by Richard Rose. New York: The Free Press, 1974.

_____. *Representation in Italy.* Chicago: University of Chicago Press, 1977.

Barnes, Samuel H., and Sani, Giacomo. "Partisan Change and the Italian Voter: Some Clues from the 1972 Election." Presented at the World Congress of the International Political Science Association, Montreal, 1973.

_____. "Mediterranean Political Culture and Italian Politics: An Interpretation." *British Journal of Political Science,* July 1974, pp. 289-313.

Barzini, Luigi. *The Italians.* New York: Bantam, 1965.

Bax, Mart. "The Political Machine and Its Importance in the Irish Republic." *Political Anthropology,* March 1975, pp. 6-20.

Benjamin, Roger W., and Ori, Kan. *Some Aspects of Political Party Institutionalization in Japan.* Tokyo: Institute of International Relations, Sophia University, 1971.

Blok, Anton. "Land Reform in a West Sicilian Town: The Persistence of a Feudal Structure." *Anthropological Quarterly,* January 1966, pp. 1-15.

_____. "South Italian Agro-Towns." *Comparative Studies in Society and History,* April 1969, pp. 121-35.

Boissevain, Jeremy. "Patronage in Sicily." *Man,* October 1966, pp. 18-33.

Boissevain, Jeremy, and Friedl, John, eds. *Beyond the Community: Social Process in Europe.* The Hague: Department of Educational Science, the Netherlands, 1975.

Borkenau, Franz. "Getting at the Facts Behind the Soviet Façade." *Commentary,* April 1954, pp. 393-400.

Brass, Paul. *Factional Politics in an Indian State.* Berkeley: University of California Press, 1965.

_____. "Party Systems and Government Stability in the Indian States." *American Political Science Review,* December 1977, pp. 1384-1405.

Browne, Eric. "Testing Theories of Coalition Formation in the European Context." *Comparative Political Studies,* January 1971, pp. 393-413.

Bueno de Mesquita, Bruce. *Strategy, Risk, and Personality.* Cambridge, England: Cambridge University Press, 1975.

Carras, Mary C. *The Dynamics of Indian Political Factions.* Cambridge, England: Cambridge University Press, 1975.

Clarke, Peter B., and Wilson, James Q. "Incentive Systems: A Theory of Organization." *Administrative Science Quarterly,* September 1961, pp. 592-615.

Conway, Margaret, and Feigert, Frank. "Motivation, Incentive Systems, and the Political Party Organization." *American Political Science Review,* December 1968, pp. 1159-73.

_____. "Incentives and Task Performances among Precinct Party Workers." *Western Political Quarterly,* December 1974, pp. 693-710.

Cornelisen, Ann. *Torregreca.* Boston: Little, Brown, 1969.

Cornelius, Wayne A. *Politics and the Migrant Poor in Mexico City.* Stanford: Stanford University Press, 1975.

Curtis, Gerald L. *Election Campaigning Japanese Style.* New York: Colombia University Press, 1971.

_____. "The Koenkai and the Liberal Democratic Party." *Japan Interpreter,* Summer 1970, pp. 206-19.

Dahl, Robert A. *Who Governs?* New Haven: Yale University Press, 1961.

_____ ed. *Political Oppositions in Western Democracies.* New Haven: Yale University Press, 1967.

Dahrendorf, Ralf. *Class and Class Conflict in Industrial Society.* Stanford: Stanford University Press, 1967.

Dalton, Richard. "Generational Change within the Italian Christian Democratic Party Elite." *European Journal of Political Research,* June 1977, pp. 155-78.

Davis, J. "Passatella: An Economic Game." *British Journal of Sociology,* September 1964, pp. 191-205.

_____. "Morals and Backwardness." *Comparative Studies in Society and History,* July 1970, pp. 340-53.

DeSwaan, Abraham, "An Empirical Model of Coalition Formation as an *N*-Person Game of Policy Distance Minimization." In *The Study of Coalition Behavior,* edited by Sven Groennings, E. W. Kelley and Michael Leiserson, pp. 420-45. New York: Holt, Rinehart and Winston, 1971.

Di Lampedusa, Giuseppe. *The Leopard.* New York: New American Library, Signet, 1961.

Di Palma, Giuseppe. *The Study of Conflict in Western Society: A Critique of the End of Ideology.* Morristown, N.J.: General Learning Press, 1973.

_____. "Institutional Rules and Legislative Outcomes in the Italian Parliament." *Legislative Studies Quarterly,* May 1976, pp. 147-80.

_____. *Surviving without Governing: The Italian Parties in Parliament.* Berkeley: University of California Press, 1977.

Dodd, Lawrence C. *Coalition in Parliamentary Government.* Princeton: Princeton University Press, 1976.

Dogan, Mattei. "Political Cleavage and Social Stratification in Italy and France." In *Party Systems and Voter Alignments,* edited by Seymour M. Lipset and Stein Rokkan, pp. 129-67. New York: The Free Press, 1967.

Dolci, Danilo. *Report from Palermo.* New York: Viking, 1970.

Eckstein, Harry, and Gurr, Ted Robert. *Patterns of Authority: A Structural Basis for Political Inquiry.* New York: Wiley Inter-Science, 1975.

Edinger, Lewis, and Searing, Donald. "Social Background in Elite Analysis: A Methodological Inquiry." *American Political Science Review,* June 1967, pp. 428-45.

Eldersveld, Samuel J.; Jaggannadham, N.; and Barnabas, A. P. *The Citizen and the Administrator in a Developing Democracy.* Glenview, Ill.: Scott, Foresman, 1968.

Evans, Robert H. *Life and Politics in a Venetian Community.* Notre Dame, Ind.: University of Notre Dame Press, 1976.

Fanfani, Amintore. *Catholicism, Protestantism, and Capitalism.* New York: Sheed and Ward, 1935.

Finer, Herman G. *Mussolini's Italy.* New York: Universal Library, 1965.

Foster, George. "The Dyadic Contract in Tzintzuntzan: Patron-Client Relations." *American Anthropologist,* December 1963, pp. 1280-94.

Frankel, Francine R. "Democracy and Political Development: Perspectives from the Indian Experience." *World Politics,* April 1969, pp. 448-68.

Fried, Robert. "Communism, Urban Budgets, and the Two Italies: A Case Study in Comparative Urban Government." *Journal of Politics,* November 1971, pp. 1008-51.

Friedmann, Frederick G. *The Hoe and the Book.* Ithaca, N.Y.: Cornell University Press, 1960.

Frolich, Norman; Oppenheimer, Joe A.; and Young, Oran. *Political*

Leadership and Collective Goods. Princeton: Princeton University Press, 1971.

Fukui, Haruhiro. *Party in Power: The Japanese Liberal-Democrats and Policy-Making.* Berkeley: University of California Press, 1970.

Gale, Roger W. "The 1976 Election, the LDP—Edge of a Precipice?" *Japan Interpreter,* Spring 1977, pp. 433-47.

Gellner, Ernest, and Waterbury, John, eds. *Patrons and Clients.* London: Duckworth, 1977.

Gerth, Hans, and Mills, C. Wright. *From Max Weber.* New York: Oxford University Press, 1958.

Giolitti, Giovanni. *Memoirs of My Life.* London: Chapman and Dodd, 1923.

Gramsci, Antonio. *Selections from the Prison Notebooks.* New York: International Publishers, 1971.

Graziano, Luigi. "Patron-Client Relationships in Southern Italy." *European Journal of Political Research,* April 1973, pp. 3-34.

———. *A Conceptual Framework for the Study of Clientelism.* Ithaca, N.Y.: Cornell University Western Societies Program, 1975.

Grindle, Merillee Serrill. *Bureaucrats, Politicians, and Peasants in Mexico.* Berkeley: University of California Press, 1977.

Groennings, Sven; Kelley, E. W.; and Leiserson, Michael, eds. *The Study of Coalition Behavior.* New York: Holt, Rinehart and Winston, 1970.

Grosser, Alfred. "The Evolution of European Parliaments." *Daedalus,* Winter 1964, pp. 153-68.

Hager, L. Michael. "Bureaucratic Corruption in India: Legal Control of Maladministration." *Comparative Political Studies,* July 1973, pp. 197-221.

Heath, Dwight. "New Patrons for Old: Changing Patron-Client Relationships in the Bolivian Yungas." *Ethnology,* January 1972, pp. 75-98.

Hendel, Charles. *David Hume's Political Essays.* New York: Liberal Arts Press, 1953.

Hobsbawm, Eric. *Primitive Rebels.* New York: Norton, 1965.

Hofstetter, C. Richard. "The Amateur Politician: A Problem in Construct Validation," *Midwest Journal of Political Science,* February 1971, pp. 31-56.

———. "Organizational Activists: The Bases of Participation in Amateur and Professional Groups." *American Politics Quarterly,* April 1973, pp. 244-76.

Hrebenar, Ronald L. "Money, the LDP, and the Symbolic Politics of Reform." *Japan Interpreter,* Winter 1976, pp. 340-50.

Ike, Nobutaka. *Japanese Politics: Patron-Client Democracy.* New York: Knopf, 1972.

Johnson, Chalmers. "Japan: Who Governs? An Essay on Official Bureaucracy." *The Journal of Japanese Studies,* Autumn 1975, pp. 1-28.

Johnson, Kenneth F. *Mexican Democracy: A Critical View.* Boston: Allyn and Bacon, 1971.

Johnston, Scott. "A Comparative Study of Intra-Party Factionalism in Israel and Japan." *Western Political Quarterly,* June 1967, pp. 288-307.

Kan'ichi, Fukuda. "Grass-roots Base of Money Politics." *Japan Interpreter,* Spring 1975, pp. 495-98.

———. "Parliamentary Democracy and Political Corruption." *Japan Interpreter,* Autumn 1976, pp. 159-66.

Kaufman, Robert R. "The Patron-Client Concept and Macro-Politics: Prospects and Problems." *Comparative Studies in Society and History,* July 1974, pp. 284-308.

Keiichi, Matsushita. "Politics of Citizen Participation," *Japan Interpreter,* Spring 1975, pp. 451-65.

Kenny, Michael. *A Spanish Tapestry.* Bloomington: Indiana University Press, 1962.

Kern, Robert, ed. *The Caciques.* Albuquerque: University of New Mexico Press, 1973.

Kochanek, Stanley A. *The Congress Party of India: The Dynamics of a One-Party Democracy.* Princeton: Princeton University Press, 1968.

Kothari, Rajni. *Politics in India.* New Delhi: Orient Longmans, 1970.

Landé, Carl H. *Leaders, Factions, and Parties: The Structure of Phillipine Politics.* New Haven: Yale University Southeast Asia Studies, 1965.

———. "Networks and Groups in Southeast Asia: Some Observations on the Group Theory of Politics." *American Political Science Review,* March 1973, pp. 103-28.

LaPalombara, Joseph. *Interest Groups in Italian Politics.* Princeton: Princeton University Press, 1964.

LaPalombara, Joseph, and Weiner, Myron, eds. *Political Parties and Political Development.* Princeton: Princeton University Press, 1966.

Legg, Keith R. *Politics in Modern Greece.* Stanford: Stanford University Press, 1972.

Leiserson, Michael. "Factions and Coalitions in One-Party Japan: An Interpretation Based on the Theory of Games." *American Political Science Review,* September 1968, pp. 770-87.

Lemarchand, René. "Political Clientelism and Ethnicity in Africa." *American Political Science Review,* March 1972, pp. 68-90.

Lemarchand, René, and Legg, Keith. "Political Clientelism and Development." *Comparative Politics,* January 1972, pp. 149-78.

Levi, Carlo. *Christ Stopped at Eboli.* New York: Farrar, Straus, 1961.

Lewis, Oscar. *Village Life in Northern India.* New York: Random House, Vintage, 1958.

Linden, Carl. *Khrushchev and the Soviet Leadership, 1957-1964,* Baltimore: The Johns Hopkins University Press, 1966.

Linz, Juan. "The Party Systems of Spain: Past and Future." In *Party Systems and Voter Alignments,* edited by Seymour M. Lipset and Stein Rokkan, pp.

197–228. New York: The Free Press, 1967.

Lipset, Seymour Martin. *Political Man.* Garden City, N.Y.: Doubleday, Anchor, 1970.

———. Revolution and Counterrevolution. Garden City, N.Y.: Doubleday, Anchor, 1970.

Lopreato, Joseph. "Social Stratification in an Italian Town." *American Sociological Review,* 1961, pp. 585-96.

———. *Peasants No More.* San Francisco: Chandler, 1967.

MacDonald, J. S. "Agricultural Organization, Migration, and Labor Militancy." *Economic Development and Cultural Change,* July 1964, pp. 368-74.

MacDonald, John, and MacDonald, Leatrice. "Institutional Economics and Rural Development: Two Italian Types." *Human Organization,* Spring 1959, pp. 113-18.

Maraspini, A. L. *The Study of an Italian Village.* The Hague: Mouton, 1968.

Marx, Karl and Engels, Friedrich. *The German Ideology.* New York: International Publishers, 1962.

Marx, Karl, and Engels, Friedrich. *Selected Works.* Moscow: Foreign Language Publishing House, 1962.

Mayer, Adrian. "Quasi-Groups in the Study of Complex Societies." In *The Social Anthropology of Complex Societies,* edited by Michael Banton, pp. 97-122. London: Tavistock, 1966.

Mayhew, David. *Congress: The Electoral Connection.* New Haven: Yale University Press, 1974.

Mosca, Gaetano. *The Ruling Class,* edited by A. Livingston. New York: McGraw-Hill, 1939.

Moss, Leonard. "The Passing of Traditional Peasant Society in the South." In *Modern Italy,* edited by Edward R. Tannenbaum and Emiliana P. Noether, pp. 147-70. New York: New York University Press, 1977.

Moss, Leonard W., and Cappannari, Stephen C. "Estate and Class in a South Italian Hill Village," *American Anthropologist,* 1962, pp. 287-300.

Moss, Leonard W., and Thompson, Walter H. "The South Italian Family: Literature and Observation." *Human Organization,* 1959, pp. 35-41.

Nakane, Chie. *Japanese Society.* Berkeley: University of California Press, 1970.

Nicholas, Ralph. "Factions: A Comparative Analysis." In *The Social Anthropology of Complex Societies,* edited by Michael Banton, pp. 21-55. London: Tavistock, 1966.

Nicholson, Norman K. "The Factional Model and the Study of Politics." *Comparative Political Studies,* October 1972, pp. 291-315.

Nicolaevsky, Boris. *Power and the Societ Elite.* New York: Praeger, 1965.

Nordlinger, Eric A. *Conflict Regulation in Divided Societies.* Cambridge: Harvard University Center for International Affairs, 1972.

Okimoto, Daniel I. "The LDP in Transition: Birth of the Miki Cabinet."

Japan Interpreter, Spring 1975, pp. 385-402.

Olson, Mancur, Jr. *The Logic of Collective Action.* New York: Schocken, 1968.

Pareto, Vilfredo. *Mind and Society.* New York: Harcourt and Brace, 1935.

_____. *The Ruling Class in Italy.* New York: Vanni, 1950.

Pempel, T. J. "The Bureaucratization of Policymaking in Postwar Japan," *American Journal of Political Science,* November 1974, pp. 647-64.

Pettigrew, Joyce. *Robber Noblemen: A Study of the Political System of the Sikh Jats.* London: Routledge and Kegan Paul, 1975.

Pinto-Duschinsky, Michael. "Theories of Corruption in American Politics." Presented to the Annual Meetings of the American Political Science Association, 1976, in Chicago.

Pitkin, Donald. "Land Tenure and Family Organization in an Italian Village." *Human Organization,* 1960, pp. 169-73.

Pitt-Rivers, Julian. *The People of the Sierra.* 2d ed. Chicago: University of Chicago Press, 1971.

Pizzorno, Alessandro. "Amoral Familism and Historical Marginality." *International Review of Community Development,* 1966, pp. 55-66.

Poggi, Gianfranco. *Italian Catholic Action.* Stanford: Stanford University Press, 1967.

Posner, Alan R. "Italy: Dependence and Political Fragmentation." *International Organization,* Autumn 1977, pp. 809-39.

Powell, John Duncan. "Peasant Society and Clientelist Politics." *American Political Science Review,* June 1970, pp. 411-26.

Putnam, Robert D. *The Beliefs of Politicians.* New Haven: Yale University Press, 1973.

_____. *The Comparative Study of Political Elites.* Englewood Cliffs, N.J.: Prentice-Hall, 1976.

Rae, Douglas, and Taylor, Michael. *The Analysis of Political Cleavage.* New Haven: Yale University Press, 1970.

Rei, Shiratori. "Conservative Rule in Japan Self-Destructs." *Japan Quarterly,* January-March 1977, pp. 44-54.

Rose, Richard, and Urwin, Derek. "Social Cohesion, Political Parties, and Strains in Regimes." *Comparative Political Studies,* April 1969, pp. 7-67.

Sachs, Paul Martin. *The Donegal Mafia: An Irish Machine.* New Haven: Yale University Press, 1976.

Salamone, A. William. *Italy in the Giolittian Era.* Philadelphia: University of Pennsylvania Press, 1960.

Sani, Giacomo. "Determinants of Party Preference in Italy: Toward the Integration of Complementary Models," *American Journal of Political Science,* 1974, pp. 315-29.

_____. "Secular Trends and Party Realignments in Italy: The 1975 Election." Presented to the Annual Meetings of the American Political Science Association, 1975, in San Francisco.

_____. "The Italian Election of 1976: Continuity and Change." Presented to the Conference Group on Italian Politics at the Annual Meetings of the American Political Science Association, 1976, in Chicago.

Sartori, Giovanni. "European Political Parties: The Case of Polarized Pluralism." In *Political Parties and Political Development*, edited by Joseph LaPalombara and Myron Weiner, pp. 136-76. Princeton: Princeton University Press, 1966.

_____. "From the Sociology of Politics to Political Sociology." In *Politics and the Social Sciences*, edited by Seymour Martin Lipset, pp. 65-100. New York: Oxford University Press, 1969.

_____. "Concept Misformation in Comparative Politics," *American Political Science Review*, December 1970, pp. 1033-53.

_____. *Parties and Party Systems: A Framework for Analysis*. Vol. 1. New York: Cambridge University Press, 1976.

Scalapino, Robert, and Masumi, Junnosuke, *Parties and Politics in Contemporary Japan*. Berkeley: University of California Press, 1962.

Schneider, Jane. "Patrons and Clients in the Italian Political System." Ph.D. dissertation, University of Michigan, 1965.

Scott, James. "Corruption, Machine Politics, and Political Change." *American Political Science Review*, December 1969, pp. 1142-58.

_____. "Patron-Client Politics and Political Change in Southeast Asia." *American Political Science Review*, March 1972, pp. 91-113.

Sethi, J. D. *India's Static Power Structure*. Delhi: Vikas, 1969.

Shefter, Martin. "The Emergence of the Political Machine: An Alternative View." In *Theoretical Perspectives in Urban Politics*, edited by Willis Hawley and Michael Lipsky, pp. 14-44. Englewood Cliffs, N.J.: Prentice-Hall, 1976.

_____. "Parties, Patronage, and Political Change." Presented to the Annual Meetings of the American Political Science Association, 1976, in Chicago.

Silverman, Sydel. "Patronage and Community Nation-Relationships in Central Italy." *Ethnology*, April 1965, pp. 172-89.

_____. "An Ethnographic Approach to Social Stratification and Prestige: A Central Italian Community." *American Anthropologist*, 1966, pp. 909-21.

_____. "Exploitation in Rural Central Italy: Structure and Ideology in a Stratification Study." *Comparative Studies in Society and History*, January 1970, pp. 321-39.

_____. *Three Bells of Civilization: The Life of an Italian Hill Town*. New York: Columbia University Press, 1975.

Sisson, Richard. *The Congress Party in Rajasthan*. Berkeley: University of California Press, 1972.

Stauffer, Robert B. *The Philippine Congress: Causes of Structural Change*. Beverly Hills: Sage Research Papers in the Social Sciences, nos. 90-024, 1975.

Stern, Alan. "Political Legitimacy in Local Politics: The Communist Party in Northeast Italy." In *Communism in Italy and France,* edited by Sidney Tarrow and Donald Blackmer, pp. 221-58. Princeton: Princeton University Press, 1976.

Stern, Alan; Tarrow, Sidney; and Williams, Mary. "Factions and Opinion Groups in European Mass Parties: Some Evidence from a Study of Italian Socialist Activists." *Comparative Politics,* July 1971, pp. 529-61.

Stewart, Philip, et al. "Political Mobility and the Soviet Political Process." *American Political Science Review,* December 1972, pp. 1269-91.

Stirling, Paul. "Impartiality and Personal Morality (Italy)." In *Contributions to Mediterranean Sociology,* edited by J. G. Peristiany, pp. 49-64. The Hague: Mouton, 1968.

Stockwin, J. A. *Japan: Divided Politics in a Growth Economy.* London: Wiedenfield and Nicolson, 1975.

Styskal, Richard A. "Philippine Legislators' Reception of Individuals and Interest Groups in the Legislative Process." *Comparative Politics,* April 1969, pp. 405-23.

Tarrow, Sidney. *Peasant Communism in Southern Italy.* New Haven: Yale University Press, 1967.

_____. "Economic Development and the Transformation of the Italian Party System." *Comparative Politics,* January 1969, pp. 161-83.

_____. "Italy: Political Integration in a Fragmented Political System." Presented to the Annual Meetings of the American Political Science Association, 1975, in San Francisco.

_____. "The Italian Party System between Crisis and Transition." *American Journal of Political Science,* May 1977, pp. 193-224.

_____. *From Center to Periphery: Alternative Models of National-Local Policy Impact and an Application to France and Italy.* Ithaca, N.Y.: Cornell University Western Societies Program, April 1976.

Tarrow, Sidney, and Blackmer, Donald, eds. *Communism in Italy and France.* Princeton: Princeton University Press, 1976.

Thayer, Nathaniel B. *How the Conservatives Rule Japan.* Princeton: Princeton University Press, 1969.

Tolchin, Martin and Susan. *To the Victor.* New York: Random House, Vintage, 1971.

Truman, David. *The Governmental Process.* New York: Knopf, 1951.

Vailland, Roger. *The Law.* New York: Knopf, 1958.

Webster, Richard. *The Cross and the Fasces.* Stanford: Stanford University Press, 1960.

Weiner, Myron. *Party Politics in India.* Princeton: Princeton University Press, 1957.

_____. *Party Building in a New Nation: The Indian National Congress.* Chicago: University of Chicago Press, 1967.

Weingrod, Alex. "Patrons, Patronage, and Political Parties," *Comparative Studies in Society and History,* July 1968, pp. 377-400.

Wildavsky, Aaron. "The Goldwater Phenomenon: Purists, Politicians, and the Two-Party System." *Review of Politics,* July 1965, pp. 386-413.

Wilson, James Q. *The Amateur Democrat.* Chicago: University of Chicago Press, 1966.

_____. *Political Organizations.* New York: Basic Books, 1974.

Wolfe, Eric. "Kinship, Friendship, and Patron-Client Relations in Complex Societies." In *The Social Anthropology of Complex Societies,* edited by Michael Banton, pp. 2-22. London: Tavistock, 1966.

Wolfinger, Raymond. *The Politics of Progress.* Englewood Cliffs, N.J.: Prentice-Hall, 1974.

Zariski, Raphael. "Party Factions and Comparative Politics: Some Preliminary Observations." *Midwest Journal of Political Science,* February 1960, pp. 372-90.

_____. "The Italian Socialist Party: A Case Study in Factional Conflict." *American Political Science Review,* June 1962, pp. 372-90.

_____. "Intraparty Conflict in a Dominant Party: The Experience of Italian Christian Democracy." *Journal of Politics,* February 1965, pp. 3-34.

_____. *Italy: The Politics of Uneven Development.* Homewood, Ill.: Dryden, 1972.

Zuckerman, Alan. "Hierarchal Social Divisions and Political Groups: Factions in the Italian Christian Democrat Party." Ph.D. dissertation, Princeton University, 1971.

_____. "Social Structure and Political Competition: The Italian Case." *World Politics,* April 1972, pp. 428-44.

_____. "Political Cleavage: A Conceptual and Theoretical Analysis." *British Journal of Political Science,* April 1975, pp. 231-48.

_____. *Political Clienteles in Power: Party Factions and Cabinet Coalitions in Italy.* Beverly Hills: Sage Professional Papers in Comparative Politics, 1975.

_____. "The Concept 'Political Elite': Lessons from Mosca and Pareto." *Journal of Politics,* May 1977, pp. 324-44.

Zuckerman, Alan, and Lichbach, Mark Irving. "Stability and Change in European Electorates." *World Politics,* July 1977, pp. 523-51.

Primary Sources in English

Italy: Documents and Notes. All volumes. Rome: Office of the Presidency of the Council of Ministers.

Books and Articles in Italian

Alberoni, Francesco, et al. *L'Attivista di Partito.* Bologna: Il Mulino, 1967.

Amato, L. *Correnti di Partito e Partito di Correnti.* Milan: Giuffre, 1965.

Caciagli, Mario, and Spreafico, Alberto, eds. *Un Sistema Politico alla Prova.* Bologna: Il Mulino, 1975.

Cantelli, Franca Cervellati, et al. *L'Organizzazione Partitica del PCI e della DC.* Bologna: Il Mulino, 1968.

Capecchi, Vittorio, et al. *Il Comportamento Elettorale in Italia.* Bologna: Il Mulino, 1968.

Cavazza, F. L., and Graubard, Stephen R., eds. *Il Caso Italiano.* Milan: Garzanti, 1974.

Cazzola, Franco. "Partiti, Correnti, e Voto di Preferenza." In *Un Sistema Politico alla Prova,* edited by Mario Caciagli and Alberto Spreafico, pp. 127-52. Bologna: Il Mulino, 1975.

Cotta, Maurizio. "Classe Politica e Istituzionalizzazione del Parlamento: 1946-1972." *Rivista Italiana di Scienza Politica,* 1976, pp. 71-110.

"La Democrazia Italiana Fra Alternativa e Confronto." Roundtable discussion. *Il Mulino,* September–October 1976, pp. 749-807.

De Rosa, Gabriele. *Storia del Movimento Cattolico in Italia.* Bari: Laterza, 1966.

Di Capua, Giovanni. *Le Chiavi Del Quirinale.* Milan: Feltrinelli, 1971.

Di Palma, Giuseppe. "Contenuti e Comportamenti Legislativi nel Parlamento Italiano." *Rivista Italiana di Scienza Politica,* 1975, pp. 3-39.

Dogan, Mattei, and Petrarca, Orazio Maria, eds. *Partiti Politici e Strutture Sociale in Italia.* Milan: Edizioni di Communità, 1968.

Franchi, Paolo. "Le Amibiguità della DC." *Rinascita,* April 8, 1977, p. 4.

Galli, Giorgio. *Il Bipartismo Imperfetto.* Bologna: Il Mulino, 1966.

Gallo, Vittorio, ed. *Antologia di "Prospettive."* Rome: EBE, 1971.

Leonardi, Robert. "Opinioni Politiche delle Correnti Democristiana in Emilia-Romagna." *Rivista Italiana di Scienza Politica,* 1974, pp. 387-408.

Lombardo, Antonio. "Sistema di Correnti e Deperimento dei Partiti in Italia." *Rivista Italiana di Scienza Politica,* 1976, pp. 139-62.

Manoukian, Agopik, et al. *La Presenza Sociale del PCI e della DC.* Bologna: Il Mulino, 1968.

Merli, Luca, ed. *Antologia de "La Base."* Rome: EBE, 1971.

Mosca, Gaetano. *Partiti e Sindacati Nella Crisi del Regime Parlamentare.* Bari: Laterza, 1949.

_____. *Teorica dei Governi e Governo Parlamentare.* new ed. Milan: Giuffre, 1968.

Nobecourt, Jacques. *Italia al Vivo.* Milan: Etas Kompass, 1971.

Pansa, Gian Paolo. *Bisaglia: Una Carriera Democristiana.* Milan: Sugarco, 1975.

Parisi, Arturo, and Pasquino, Gianfranco. "20 Giugno: Struttura Politica e Comportamenti Elettorali." *Il Mulino,* May–June 1976, pp. 342-86.

_____. "Relazioni Partiti-Elettori e Tipi di Voto." In *Continuità e Mutamento Elettorale in Italia,* pp. 215-49. Bologna: Il Mulino, 1977.

Pasquino, Gianfranco. "Le Radici del Frazionismo e Il Voto di Preferenza." *Rivista Italiana di Scienza Politica,* 1972, pp. 353-68.

_____. "Il Sistema Politico Italiano Tra Neo-Trasformismo e Democrazia

Consociativa." *Il Mulino,* July–August 1973, pp. 549–66.

_____. "Contro il Finanzimento dei Questi Partiti." *Il Mulino,* March–April 1974, pp. 233–55.

_____. "Crisi della DC e Evoluzione del Sistema Politico." *Rivista Italiana di Scienza Politica,* 1975, pp. 443–72.

_____. "Ricambio Parliamentare e Rendimento Politico." *Politica del diritto,* September–October 1976, pp. 543–65.

_____. "Per Un'Analisi Delle Coalizioni di Governo in Italia." In *Continuità e Mutamento Elettorale in Italia,* edited by Arturo Parisi and Gianfranco Pasquino, pp. 251–79. Bologna: Il Mulino, 1977.

Passigli, Stefano. "Proporzionalismo, Frazionismo e Crisi dei Partiti: Quid Prior?" *Rivista Italiana di Scienza Politica,* 1972, pp. 126–39.

Pellicani, Luciano. "Verso il Superamento del Pluralismo Polarizzato?" *Rivista Italiana di Scienza Politica,* 1974, pp. 645–74.

Poggi, Gianfranco. *Le Preferenze Politiche Italiane.* Bologna: Il Mulino, 1968.

Prandi, Alfonso. *Chiesa e Politica.* Bologna: Il Mulino, 1968.

Predieri, Alberto. "Mediazione e Indirizzo Politico nel Parlamento Italiano." *Rivista Italiana di Scienza Politica,* 1975, pp. 407–41.

Sani, Giacomo. "Ricambio Elettorale e Indicazioni Partitiche: Verso Una Hegemonia delle Sinistre?" *Rivista Italiana di Scienza Politica,* 1975, pp. 515–44.

Sartori, Giovanni. "Proporzionalismo, Frazionismo e Crisi dei Partiti." *Rivista Italiana di Scienza Politica,* 1971, pp. 629–55.

_____. "Il Caso Italiano: Salvare il Pluaralismo e Superare La Polarizzazione." *Rivista Italia di Scienza Politica,* 1974, pp. 675–88.

_____. "Rivisitando il 'Pluralismo Polarizzato." In *Il Caso Italiano,* edited by F. L. Cavazza and Stephen R. Graubard, pp. 196–223. Milan: Garzanti, 1974.

Schepis, Giovanni. "Analisi Statistica dei Resultati," In *Elezioni e Comportamento Politico in Italia,* edited by Alberto Spreafico and Joseph LaPalombara, pp. 329–406. n.p.: Edizioni di Communità, 1963.

Sernini, Michele. *Le Correnti nel Partito.* Milan: Cisalpino, 1966.

Spreafico, Alberto, and LaPalombara, Joseph, eds. *Elezioni e Comportamento Politica in Italia.* n.p. Edizioni di Communità, 1963.

Tamburrano, Giuseppe. *L'Iceberg Democristiano.* Milan: Sugarco, 1974.

_____. *Storia e Cronaca del Centro-Sinistra.* Milan: Feltrinelli, 1974.

Wollemborg, Leo. *Italia al Ralentore.* Bologna: Il Mulino, 1966.

Zincone, Giovanna. "Accesso Autonomo alle Resorse: le Determinanti del Frazionismo." *Rivista Italiana di Scienza Politica,* 1972, pp. 239–59.

Primary Sources in Italian

Atti e Documenti della Democrazia Cristiana: 1943–1967. Rome: Edizioni Cinque Lune, 1968.

I Deputati e Senatori del Quinto Parlamento. Rome: La Navicella, 1968.

Diritti e Doveri dei Soci e Relative Garanzie. Assemblea Nazionale della Democrazia Cristiana. Sorrento, 1965.

_____. *Dopo Firenze: Azione per lo Sviluppo Democratico dell'Italia.* Milan: Garzanti, 1963.

_____. *Centro Sinistra '62.* Milan: Garzanti, 1963.

Granelli, Luigi. *Politica di Potenza e Strategia di Pace.* Milan: Centro di Carlo Puecher, 1968.

_____. *Per un Mondo della Liberta Scelta.* Milan: Centro di Carlo Puecher, 1968.

_____. *Nuova Frontiera in Europa.* Milan: Centro di Carlo Puecher, 1968.

_____. *Il XII Congresso del PCI.* Milan: Centro di Carlo Puecher, 1968.

Libro Bianco Sullo Scioglimento di "Impegno Democratico": No a Queste Correnti. Rome: Edizioni N.P., 1969.

Moro, Aldo. *Una Politica per I Tempi Nuovi.* Rome: Agenzia "Progetto," 1967.

Il Partito e Le Sue Rappresentanze. Assemblea Nazionale della Democrazia Cristiana. Sorrento, 1965.

Statuto del Partito: Democrazia Cristiana. Rome, 1968.

Taviani, Paolo Emilio. *Principi Cristiani e Metodo Democratico.* Florence: Le Monnier, 1965.

_____. *Per Il Progresso e la Liberta D'Italia,* Rome: Eliograf, 1972.

Traverso, C. E., et al. *I Partiti Politici: Leggi e Statuti.* Milan: Cisalpino, 1966.

Newspapers and Newsweeklies

Corriere della Sera
L'Espresso
Il Messagero
Il Popolo
Panorama

Index